# iOS 7 Programming:

## *A Quantitative Approach*

Henry H. Liu

*P* **PerfMath**

ISBN-13: 978-1500728496

ISBN-10: 1500728497


10 9 8 7 6 5 4 3 2 1

09062014

*To My Family*

# Table of Contents

# List of Programs and Scripts

# Table of Figures

# Preface

## WHY THIS BOOK

Over half a billion Apple mobile devices (iPhone, iPad and iPod Touch) run on iOS. Apple pays billions of dollars a year for the apps made available to consumers on the iTunes Store. Such simple facts purport numerous opportunities for businesses, software developers, and researchers as well. Fundamentally, such unprecedented phenomena are powered by iOS programming behind the scene.

On the other hand, Apple provides tons of programming guides in its developer libraries. These guides are well-written, but not necessarily suitable for those who are new to iOS programming. Available texts help, but have various limitations. Some are excessively overwhelming and intimidating, and some are filled with piecemeal examples without a consistent context. They either made iOS programming unnecessarily over-complicated or over-simplified. This book serves as a single source for a software developer to learn how to master iOS programming in a matter of weeks rather than months. After having worked through this book, you will be equipped with all knowledge and skills, ranging from using Xcode, Objective-C, Apple-recommended design patterns and best coding practices, etc., and more importantly, you will be able to plough along yourself for developing commercial grade iOS apps by referencing Apple's iOS programming guides on an as-needed basis. Essentially, this book provides an easy entry for you to get into the door of iOS programming – *effectively* and *efficiently*.

## SOFTWARE AND HARDWARE

Unlike Java, Objective-C programs are machine dependent, which means that they might need to be recompiled and linked on a device different than the one on which the initial compilation and linking were carried out. For this book, we will use either Xcode or a command-line compiler named *clang*. Xcode is Apple's iOS and OS X integrated development environment (IDE), while clang is a compiler front end for the C, C++, Objective-C and Objective-C++ programming languages. Clang uses LLVM, which is a collection of modular and reusable compiler and toolchain technologies, as its back end and has been part of the LLVM release cycle since LLVM 2.6. Clang is designed to replace the GNU Compiler Collection (GCC). It is open-source, developed mainly by Apple.

You will learn how to use Xcode and clang to build Objective-C programs and iOS apps throughout this book.

## HOW TO USE THIS BOOK

For each feature, first, try to understand all the concepts associated with it. Then, I strongly encourage you to carefully study and actually run all the examples on your machine to see the output of each program yourself. (All the examples presented in the book have been thoroughly tested and expected to work without tweaking.) For some special purposes such as preparing for an examination or a job interview coding test, you might want to memorize some examples in order to succeed, although in general mechanically memorizing certain specifics of a subject is not a recommended way to learn. Don't hesitate to memorize certain coding specifics, as your success is the *only* thing that matters to you under certain circumstances. Of course, merely mechanically memorizing something without trying to understand it first is not recommended under any circumstances.

## TYPOGRAPHIC CONVENTIONS

Times New Roman indicates normal text blocks.

*Italic* indicates *file names*, *directory paths*, *class names*, *emphasis*, *definitions*, and *references* in general.

Calibri font indicates code listings, scripts, and all other types of programming segments.

Courier indicates programming elements outside a program or script as well as everything related to executing a program or script such as variable names, method names, commands, entries on an HTML form, etc.

## HOW TO REACH THE AUTHOR

All typos and errors in the text are the author's responsibility. You are welcome to email your questions and comments to me at *henry_h_liu@perfmath.com*. Your valuable feedback will be greatly appreciated.

## THE BOOK'S WEB SITE

This book has a companion website at http://www.perfmath.com. For downloads and updates, please visit the book's web site.

Henry H. Liu, PH. D.

Cupertino, California

August, 2014

# Acknowledgements

First, I would really like to thank the self-publishing vendors I have chosen for making this book available to you. This is the most cost-effective and efficient approach for both you as my audience and myself as author. Computer and software technologies evolve so fast that a more timely publishing approach is beneficial for all of us. In addition, my gratitude extends to my wife Sarah and our son William, as I could have not been able to complete this book without their support and patience.

I would also like to thank my audience for valuable feedback and comments, which I always take whole-heartedly and include every time the book is updated.

Finally, the cover image shows the Iberian Peninsula at Night , taken by NASA and made available to public at http://www.nasa.gov/content/iberian-peninsula-at-night/. To learn more about this image, here is the NASA's notation: *One of the Expedition 40 crew members aboard the International Space Station recorded this early evening photo of the entire Iberian Peninsula (Spain, Portugal and Andorra) on July 26, 2014. Part of France can be seen at the top of the image and the Strait of Gibraltar is visible at bottom, with a very small portion of Morocco visible near the lower right corner.* I chose this image as the book's cover image, as it pleasantly reminds us of the amazing things beyond the bits and bytes we struggle with every day while we program.

# 1 Introducing iOS 7

iOS is the operating system that runs on Apple's iPhone, iPad, and iPod Touch mobile devices. Like every other OS, it manages the underlying hardware and provides the technologies for running various system software such as Phone, Mail, Safari, and so on to provide standard system services to the user.

Apple also provides the iOS SDK (Software Development Kit) for developing native apps to run on iOS. Such native apps are built using the iOS system frameworks and Objective-C language and run directly on iOS, while web apps run on Apple's browser, Safari, which depends on Internet connections. This book is concerned with developing native apps to run on iOS.

Next, we take a look at the resources the iOS SDK provides for building iOS apps.

## 1.1 OVERVIEW OF THE iOS TECHNOLOGIES

iOS has a layered architecture as shown in Figure 1.1. At the highest level, iOS acts as an interface between apps and the underlying hardware, as apps are not allowed to access the hardware directly. Developers use that interface, which is exposed as a collection of frameworks, to build apps. There are high-level frameworks and low-level frameworks. In general, developers should use high-level frameworks as much as possible, as the high-level frameworks provide object-oriented abstractions for low-level constructs. Thanks to the concept of abstractions, high-level frameworks make it much easier to write code as they drastically reduce the amount of code to write by encapsulating complex building blocks such as sockets and threads.

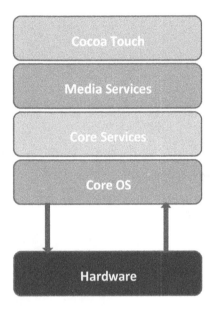

**Figure 1.1** iOS architecture

In fact, "*framework*" is an overloaded term in software parlance. A framework essentially is a bundle or package or a structured directory that contains a dynamically shared library along with relevant resources or assets such as image files, header files, property files, meta-data files, and so on. During development, required frameworks are linked to the project – mostly conveniently through an Integrated Development Environment (IDE) such as Xcode, which is the IDE for developing apps for iOS and OS X. As an example, Figure 1.2 shows how the AppKit.framework is used for building apps, such as the *Mail.app* and *MyApp.app*. As you see, the AppKit framework contains mainly code and resources.

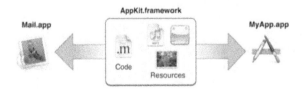

**Figure 1.2** An example use of the AppKit.framework

**☑ Xcode**: This is the all-in-one IDE for creating, debugging, testing, and tuning your apps. You use Xcode to write your code and run your apps on iOS simulator or directly on an attached iOS device. To measure your app's performance, use Xcode to launch instruments. How to use Xcode effectively and efficiently is covered throughout the remainder of this book.

You can also view a framework as an application programming interface (API), which is defined through its header files. Because a framework library is dynamically shared, multiple applications can access the framework code and resources simultaneously. The system loads a framework into memory and shares only one copy among all apps.

One good example of using frameworks is that iOS application projects link by default to the *Foundation*, *UIKit*, and *Core Graphics* frameworks. All these and other frameworks are provided by Apple, and third-party frameworks are not allowed to run on iOS and OS X.

Next, let us take a look at various iOS layers as shown in Figure 1.1 as well as frameworks associated with them.

## 1.1.1   Cocoa Touch Layer

The Cocoa Touch layer contains frameworks that support defining the appearance of your app, multitasking, touch-based input, push notifications, and many other high-level system services, including:

- AirDrop: Lets users share documents, media files, URLs, and other kinds of data with nearby devices. It's built into the UIActivityViewController class.
- Text Kit: For handling text and fine typography. It is integrated with all UIKit text based controls to enable apps to manipulate text more easily.
- UIKit Dynamics: Allows apps to specify dynamic behaviors for UIView objects and for other objects that conform to the UIDynamicItem protocol.
- Multitasking: Is designed to maximize battery life while giving apps execution time needed to perform various tasks.
- Auto Layout: Used for developing dynamic interfaces with little code. It allows apps to define rules for how to lay out the elements in a UI view.
- Storyboards: A simpler way for designing a user interface. A storyboard allows you to design an entire user interface in one place for all views and view controllers. The transitions from one view controller to another are managed with *segues*, which allow you to capture the flow of your user interface in addition to the content.
- UI State Preservation: This is for providing smooth user experiences in situations that some apps have to be halted and restored later. For example, if the system is under memory pressure, it may be forced to terminate some background apps quietly. When an app moves from the foreground to the background, it can preserve the state of its views and view controllers. During the next launch cycle, it can use the preserved state information to restore its views and view controllers to their previous configurations and make it appear as if the app had never quit.

- Apple Push Notification Service: Provides a way to alert users about new information even when the app is not actively running. It allows an app to push text notifications, add a badge to its icon, and trigger audible alerts on user devices at any time.
- Local Notifications: Allow apps to generate notifications locally instead of relying on an external server.
- Gesture Recognizers: Allow gestures such as swipes, taps, rotations, and pinches in an app's views recognized. To use it, you attach a gesture recognizer to your view and specify an action method to perform when the gesture occurs.
- Standard System View Controllers: Allow developers to use system-provided view controllers rather than their own to present a consistent user experience. For example, the following common tasks all have well-defined view controllers:

  o Display or edit contact information: Use the view controllers in the Address Book UI framework.
  o Create or edit calendar events: Use the view controllers in the Event Kit UI framework.
  o Compose an email or SMS message: Use the view controllers in the Message UI framework.
  o Open or preview the contents of a file: Use the UIDocumentInteractionController class in the UIKit framework.
  o Take a picture or choose a photo from the user's photo library: Use the UIImagePickerController class in the UIKit framework.
  o Shoot a video clip: Use the UIImagePickerController class in the UIKit framework.

If some of those technical jargons sound unfamiliar to you, don't worry as we'll learn them later in the main text.

## 1.1.2   Media Services Layer

The media services layer supports imaging, audio and video processing through the following frameworks:

- UIKit graphics framework: Provides a fast way to render images and text-based contents.
- Core Graphics framework (also known as Quartz): Is the native drawing engine for iOS apps to render 2D images. Although not as fast as OpenGL ES rendering, it's well suited for rendering custom 2D shapes and images dynamically.
- Core Animation: Optimizes the animation experience of iOS apps as part of the Quartz Core framework.
- Core Image: Supports manipulating video and still images in a nondestructive manner.
- OpenGL ES and GLKit: OpenGL ES handles advanced 2D and 3D rendering using hardware-accelerated interfaces. This framework is traditionally used by game developers. GLKit framework (GL.framework) contains a set of Objective-C based utility classes that simplify the effort required to create an OpenGL ES app.
- Text Kit and Core Text: Text Kit is part of UIKit used to perform fine typography and text management. Core Text is a lower-level C-based framework for handling advanced typography and layout.

- Image I/O: Provides interfaces for reading and writing most image formats.
- Assets Library: Provides access to user's photos, videos, and media.

Next, we explore core services layer.

## 1.1.3   Core Services Layer

The Core Services layer contains fundamental system services for building both native and web apps. It includes the following frameworks:

- Accounts Framework: (Accounts.framework): Provides user account services such as single sign-on (SSO).
- Address Book Framework (AddressBook.framework): Provides programmatic access to user's contacts database.
- Ads Support Framework (AdSupport.framework): Provides access to an identifier that apps can use for advertising purposes. It also provides a flag to indicate whether the user has opted out of ad tracking.
- CFNetwork Framework (CFNetwork.framework): Is a set of high-performance C-based interfaces for supporting various network protocols. It is based on BSD sockets and supports communications with FTP and HTTP servers.
- Core Data Framework (CoreData.framework): Manages the data model of an app based on the MVC design pattern. It significantly reduces the amount of code you have to write for your app. It also provides the following features:

  o   Storage of object data in a SQLite database for optimal performance
  o   An NSFetchedResultsController class to manage results for table views
  o   Support for validating property values
  o   Support for grouping , filtering, and organizing data in memory
  o   Support for propagating changes and ensuring that the relationships between objects remain consistent

- Core Foundation Framework (CoreFoundation.framework): Is a set of C-based interfaces that provide basic data management and service features for iOS apps. It supports the following:

  o   Collection data types (arrays, sets and so on)
  o   Bundles
  o   String management
  o   Date and time management
  o   Raw data block management
  o   Preferences management
  o   URL and stream manipulation
  o   Threads and run loops
  o   Port and socket communication

- Core Location Framework (CoreLocation.framework): Provides location and heading information to apps. It uses the onboard GPS, cell or Wi-Fi radios to find the user's current longitude and latitude. It also provides access to compass-based heading information on iOS devices that have a magnetometer installed.

- Core Motion Framework (CoreMotion.framework): Provides interfaces for accessing motion-based data available on a device that has an accelerometer and/or gyroscope installed.
- Core Telephony Framework (CoreTelephony.framework): Provides services for interacting with phone-based information on devices that have a cellular radio.
- Event Kit Framework (EventKit.framework): Provides an interface for accessing calendar events on a user's device.
- Foundation Framework (Foundation.framework): provides Objective-C wrappers to many of the features found in the Core Foundation framework.
- JavaScript Core Framework (JavaScriptCore.framework): Provides Objective-C wrappers for many standard JavaScript objects. Use this framework to evaluate JavaScript code and to parse JSON data.
- Mobile Core Services Framework (MobileCoreServices.framework): Defines the low-level types used in uniform type identifiers (UTIs).
- Pass Kit Framework (PassKit.framework): Provides a place for users to store coupons, boarding passes, event tickets, and discount cards for businesses. This would help eliminate the need of carrying a physical representation of such items.
- Quick Look Framework (QuickLook.framework): Provides a direct interface for previewing the contents of files that your app does not support directly.
- Safari Services Framework (SafariServices.framework): Provides support for programmatically adding URLs to the user's Safari reading list.
- Social Framework (Social.framework): Provides an interface for accessing the user's social media accounts such as Twitter, Facebook, and so on.
- Store Kit Framework (StoreKit.framework): Provides support for purchasing from within your iOS apps, a feature also known as *In-APP Purcahse*.
- System Configuration Framework (SystemConfiguration.framework): Provides the reachability interfaces for determining the network configuration of a device, e.g., whether a Wi-Fi or cellular connection is in use and whether a particular host server can be accessed.

Next, we discuss the Core OS layer.

## 1.1.4   Core OS Layer

The Core OS layer contains the low-level features for other higher-level layers. It includes the following frameworks:

- Accelerate Framework (Accelerate.framework): Contains interfaces for performing digital signal processing (DSP), linear algebra, and image-processing calculations. It is optimized for all of the hardware configurations present in iOS devices so that you don't have to develop your own.
- Core Bluetooth Framework (CoreBluetooth.framework): Allows developers to interact specifically with Bluetooth low energy (LE) accessories.
- External Accessory Framework (ExternalAccessory.framework): Provides support for communicating with hardware accessories attached to an iOS-based device.

- Generic Security Services Framework (GSS.framework): Provides a standard set of security-related services to iOS apps.
- Security Framework (Security-framework): Provides an explicit security framework in addition to other built-in security features to guarantee the security of the data your app manages.

Next, we explore the history of iOS.

## 1.2   THE HISTORY OF IOS

iOS powers Apple's iPhone, iPad and iPod Touch. It has been maintained through over-the-air software updates since iOS 5.0 released in June 2011. It was named iPhone OS initially, but was renamed iOS on June 7, 2010, as the iPhone was no longer the only device on which it runs. Interestingly, "iOS" was a Cisco trademark and Apple licensed it from Cisco.

Here is a summary of the history of iOS since its first release on June 29, 2007:

- March 8, 2008 (iPhone OS 1.x): First release of Apple's touch-centric mobile OS.
- July 11, 2008 (iPhone OS 2.x): Second release with iPhone 3G. Apple also introduced the *App Store*, making third-party applications available to the iPhone and iPod Touch devices.
- June 17, 2009 (iPhone OS 3.x): Third release with the iPhone 3GS. This release introduced features such as *copy/paste*, and *multimedia messaging service* (MMS).
- June 21, 2010 (iOS 4.x): Fourth release with the iPhone and iPod Touch.
- June 6, 2011 (iOS 5.x): Fifth release with iPhone 3GS, iPhone 4 (GSM and CDMA), iPhone 4S, iPod Touch ($3^{rd}$ and $4^{th}$ generations), iPad ($1^{st}$ generation), and iPad 2 on October 12, 2011.
- September 19, 2012 (iOS 6.x): Released through iTunes and over-the-air updates.
- September 18, 2013 (iOS 7.x): Seventh release with the iPad mini introduced.

At the time of this writing, Apple announced iOS 8 to be released in the fall of 2014. However, regardless of the version of a specific iOS release, it's universally true that not only the iOS and OS X but also all frameworks are written in Objective-C. Therefore, it's obvious that if you are interested in iOS programming, you have to become conversant with Objective-C. In case you're not familiar with Objective-C, the next section gives you an overview of the programming language Objective-C. If you're not familiar with Objective-C, I suggest that you spend one – two weeks to become familiar with Objective-C by taking a quick training using Appendix B of this book or any other resources.

## 1.3   OBJECTIVE-C

Dennis Ritchie created the C programming language in the early 1970s. C became popular in late 1970s, mainly because of the popularity of the UNIX operating system, which was almost entirely written in C.

Then, in the early 1980s, Brad J. Cox designed the Objective-C language, which was layered on C with extensions added to create a new object-oriented language. This might remind you of the

C++ programming language, but Objective-C was patterned on another language called SmallTalk-80, which has a totally different style in enabling object definition and instantiation.

In 1998, NeXT Software licensed Objective-C and developed its libraries and a development environment called NEXTSTEP. In 1992, Objective-C support was added to the Free Software Foundation's (FSF) GNU development environment. In 1994, NeXT Computer and Sun Microsystem released a standardized spec of the NEXTSTEP system, called OPENSTEP. The FSF's implementation of OPENSTEP was called GNUStep.

On December 20, 1996, Apple acquired NeXT Software, and the NEXTSTEP/OPENSTEP environment became the basis for the subsequent release of Apple's operating system, OS X. Apple's development environment was called Cocoa. Apple also developed its own development tools Project Builder (and its successor Xcode) and Interface Builder, making it a powerful development environment on Mac OS X.

In 2007, Apple released Objective-C 2.0. In the same year, Apple released a revolutionary device - iPhone. At first, Apple did not welcome 3$^{rd}$-party application development. Developers could only develop Web apps that ran in iPhone's built-in Safari Web browser. To overcome many limitations associated with Web apps, Apple announced support for developing *native* apps that could run on iPhone directly. Apple also provided an iPhone simulator so that developers could test their software using the simulator instead of a physical iPhone or iPod touch device.

In 2010, Apple introduced its iPad and expanded their simulator to accommodate mobile devices with different sizes and resolutions. In the meanwhile, the iPhone OS, which was actually a specialized version of OS X, was renamed as iOS that powers iPhone, iPod Touch and iPad, as we mentioned in the previous section. However, at WWDC 2014, Apple announced plans to replace Objective-C for Cocoa development with its new Swift language, which it characterized as "Objective-C without the C". We'll have to see how this would work out, though.

To give you an idea of how Objective-C looks like or works, Listing 1.1 shows the "Hello, World!" program in Objective C. As you see, it's similar to C, but not exactly the same. First, note its `import` statement, which imports the `Foundation` interface. Next, note its output statement in the form of `NSLog (@"Hello, World!")`. Here, the @ sign that immediately precedes a string of characters enclosed in a pair of double quotes designates a constant `NSString` object, whereas `NSLog` is simply a function that logs its argument. (If it were in C++, it would have been in the form of `cout << "Hello, World!" << endl`.) At last, note the structure of `@autorelease { … }`, which means that the statements enclosed in that block are executed within a context known as *autorelease pool* or *automatic garbage collection*.

### Listing 1.1 The HelloWord program in Objective-C

```
#import <Foundation/Foundation.h>

int main(int argc, const char * argv[])
{
    @autoreleasepool {
        NSLog (@"Hello, World!");
```

```
    }
    return 0;
}
```

However, whether a program is written in C or Objective C, it is executed similarly. The program has to go through a process as shown in Figure 1.3 that the final form of the program would be translated into assembly language code that the hardware can understand.

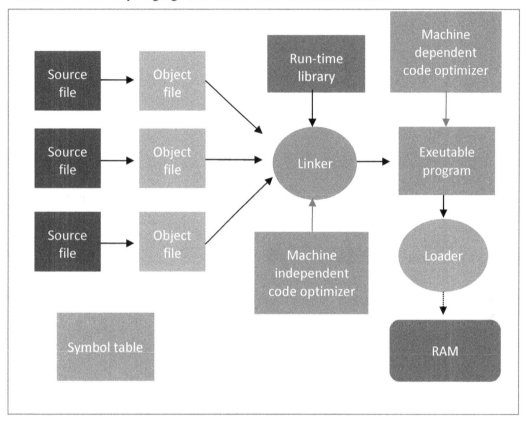

**Figure 1.3** The process of translating high-level language source code to machine language code

In fact, after learning how to set up Xcode and create iOS or OS X projects in the next chapter, you could use Xcode to create the "Hello, World!" program shown in Listing 1.1 by choosing the OS X/Application/CommandLine Tool template. Figure 1.4 shows the same "Hello, World!" program created in Xcode, along with the output shown at the bottom after the program was executed. You might want to take a cursory look at Figure 1.5, which shows the overall structure of the Xcode workspace window with various areas, such as the Navigator area, Editor area, Debug area, and Utility area. We cover Xcode more in the next chapter.

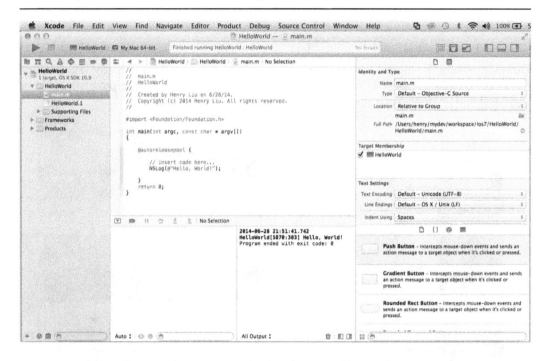

**Figure 1.4** The "Hello, World!" program created and executed in Xcode

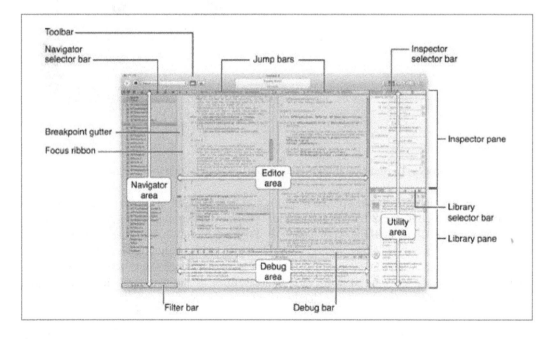

**Figure 1.5** Overall structure of an Xcode workspace window

However, my purpose here is not to show you how to create a project in Xcode. Instead, I wanted to show you that by selecting *Product/Perform Action/Assemble "main.m"* on the Xcode's top menu bar as shown in Figure 1.4, you could actually see the assembly code of this program as shown in Figure 1.6. Without going into too much detail of the assembly code therein, notice that those `movq`, `subq`, and `movl` are assembly instructions, while those `%rbp`, `%rsp`, `%edi`, and `%rsi` represent registers. It is unimaginable if we have to program in assembly language like that. It's even hard to program everything using a high-level programming language from scratch, which is why every product has its own frameworks to help hide complexity through abstractions and encapsulations. To some extent, learning iOS programming is learning how to use those frameworks as we covered previously.

```
≡   ◄   ►    .m  main.m (Assembly)
# Assembly output for main.m
# Generated at 9:42:59 PM on Saturday, June 28, 2014
# Using Debug configuration, x86_64 architecture for HelloWorld target of HelloWorld
    project

        .section      __TEXT,__text,regular,pure_instructions
        .section      __DWARF,__debug_info,regular,debug
Lsection_info:
        .section      __DWARF,__debug_abbrev,regular,debug
Lsection_abbrev:
        .section      __DWARF,__debug_aranges,regular,debug
        .section      __DWARF,__debug_macinfo,regular,debug
        .section      __DWARF,__debug_line,regular,debug
Lsection_line:
        .section      __DWARF,__debug_loc,regular,debug
        .section      __DWARF,__debug_str,regular,debug
Linfo_string:
        .section      __DWARF,__debug_ranges,regular,debug
Ldebug_range:
        .section      __DWARF,__debug_loc,regular,debug
Lsection_debug_loc:
        .section      __TEXT,__text,regular,pure_instructions
Ltext_begin:
        .section      __DATA,__data
        .file   1 "/Users/henry/mydev/workspace/ios7/HelloWorld/HelloWorld/main.m"
        .section      __TEXT,__text,regular,pure_instructions
        .globl  _main
        .align  4, 0x90
_main:                                    ## @main
        .cfi_startproc
Lfunc_begin0:
        .loc    1 12 0                    ## /Users/henry/mydev/workspace/ios7/HelloWorld/
            HelloWorld/main.m:12:0
## BB#0:
        pushq   %rbp
Ltmp2:
        .cfi_def_cfa_offset 16
Ltmp3:
        .cfi_offset %rbp, -16
        movq    %rsp, %rbp
Ltmp4:
        .cfi_def_cfa_register %rbp
        subq    $32, %rsp
        movl    $0, -4(%rbp)
        movl    %edi, -8(%rbp)
        movq    %rsi, -16(%rbp)
        .loc    1 14 0 prologue_end       ## /Users/henry/mydev/workspace/ios7/HelloWorld/
```

**Figure 1.6** The partial assembly code of the "Hello, World!" program created in Xcode

## 1.4  SUMMARY

In this chapter, we introduced the overall architecture of iOS with multiple layers consisting of the Cocoa Touch layer, the media services layer, the core services layer, and the core OS layer. We also covered the history of iOS to set the context for this book. We illustrated the Objective-C language with a simple example and explained how a program like that written in a high-level programming language is built and run in general. That way, you can learn some general concepts associated with a development environment with a proper combination of a platform, a compiler, and a source code editor, and so on. This preparation helps lay the foundation for learning programming in iOS as presented throughout the remainder of this book. You have achieved your objectives for this chapter if you have learnt those concepts associated with various iOS frameworks as well as the programming elements illustrated in that simple `HelloWorld` program – even if you may not fully understand it yet. The rest of this book helps you learn iOS programming within a matter of weeks.

# 2 Setting up an Xcode IDE on Mac OS X

In this chapter, we illustrate how to set up an Xcode IDE on a Mac OS X machine to get started with developing iOS applications. Along the way, you'll learn what you can do with Xcode, which is one of the best IDEs I've used. You will also learn how to get around on an Xcode IDE.

## 2.1 INSTALLING XCODE

If you do not have an Apple ID yet, follow the below steps to create an Apple ID:

1  Access the website `appleid.apple.com` or search online for "Create an Apple ID" and create an Apple ID. Put your ID and password in a safe place to be used next and in future.
2  Access the website `developer.apple.com` and you should see a screen similar to Figure 2.1. Note the advertisement text for iOS 8, OS X Yosemite, and the new programming language, Swift, available in Xcode 6.
3  Click on the "Member Center" link at the upper right corner and you should see a screen similar to Figure 2.2. Enter your own AppleID and password and click Register.
4  Accept license terms and click Next.
5  Fill in the "Tell us about yourself" section and check whatever items you like about "What are you developing?" and "What other platforms do you develop for?" sections as shown in Figure 2.3. Take this opportunity and learn the applications you can develop with Xcode for iOS, OS X and Web on mobile devices and desktop/notebook machines. You can make your own list of interests by checking the items that you're most interested in.
6  Click Register and you should see a screen similar to Figure 2.4. As you see, Registered Apple Developer Resources include accesses to Dev Centers, Development Videos, Apple Development Forum, and Bug Reporting. You might want to come back later and check out these great resources.

7    Click on iOS under Dev Centers (upper left icon) and you should see a screen similar to Figure 2.5. As you see, this is the site dedicated to iOS 7 with pointers to Resources for iOS 7, Featured Content, Downloads, Custom B2B Apps, Developers in Action, iOS Developer Opportunities, Promote Your Apps, which empowers you to use the App Store badge and Apple product images to promote your apps on the Apple Store. Also note the iOS Developer Program at the upper right corner, which offers a complete process for developing and distrusting iOS apps. This kind of benefit is unique and available through Apple only.

8    Click the "Download Xcode 5" icon, which might redirect you to a different site similar to Figure 2.6. Note that this release of Xcode includes not only Xcode IDE, but also iOS simulator, the latest OS X and iOS SDKs, etc.

9    Click "View on the Mac Apple Store" link and then Install button. After the installation is complete, you should see a screen similar to Figure 2.7 with "Install" changed to "Installed."

**Figure 2.1** Apple's developer website

**Figure 2.2** Register or sign in to Apple's developer website

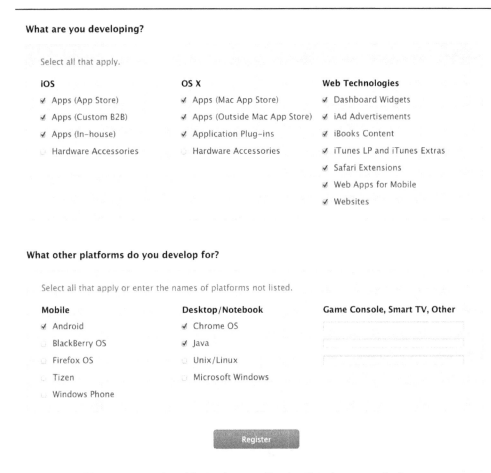

Figure 2.3 Things you can do with Apple's application development platform

Figure 2.4 Registered Apple Developer Resources

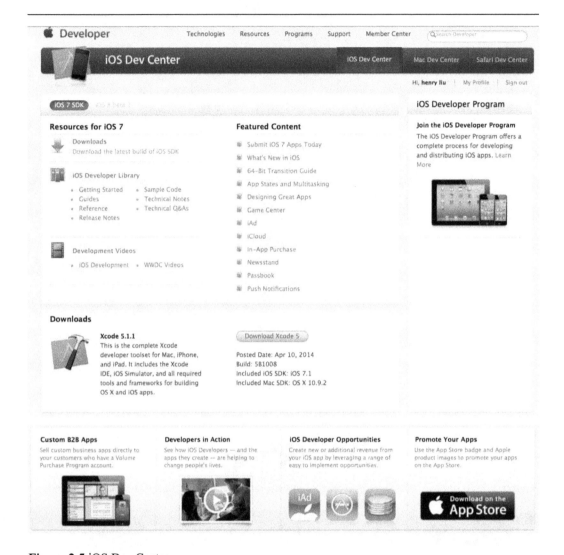

**Figure 2.5** iOS Dev Center

◀ **Mac OS X**: Whether you're new to Mac OS X, I suggest that you review Appendix *A Getting around on Mac OS X* to learn some of the easier ways to work on OS X. The shortcuts listed there may help you get through the projects presented in this book significantly faster.

**Figure 2.6** Xcode download link

**Figure 2.7** Installing Xcode

## 2.2   Getting Around on an Xcode IDE

Assuming that you have installed Xcode on your OS X, let's take a moment and learn how to get around on an Xcode IDE by creating a simple Hello-iOS program.

In order to achieve the objective stated above, press F4, locate the Xcode and click on it to open it. Then, you can right-click on its icon on the Dock, select Options -> Keep in Dock so that next time you just need to click on it on the Dock to open it.

When your Xcode is opened the first time, you should see a screen similar to Figure 2.8 with no pre-existing projects. As is seen, there are two options: one is Create a new Xcode project and the other is Check out an existing project from an SCM repository. Since we'll work on a new project, click on the first option, which should bring up a dialog similar to Figure 2.9.

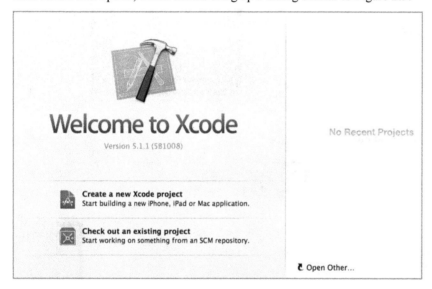

**Figure 2.8** Initial Welcome to Xcode

As is shown in Figure 2.9, there are two categories: iOS and OS X, with several sub-categories for each. Both have Application, Framework & Library and Other, but the OS X has more: the Application Plug-in and System Plug-in sub-categories. It's desirable to learn the full spectrum of power of Xcode for developing all kinds of applications, but I'll leave it to the next section so that we would not digress too much from our goal set for this section. Now, click on iOS/Application and select Single View Application to start our journey for developing a simple "Hello, iOS!" sample. When you're done, you should see a dialog similar to Figure 2.10. You can choose your own entries except that the Class Prefix entry should be a unique three-letter entry to help classify a class of application type. We'll get to this more later, and for now, just click on Next, which should bring up a screen similar to Figure 2.11. Next, we explain how to get around on Xcode for a project similar to what we have created here.

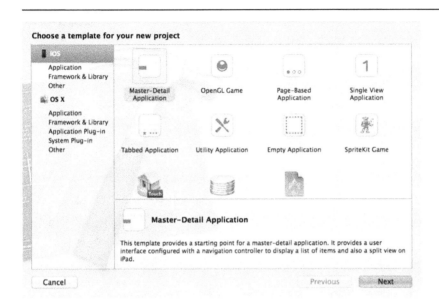

**Figure 2.9** Create a new Xcode project

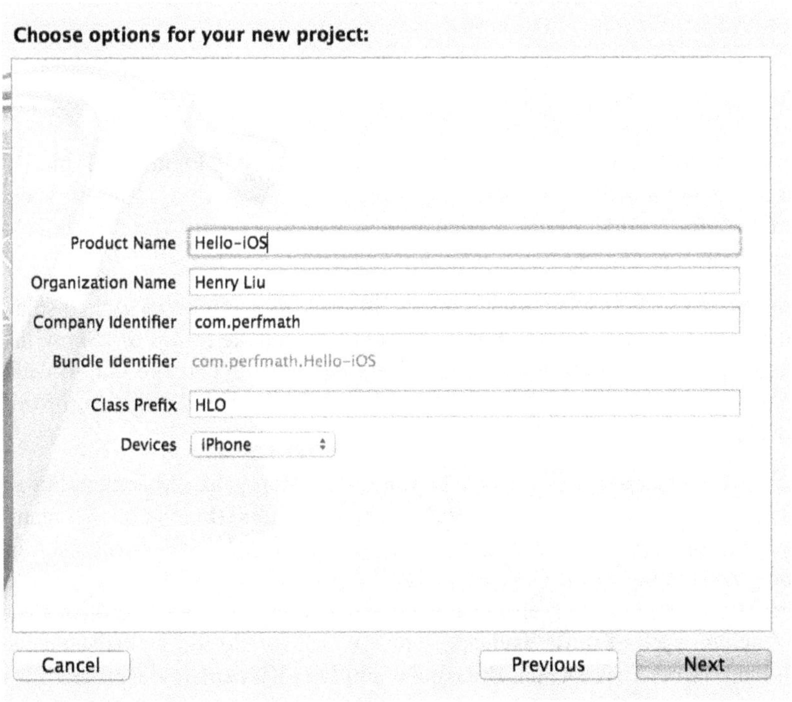

| | |
|---|---|
| Product Name | Hello-iOS |
| Organization Name | Henry Liu |
| Company Identifier | com.perfmath |
| Bundle Identifier | com.perfmath.Hello–iOS |
| Class Prefix | HLO |
| Devices | iPhone |

Choose options for your new project:

Cancel    Previous    Next

**Figure 2.10** Choose options for your new project

**Figure 2.11** Workspace for a typical Xcode project

Apparently, there are many things to go through in the workspace as shown in Figure 2.11, but I'll show some general tips at this point and you'll learn more later as we move along. I'll also leave explaining how this simple sample works to the next chapter so that we can just focus on how to get around on Xcode for a project in general.

First, there are many icons and if you place your pointer on each of them, a tip will display showing what it's used for. For example, at the upper right corner, I marked a tip of "Show the File inspector" associated with that icon on which I placed my pointer. I encourage you to walk through all those icons at least once later, after I walk you through the general structure of this project workspace as follows:

1    The **Tool bar**: The top most part shows the icons for Build/Run/Stop your application, Set an active scheme for your application, project status, various Editors (Standard, Assistant, Version) and Show/Hide several views (Navigator, Debug, Utilities). Please try out each of them to verify the information I described above.

2    The **Navigator** bar: Beneath the tool bar left most is the Navigation area with a navigator bar located on its top. Click on each of those navigator icons, which should follow the sequence of Project, Symbol, Find, Issue, Test, Debug, Breakpoint and Log. I'll explain the project files later.

3    The **Content** or **Editing** area: The center area beneath the tool bar and next to the navigation area is the content or editing area. Depending on what is selected on the left navigation area, you may see a different view there. We leave it to our exploration in future.

4    The **Utility** area: Beneath the tool bar at right most is the Utility area for making auxiliary features available to your project. Try out the top two icons for File Inspector and Quick Help Inspector and four more in the middle for File template, Code snippet, Object library and Media library. You don't need to memorize them now as you will get used to them as we use them more often later.

You can also learn how to get around on Xcode by accessing menus located at the Xcode menu bar as shown in Figure 2.12. For example, clicking on View / Navigators brings up many options for showing/hiding various Navigators, but accessing directly through icons on the workspace as described above is more convenient.

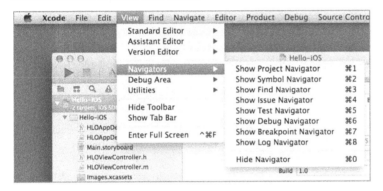

**Figure 2.12** Options available from Xcode menus

Next, I suggest that you take a cursory look at what you can do with Xcode as described in the next section, or you can skip it and go to Chapter 3, which explains more about some specifics relating to this simple "Hello, iOS!" sample.

## 2.3   PROJECT TEMPLATES ON XCODE 5.1.1

In addition to enhancing productivity, Xcode has many built-in project templates to help you get bootstrapped when you start developing a new application. In this section, we take a look at what templates are available from Xcode 5.1.1, which helps us appreciate Xcode even more for its power in assisting us to develop applications on iOS and OS X.

### 2.3.1   Project Templates for iOS

In this section, we explore templates from Xcode 5.1.1 for developing iOS applications. We briefly describe what each of the templates is meant for so that you would get an idea about which template to use when you decide to develop something for iOS.

Templates are available when you start creating a new project, as shown in Figure 2.9. First, according to whether your application will run on iOS (iPhone, iPad, and iPod) or OS X (Mac computers), you select proper sub-category and all available templates for that sub-category would show up in the content pane for you to choose. For example, when you select iOS/Application, the first available template would be the Master-Detail Application template. When you single click on that template, a description about that template is displayed at the bottom, displaying a description like *"This template provides a starting point for a master-detail application. It provides a user interface configured with a navigation controller to display a list of items and also a split view on iPad."*

In addition to the Master-Detail Application template, the *iOS/Application* sub-category includes the following templates:

1    **OpenGL Game** template. This template is for developing OpenGL based games. The Open Graphics Library (OpenGL) is used for processing data to render 2D and 3D images. It's used widely for 2D/3D digital content creation, virtual prototyping, video games, mechanical and architectural design, and so on. One can use OpenGL to configure a 3D graphics pipeline and submit data to it. Vertices are transformed and lit to create rasterized images. Behind the scene, OpenGL is used to translate function calls into graphics commands, which are sent to the underlying graphics hardware. For mobile graphics hardware, OpenGL for Embedded Systems (ES) is used, instead, which is a simplified version of OpenGL with significantly reduced footprint. Figure 2.13 shows how OpenGL ES framework works. It is seen that it runs in OpenGL Client to interact with both graphics hardware or GPU (graphics processing units) and applications such as games, which run on CPU. OpenGL-based games usually require specific performance tuning so that the CPU and GPU do not wait for each other to finish processing commands. You can refer to OpenGL ES Programming Guide for iOS from Apple's iOS Developer Library for more details about developing OpenGL games for iOS.

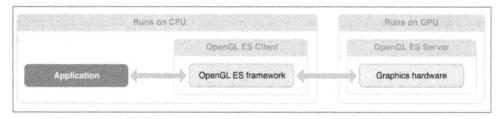

**Figure 2.13** How OpenGL-based games work on iOS

2    **Page-Based Application** template. This template is for developing applications that are page –based, for example, books or phablets that the user can read by turning page by page. It uses pageViewController to enable users to swipe from page to page like reading an e-book.
3    **Single-View Application** template. Contrary to the page-based application template, single-view application template is for developing applications of mainly one view on which you can place various views and controls. Our simple "Hello, iOS!" sample belongs to this type of applications that it uses one single view to display a "Hello, iOS!" message.

4    **Tabbed Application** template. This template is for developing tab bar based applications through a tab bar interface. With the same set of data or resources, different tabs provide different views to the user, such as the Tab bar items of the iPod app as shown in Figure 2.14, illustrated in the article, *ViewController Catalog for iOS*, from Apple's iOS Developer Library.

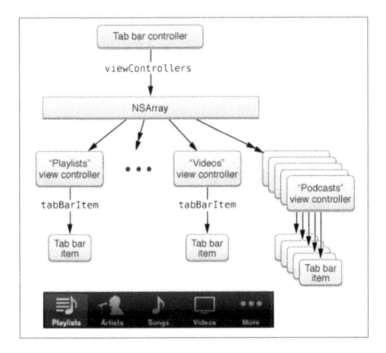

**Figure 2.14** An example of a tabbed application on iOS

5    **Utility Application** template. This template is for developing utility applications by setting up a main view and an alternate view. For iPhone, it sets up an Info button to flip the main view to the alternate view. For iPad, it sets up an Info bar button that shows the alternate view in a popover, which is like a popup over the main view without taking extra space.

6    **Empty Application** template. This template is for creating a bare-minimum boilerplate so that you can run your iOS app with just an application delegate and a window. Such an example is presented in Chapter 3 and you can take a look at it later.

7    **SpriteKit Game** template. This template is for developing a SpriteKit Game. What's SpriteKit after all? The Sprite Kit framework provides a hardware-accelerated animation system optimized for creating 2D games. It is a graphics rendering and animation infrastructure that can be used to animate arbitrary textured images, or *sprites*, on a frame-by-frame basis. It uses a traditional rendering loop where the contents of each frame are processed before the frame is rendered. For more details about developing SpriteKit games,

refer to the articles *SpriteKit Programming Guide* and *code:Explained Adventure* from Apple's iOS Developer Library.

The *iOS/Framework & Library* sub-category has only one template: **Cocoa Touch Static Library**. What is Cocoa Touch? It's a complete assortment of frameworks that provide touch-based interfaces and optimization. It is implemented in Objective-C, an object-oriented language that is compiled to run at incredible speed, yet employs a truly dynamic runtime for much-needed flexibility. Because Objective-C is a superset of C, it is possible to mix C and even C++ into your Cocoa Touch applications. When an application runs, the Objective-C runtime instantiates objects based on executing logic – not just in ways defined during compilation. For example, a running Objective-C application can load an interface (a nib file created by Interface Builder), connect the Cocoa objects in the interface to your application code, then run the correct method once the UI button is pressed. That way, no recompiling is necessary.

Cocoa Touch includes powerful Objective-C frameworks that perform entire tasks in only a few lines of code, while providing the foundational C-language APIs to give direct access to the system when needed. In addition to UIKit, which provides the basic tools you need to implement graphical, event-driven applications in iOS, the other Cocoa Touch frameworks such as Core Audio, Core Video, and Core Data are available for creating iOS apps, from 3D graphics, to professional audio, to networking, and even special device access APIs to control the camera, or get location from the GPS hardware. You can learn more about Cocoa Touch at https://developer.apple.com/technologies/ios/cocoa-touch.html, which has more details about those three major Cocoa Touch frameworks of Core Animation, Core Video and Core Data. Figure 2.15 summarizes Cocoa Touch frameworks by category, provided by Apple at that website. It gives us an idea about what frameworks to use for developing a particular type of applications of interest. The Data Management and Networking and Internet frameworks are very relevant for developing mobile enterprise applications targeting iOS devices. We will touch upon some of the frameworks such as Core Data later.

**Features List: Frameworks by Category**

Below is a small sampling of the available frameworks included in Cocoa Touch:

| Audio and Video | Graphics and Animation | User Applications |
|---|---|---|
| Core Audio | Core Animation | Address Book |
| OpenAL | OpenGL ES | Core Location |
| Media Library | Quartz 2D | Map Kit |
| AV Foundation | | Store Kit |
| | **Networking and Internet** | |
| **Data Management** | Bonjour | |
| Core Data | WebKit | |
| SQLite | BSD Sockets | |

**Figure 2.15** Some commonly used Cocoa Touch frameworks

The *iOS/Other* sub-category contains the following two templates:

1   **In-App Purchase Content** template. This template builds an In-App Purchase Content package. As is shown in Figure 2.16, In-App Purchase allows you to embed a store inside your app using the StoreKit framework. Remember those teaser apps that are free, but require purchase for more features or contents? If you plan to develop something to sell on Apple Store, this is the technology you need to handle payment processing through Apple Store. For more information about In-App Purchase, refer to the article *In-App Purchase Programming Guide* from Apple's iOS Developer Library.

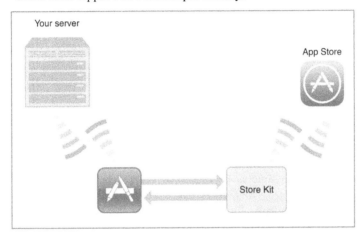

**Figure 2.16** In-App Purchase framework

2   **Empty** template. This template creates an empty project with no files, targets, or build configurations. It just creates a dummy project. Unless for very experienced developers, this template should be avoided in general.

Next, we explore project templates for OS X applications. Since we are less concerned with OS X, the purpose for the next section is for completeness only, rather than a detailed explanation of any template therein. Therefore, expect very light coverage for each template.

### 2.3.2   Project Templates for OS X

An OS X application falls into one of the following sub-categories:

■   Application
■   Framework & Library
■   Application Plug-in
■   System Plug-in
■   Other

The OS X/Application sub-category contains the following templates:

1   Cocoa Application template. Cocoa frameworks use Model-View-Controller (MVC) design pattern for developing applications on OS X, as shown in Figure 2.17. It's the counterpart

technology of iOS Cocoa Touch on OS X. You can learn more about it at Apple's website https://developer.apple.com/technologies/mac/cocoa.html.

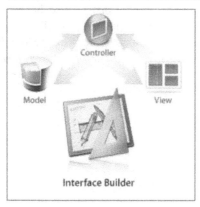

**Figure 2.17** The MVC pattern that Cocoa and Cocoa Touch depend on

2    SpriteKit Game template. This is the same as we described in the previous section for iOS except that it's for OS X.
3    Cocoa AppleScript Application template. This template is for developing Cocoa-based application using AppleScript, which is Apple's scripting language for MACs.
4    CommandLine Tool template. This template is for building a command-line tool on OS X.

The OS X/Framework & Library sub-category contains the following templates:

1    Cocoa Framework template. This template builds a framework that links against the Cocoa framework.
2    Cocoa Library template. This template builds a library that links against the Cocoa framework.
3    Bundle template. This template builds a bundle that links against the Cocoa or Cocoa Foundation framework.
4    XPC Service template. This template builds an XPC service. The XPC Services API provides a lightweight mechanism for basic inter-process communication that allows you to create lightweight helper tools, called XPC services, that perform work on behalf of your application.
5    C/C++ Library. This template builds a library written in C or C++.
6    STL C++ Library. This template builds a C++ dynamic shared library.

The OS X/Application Plug-in sub-category contains the following templates:

1    Automator Action template. This template builds an Automator action.
2    Address Book Action Plug-in. This template builds an Address Book action.
3    Installer Plug-in. This template builds a plugin to provide additional UI in an Installer application.

4    Quartz Composer Plug-in. This template builds a custom patch Quartz Composer as a
     QCPlugin subclass. Quartz Composer is a development tool for processing and rendering
     graphical data. Its visual programming environment lets you develop graphic processing
     modules, called compositions, without writing a single line of code.

The OS X/System Plug-in sub-category contains the following templates:

1    Generic C++ Plug-in. This template builds a generic C++ plug-in.
2    Generic Kernel Extension. This template builds a kernel extension.
3    Image Unit Plug-in. This template builds an Image Unit for Core Image.
4    IOKit Driver. This template builds an IOKit driver. The I/O Kit is a collection of system
     frameworks, libraries, tools, and other resources for creating device drivers in OS X. It is
     based on an object-oriented programming model implemented in a restricted form of C++.
5    Preference Pane. This template builds a preference pane bundle that can be used with the
     System Preference application.
6    Quick Look Plug-in template. This template builds a Quick Look generator plug-in.
7    Screen Saver template. This template builds a screen saver bundle that can be used with the
     Desktop & Screen Saver panel in the System Preferences application.
8    Spotlight Importer template. This template builds a Core Data Spotlight Importer. Core Data
     helps you manage a graph of objects in your program and save the graph to a persistent store,
     while Spotlight is a fast desktop search technology that allows users to organize and search
     for files based on metadata. To integrate a Core Data-based program with Spotlight, you have
     to provide the Spotlight importer to index the data in your persistent store.

The OS X/Other sub-category includes the following templates:

1     In-App Purchase Content template. Same as for iOS except it's for OS X.
2    Empty template. This template creates a dummy project with no files, targets, or build
     configurations.
3    External Build System template. This template builds a build tool using an external build
     system.

This concludes our introduction to various iOS and OS X project templates. We certainly will not
cover all of them, but it's good to know what templates exist on Xcode that can assist you
developing various types of applications on iOS and OS X.

## 2.4  SUMMARY

In this chapter, we focused on setting up an Xcode IDE and becoming familiar with various
project templates to help you get up to speed with iOS programming quickly. In the next chapter,
we anatomize a simple iOS program to help you learn some of the most basic concepts and
building blocks that apply to every iOS program. That would be more beneficial than having you
dive into coding immediately without understanding some of the fundamental elements associated
with iOS programming.

# 3 The Anatomy of a Simple iOS Program

In the previous chapter, we learnt how to set up and how to get around on an Xcode IDE. We also explained various templates for creating different kinds of applications. In this chapter, we anatomize the simple "Hello, iOS!" application we created in the previous chapter and explore the most basic building blocks that an iOS app must have. This is a common set of basic elements that many other iOS apps must have as well; therefore, although this sample is simple, it will help establish a solid base for us to explore examples that are more complex later.

Let us start with the files created by Xcode for that simple "Hello, iOS!" sample first.

## 3.1 BASIC BUILDING BLOCKS OF AN IOS APP

I assume that you once followed the instructions in the preceding chapter and created the "Hello, iOS!" app as shown in Figure 2.11. If not, please create it by following the instructions given there. Either way, you should see a project created with Xcode on your Mac OS X similar to Figure 3.1.

As is seen in Figure 3.1, under the project "Hello-iOS," there are four folders created:

- Hello-iOS
- Hello-iOSTests
- Frameworks
- Products.

Since we did not enter any code ourselves, the files created in those folders are all boilerplate code. In this section, we explain what those files are meant for.

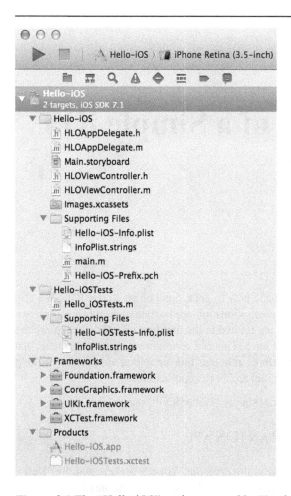

**Figure 3.1** The "Hello-iOS" project created by Xcode

However, before we proceed, make sure that the project has been created by Xcode correctly. To verify it, click the icon ▶ located left most on the Xcode tool bar (or if you place your pointer over it, it should display *Build and then run the current scheme*); then you should see a brief message "Build succeeded" and then a screen similar to Figure 3.2(a) generated from the iOS simulator as part of Xcode. If you own an iPhone, it should look familiar to you except that it does not have any apps on its Home screen. A few things to explain here:

■   This simulator displayed a time of "9:06 PM," which was actually the time when the screenshot was taken. The left-hand side is a carrier icon and the right-hand side is a battery icon. You can also easily identify all other parts on an iPhone device specifically.

■   It's important to know that the iOS simulator can only simulate one *scheme* a time. (In this case, it was *iPhone Retina (3.5-inch)*. If you locate the '*Set the active scheme*" icon and click on it, you could get more schemes as shown in Figure 3.2 (b). As you see, this simulator can simulate three iPhone schemes and three iPad schemes. You can close the current run by clicking om the icon ■ there on the tool bar and try different schemes if you want.

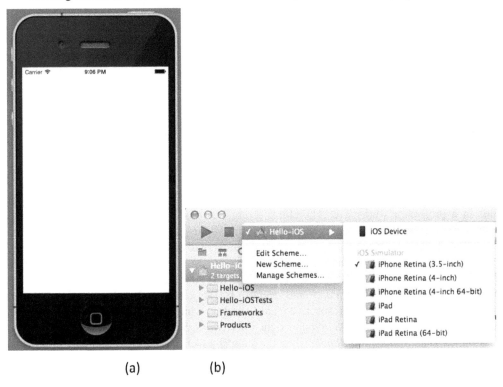

(a)                    (b)

**Figure 3.2 (a -left)** An empty iPhone screen from the iOS simulator; (**b-right**) Various iOS device schemes

Next, we explore those four project folders as shown in Figure 3.1 above.

## 3.1.2    Products/Bundles

You might already know that the newest fashion with building software is based on the concept of *bundles*. This is especially true with building enterprise software by adopting the OSGi technologies with loosely coupled components, which are dynamic and flexible. The three pillars of OSGi are *modules*, *services* and *life cycle*, as shown in Figure 3.3. However, that OSGi model runs on a Java VM (virtual machine), while iOS apps and bundles run natively on iOS directly without relying on a VM, and the end result of it is superior performance with iOS. (You can learn more about OSGi at http://www.osgi.org/Technology/WhatIsOSGi ). Sorry for the digression and let's continue exploring the concept of bundles for iOS apps.

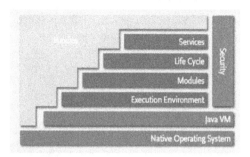

**Figure 3.3** OSGi bundles built on a layered model for building dynamic, modular software

In order to explain what an iOS *bundle* is, we need to explain the concept of an iOS *target* first. According to an article named *Xcode Concepts* that can be found in the *iOS Developer Library*, a target specifies a product to build and contains the instructions for building the product from a set of files in a project or workspace. Therefore, a target is basically a product and a bundle is basically a product built from a specified target. For this simple sample, you can identify in Figure 3.1 that this project has two targets, because of which two products are displayed under the *Products* folder: *Hello-iOS.app* and *Hello-iOSTests.xctest*. (XC Test is a test framework for iOS, which makes it possible for us to click the Run tab and test this sample as demonstrated in Figure 3.2.) If you click on *Hello-iOS.app* and *Hello-iOSTests.xctest* under the *Products* folder, respectively, you would see their respective identity and type under the *file inspector* as shown in Figure 3.4 – left for the *Hello-iOS.app* and right for *Hello-iOSTests.xctest*, respectively. As you see, the former is an *Application Bundle* while the latter is a *Core Foundation Bundle*.

**Identity and Type**

| | |
|---|---|
| Name | Hello-iOSTests.xctest |
| Type | Core Foundation Bundle |
| Location | Relative to Build Products |
| | Hello-iOSTests.xctest |
| Full Path | /Users/henry/Library/Developer/Xcode/ DerivedData/Hello-iOS- bogkhxpykhknyoctlfkyglhkdeai/Build/ Products/Debug-iphoneos/Hello- iOSTests.xctest |

**Localization**

Localize...

**Identity and Type**

| | |
|---|---|
| Name | Hello-iOS.app |
| Type | Application Bundle |
| Location | Relative to Build Products |
| | Hello-iOS.app |
| Full Path | /Users/henry/Library/Developer/Xcode/ DerivedData/Hello-iOS- bogkhxpykhknyoctlfkyglhkdeai/Build/ Products/Debug-iphoneos/Hello- iOS.app |

**Target Membership**

☐ Hello-iOS
☐ Hello-iOSTests

**Target Membership**

☐ Hello-iOS
☐ Hello-iOSTests

**Figure 3.4** Two iOS bundles created by Xcode

I hope we have clearly explained what iOS bundles are. Specific to the "Hello, iOS" project, those two bundles enable us to test a target when we clicked on the Run tab.

Next, we explore the Framework folder.

### 3.1.3    Linked Frameworks and Libraries

As we explained in Chapters 1 and 2, we do not develop iOS apps from scratch. Instead, we build apps by using some of the built-in iOS frameworks offered by Apple. To confirm that recommended practice, Figure 3.5 shows the frameworks added automatically by Xcode to this sample project. (I hope this also helps convince you the advantage of developing an iOS using a fully-fledged IDE like Xcode.) As is seen, under the *General* tab in the content area, three frameworks were added:

- CoreGraphics.framework
- UIKit.framework
- Foundation.framework.

Note that each framework can be made *Required* or *Optional*.

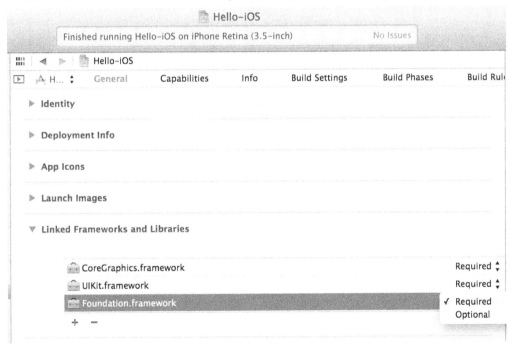

**Figure 3.5** Automatically added frameworks by Xcode for the "Hello, iOS!" project

In fact, you can explore each framework by opening it in the Frameworks folder shown in Figure 3.1 and expanding the *Headers* folder. For example, if you open the

*Foundation.framework/Headers* folder, you would see many header files with the .h extension, which are the interfaces defined by that framework. We'll come back to those frameworks later when we discuss the remaining two folders of *Hello-iOSTests* and *Hello-iOS*.

## 3.1.4    The Hello-iOSTets bundle

As you can see in Figure 3.1, under the *Hello-iOSTests* folder, there is a *Hello_iOSTests.m* file and a folder, *Supporting Files* with two files: *Hello-iOSTests-Info.plist* and *InPlist.strings*. In iOS, every file with a *.plist* extension is a *property list* file, which is a structured test file containing essential configuration for a bundled executable. The file with the *.strings* extension contains localized values, which are separated from the *Info.plist* file. If you're curious about the contents of the *Hello-iOSTests-Info.plist* file for this sample, refer to Figure 3.6. Otherwise, let us focus on explaining the *Hello_iOSTests.m* file next, which contains the test code logic to be executed.

| Key | Type | Value |
|---|---|---|
| ▼ Information Property List | Dictionary | (8 items) |
| Localization native develop... | String | en |
| Executable file | String | ${EXECUTABLE_NAME} |
| Bundle identifier | String | com.perfmath.${PRODUCT_NAME:rfc1034identifi( |
| InfoDictionary version | String | 6.0 |
| Bundle OS Type code | String | BNDL |
| Bundle versions string, short | String | 1.0 |
| Bundle creator OS Type code | String | ???? |
| Bundle version | String | 1 |

**Figure 3.6** Property list file added by Xcode automatically to the sample

Finally, we come to a point that we could look at some source files. First, if you have never learnt Objective-C, note that Objective-C is rooted in C, both of which use .h extension to define header files, but C uses *.c* extension for C implementation files, whereas Objective-C uses *.m* extension for Objective-C implementation files. (Regarding why letter *m*, some say it stands for "*methods*" while some say it stands for "*messages*," as the *class* part of Objective-C is patterned on SmallTalk, which invokes the methods of an object by passing messages. Nevertheless, from our perspective of learning iOS programming, it doesn't matter much what it stands for after all.)

Now let's explain the test file named Hello_iOSTests.m, as shown in Listing 3.1. This file contains the following basic Objective-C constructs:

■    **The** #import **statement**: As explained earlier, application developers rarely need to develop an app from scratch. Instead, they need to try to use relevant, existing frameworks and libraries as much as possible; so a large part of the learning curve is to get familiar with the applicable frameworks. In this sample, the beginning statement of #import <XCtest/XCTest.h> does just that. Note the general statement syntax for importing a framework is:

```
#import <FrameworkName/FrameworkName.h>
```

- **The @interface section**: The next block marked by the @interface and @end keywords defines an interface section for the class being defined and implemented. The general syntax for defining an interface is:

```
@interface ClassName : ParentClassName
    propertyAndMethodDeclarations
@end
```

- **The @implementation section**: This is the section that implements the class defined by the @interface section. Once again, it's defined by the two markers of @implementation and @end, with the following general syntax:

```
@implementation ClassName
{
    //Properties;
}
// methodDeclarations
(<methodType>) <methodName> : (<parameter type>) paramName
{
    //Method body;
}
@end
```

A few more things to note:

1   **The "–" sign at the beginning of each method definition**: The leading minus sign (–) signifies to the Objective-C compiler that the method is an instance method. If a "+" sign is there, it signifies a class method. An instance method performs operations on the instances of a class, while a class method performs operations on the class itself, for example, creating a new instance of the class.

2   **How an Objective-C method is called**: Objective-C has its unique way of calling a method. The general syntax is shown as follows for a class or an instance, where the whole thing is enclosed by a pair of square brackets with <className> or <instanceName> <space> followed by the <methodName> to be called, which is further followed by a colon sign ":" and a comma-separated parameter list if any (this may look strange if you have gotten used to C++ or Java, but you need to get used to it for obvious reasons):

    ```
    [className methodName : <paramList>];
    [instanceName methodName : <paramList>];
    ```

3   **How a method from the parent class is called**: Note the [super setup] and [super teardown] methods are called in the Hello_iOSTests class, which is how the setup and tearDown methods of its parent class are called. These two methods are parameter-less, so they are called with no parameters provided.

4   **About the XCTFail method call**: If you want to find out about the XCTFail method call in the testExample method, you can find it out in the XCTestAssertions.h file in the XCTestFramework/Headers folder. Xcode provides self-documenting for all frameworks

that way, which really is convenient. Specifically for this method, that header file says it's for logging an error message, which is already obvious from that statement itself.

**Listing 3.1 Hello_iOSTests.m**

```objc
#import <XCTest/XCTest.h>

@interface Hello_iOSTests : XCTestCase

@end

@implementation Hello_iOSTests

- (void)setUp
{
    [super setUp];
    // Put setup code here. This method is called before the
    // invocation of each test method in the class.
}

- (void)tearDown
{
    // Put teardown code here. This method is called after the
    // invocation of each test method in the class.
    [super tearDown];
}

- (void)testExample
{
    XCTFail(@"No implementation for \"%s\"", __PRETTY_FUNCTION__);
}

@end
```

Next, we discuss the Hello-iOS bundle, which is the main part that we are most interested.

## 3.1.5    The Hello-iOS Bundle

The Hello-iOS bundle has quite a few files, such as:

- HLOAppDelegate.h/HLOAppDeletegate.m
- Main.storyboard
- HLOViewController.h/HLOViewController.m
- main.m in the *Supporting Files* folder

We examine these files one by one next to understand what they do. Let's start with the main.m file first.

Listing 3.2 shows the contents of the main.m file. It consists of the following sections:

- #*import*: It imports the UIKit framework, which is required for all view-based apps. It also imports the HLOAppDelegate interface, which is required by the UIApplicationMain method call to be explained below.

- *UIApplicationMain call*: This function call is for Application Launch, as explained in the article UIKit Function Reference from the iOS Developer Library. Its first two parameters, `argc` and `argv`, are from the main function; the third parameter is supposed to be an NSString like `NSString *principalClassName`, which is assumed to be `UIApplication` when a `nil` is specified. (See the following note for more about `UIApplication`.) The last parameter `NSStringFromClass` is explained below.

- *NSStringFromClass*: This method returns the name of a class as a string. In this case, it returns the name of the class HLOAppDelegate by calling `[HLOAppDelegate class]`. See the following note for more about the `UIApplication` function.

**Listing 3.2 main.m**

```
#import <UIKit/UIKit.h>
#import "HLOAppDelegate.h"

int main(int argc, char * argv[])
{
    @autoreleasepool {
    return UIApplicationMain(argc, argv, nil,
      NSStringFromClass([HLOAppDelegate class]));
    }
}
```

☛ **More about UIApplication**: According to the article *UIApplicatoin Class Reference* from the iOS Developer Library, the `UIApplication` class provides a centralized point of control and coordination for apps running on iOS. Every app must have exactly one instance of a `UIApplication` (or a subclass of `UIApplication`). When an application is launched, the `UIApplicationMain` is called, which creates a singleton `UIApplication` object, among its other tasks. Thereafter this object is accessed by invoking the `sharedApplication` class method.

A major role of a `UIApplication` object is to handle the initial routing of incoming user events. It also dispatches action messages forwarded to it by control objects (`UIControl`) to the appropriate target objects. In addition, the `UIApplication` object maintains a list of all the windows (`UIWindow` objects) currently open in the application so that it can retrieve any of the application's `UIView` objects. The application object is typically assigned a delegate, an object that the application informs of significant runtime events—for example, application launch, low-memory warnings, and application termination—giving it an opportunity to respond appropriately.

☛ **More about NSStringFromClass**: This class is declared in NSObjCRuntime.h from the Foundation framework. In addition to support C-strings, which are a series of characters terminated with a null character, Objective-C has its own String object, which is NSString. A C-string is output with the format "%s" while an NSString object is output with the format "%@", as is shown in a modified version of the HelloWorld program in Listing 3.3. This program would not run if "%@" were changed to "%s".

**Listing 3.3 A program illustrating NSString and NSStringFromClass**

```
#import <Foundation/Foundation.h>

int main(int argc, const char * argv[])
{

    @autoreleasepool {

        NSLog(@"Hello, World!");
        NSLog(@"className of NSCache: \"%@\"",
            NSStringFromClass([NSCache class]));
    }
    return 0;
}
```

As is shown in Listing 3.2, the HLOAppDelegate object is passed to the UIApplicationMain object. We now explore what this delegate class is about.

Listings 3.4 and 3.5 show the pair of HLOAppDelegate interface and implementation files. First, as is seen from the interface definition file, HLOAppDelegate.h file, it imports the UIKit framework. Then, it is seen that the HLOAppDelagate class extends the UIResponder class, which defines an interface for objects that respond to and handle events – both touch events and motion events. UIResponder is the superclass of UIApplication, UIView and its subclasses such as UIWindow. Instances of these classes are referred to as responder objects or, simply, responders. A responder object's responsibilities include:

- Managing the responder chain
- Managing input views
- Responding to touch events
- Responding to motion events
- Responding to remote-control events
- Getting the undo manager
- Validating commands
- Accessing available key commands
- Managing text input mode

The UIApplicationDelegate protocol declares methods that are implemented by the delegate of the singleton UIApplication object. Those methods provide you with information about key events in an app's execution such as when it finished launching, when it is about to be terminated, when memory is low, and when important changes occur. Implementing these methods gives you a chance to respond to these system events and respond appropriately.

One of the main jobs of the app delegate is to track the state transitions an app goes through while it is running. Apps can be in the not running, inactive, active, background or suspended state. Transitions between these states often require a response from your app to ensure that it is doing the right thing. For example, a background app would need to stop updating its user interface. You provide the response to these transitions using the methods of the app delegate.

Launch time is also a particularly important point in an app's life cycle. In addition to the user launching an app by tapping its icon, an app can be launched in order to respond to a specific type of event. For example, it could be launched in response to an incoming push notification, it could be asked to open a file, or it could be launched to handle some background event that it had requested. In all of these cases, the options dictionary passed to the application:didFinishLaunchingWithOptions: method provides information about the reason for the launch.

In situations where the app is already running, the methods of the app delegate are called in response to key changes. Although the methods of this protocol are optional, most or all of them should be implemented.

In iOS 6 and later, the app delegate also plays an important role in restoring and preserving the state of your app. The delegate tells UIKit whether state restoration and preservation should proceed at all. It may also provide view controller objects in some cases, acting as the last chance for your app to provide a view controller object during restoration.

For more information about the launch cycle of an app and how to manage state transitions using the methods of an app delegate, see *iOS App Programming Guide*. For more information about the UIApplication singleton class, see *UIApplication Class Reference*.

The UIWindow class defines an object known as a *window* that manages and coordinates the views an app displays on a device screen. Unless an app can display content on an external device screen, an app has only one window.

The two principal functions of a window object are to provide an area for displaying its views and to distribute events to the views. To change the content your app displays, you can change the window's root view; you don't create a new window. A window belongs to a level—typically, UIWindowLevelNormal—that represents where it sits on the z-axis relative to other windows. For example, a system alert window appears above normal app windows.

A UIWindow's responsibilities include:

- Configuring windows
- Making key windows (A key window is the one that is designated to receive keyboard and other non-touch related events. Only one window at a time can be the key window.)
- Converting coordinates
- Sending events

◀ **More about UIWindow**: When you use storyboards and an Xcode app template to create an app, a window is created for you. If you choose to create a window in Interface Builder, be sure to select the Full Screen at Launch option in the Attributes inspector so that the window is sized appropriately for the current device. Because a window doesn't receive touch events outside of its bounds and views aren't clipped to the window's bounds by default, an improperly sized window might not be able to deliver touch events to all its views.

Also, note in Listing 3.4 that the HLOAppDelegate adopts the <UIApplicationDelegate> protocol. We'll talk more about delegate and protocol later. In addition, note how the window property is declared using one of the possible modifiers of ([weak|strong], [atomic|nonatomic]), with the following implications:

- *weak* – reference count will not increase
- *strong* – reference count will increase
- *atomic* – thread-safe
- *nonatomic* – non-thread-safe but faster

### Listing 3.4 HLOAppDelegate.h

```
#import <UIKit/UIKit.h>

@interface HLOAppDelegate : UIResponder <UIApplicationDelegate>

@property (strong, nonatomic) UIWindow *window;

@end
```

The implementation of HLOAppDelegate class has the following six methods:

- application: didFinishLaunchingWithOptions
- applicationWillResignActive
- applicationDidEnterBackground
- applicationWillEnterForground
- applicationDidBecomeActive
- applicationWillTerminate

It's obvious what each of these methods do according to the comments generated by Xcode automatically, so we would not spend more time to explain here.

### Listing 3.5 HLOAppDelegate.m

```
#import "HLOAppDelegate.h"

@implementation HLOAppDelegate

- (BOOL)application:(UIApplication *)application
didFinishLaunchingWithOptions:(NSDictionary *)launchOptions
{
    // Override point for customization after application launch.
    return YES;
```

```
}

- (void)applicationWillResignActive:(UIApplication *)application
{
    // Sent when the application is about to move from active to inactive
    // state. This can occur for certain types of temporary interruptions
    // (such as an incoming phone call or SMS message) or when the user
    // quits the application and it begins the transition to the
    // background state.
    // Use this method to pause ongoing tasks, disable timers, and
    // throttle down OpenGL ES frame rates. Games should use this method
    // to pause the game.
}


- (void)applicationDidEnterBackground:(UIApplication *)application
{
    // Use this method to release shared resources, save user data,
    // invalidate timers, and store enough application state information
    // to restore your application to its current state in case it is
    // terminated later.
    // If your application supports background execution, this method is
    // called instead of applicationWillTerminate: when the user quits.
}


- (void)applicationWillEnterForeground:(UIApplication *)application
{
    // Called as part of the transition from the background to the
    // inactive state; here you can undo many of the changes made on
    // entering the background.
}

- (void)applicationDidBecomeActive:(UIApplication *)application
{
    // Restart any tasks that were paused (or not yet started) while the
    // application was inactive. If the application was previously in the
    // background, optionally refresh the user interface.
}

- (void)applicationWillTerminate:(UIApplication *)application
{
    // Called when the application is about to terminate. Save data if
    // appropriate. See also applicationDidEnterBackground:.
}

@end
```

Listing 3.6 defines the HLOViewController interface. It just inherits the UIViewController interface from the UIKit framework, since our HelloWorld app is just an empty app and doesn't say "Hello, World!" yet. We'll see how it would change later after we add a label to enable it to say "Hello, World!" or something else.

**Listing 3.6 HLOViewController.h**

```
#import <UIKit/UIKit.h>

@interface HLOViewController : UIViewController

@end
```

Listing 3.7 shows the implementation of the HLOViewController class. It has only two methods: viewDidLoad and didReceiveMemoryWaring. They don't do anything other than call the respective methods from its parent class.

**Listing 3.7 HLOViewController.m**

```
#import "HLOViewController.h"

@interface HLOViewController ()

@end

@implementation HLOViewController

- (void) viewDidLoad
{
    [super viewDidLoad];
    // Do any additional setup after loading the view, typically from a
    // nib.
}

- (void) didReceiveMemoryWarning
{
    [super didReceiveMemoryWarning];
    // Dispose of any resources that can be recreated.
}

@end
```

The next file is named *Main.storyboard*. Because of its uniqeness, we dedicate a section to it next.

## 3.2  MAIN.STORYBOARD

Storyboard is a powerful feature available from Xcode since iOS 5. Its purpose is for saving time for developers when they build a view-centric app. A storyboard is a visual representation of the app's user interface, with explicit expressions of content and transitions from one view to another. In this section, I'll help you get familiar with the concept and usage of a storyboard using the simple Hello World program so that you will be able to build more complex apps using storyboards, rather than coding all UIs with bare-hands from scratch.

## 3.2.1    Initial Empty Storyboard

First, refer to Figure 3.7 for how the initial empty storyboard looks like.  It doesn't contain anything as we have not put anything on it yet. However, it's important to learn some common attributes with a storyboard as follows:

■   First, if you have not created this simple "Hello, iOS!" sample in your Xcode yet, create it now by following the instructions given in the previous chapter. Then click on the Main.storyboard file under the Hello-iOS folder in the left most navigation area, and you should get a similar content area and utility area as shown in Figure 3.7.

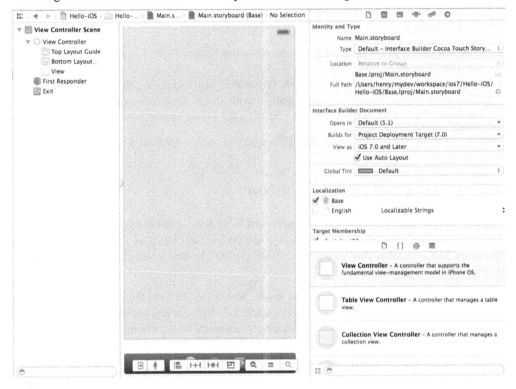

**Figure 3.7** The initial empty storyboard for the "Hello, iOS!" example

■   Now, expand the View Controller Scene around the upper left corner in the outline so that you could see the Top Layout Guide, Bottom Layout Guide, View, First Responder and Exit items beneath it.

■   Next, locate the icons at the bottom below the simulated iPhone screen. Identify the following icons by clicking on them:

o   Show/Hide Document Outline. This is the left-most icon with a symbol ◀ in it. By keeping clicking on it, it will toggle between showing/hiding the document outline.

- o   Apply … Form Factor. This is the icon with a symbol like 📱 in it. Keeping clicking on it will toggle between Retina 3.5-inch and 4-inch form factors.
- o   Align. This icon resembles a ▤ symbol, which allows us to add new alignment constraints.
- o   Pin. This icon resembles a ⊢⊣ symbol, which allows us to add new constraints.
- o   Resolve Auto Layout Issues. This icon resembles a ⊢●⊣ symbol, which helps resolve auto layout issues.
- o   Resizing Behavior. This icon resembles a square with a smaller square embedded, which decides when applying constraints to Siblings and Ancestors or Descendants when resizing views. The default is to apply constraints to Descendants.
- o   Zooming. The last three icons there, ⎡ 🔍 = 🔍 ⎤, are for Zoom out (-), Toggling Zoom (=), and Zoom in (+).

- ■   The last part is at the upper right corner showing Name, Type, Location, Full Path, Interface Builder Document, etc.
- ■   Finally, if you click on the Apply form factor icon, you should see those three icons below the simulated iPhone screen that are identical with those three icons of View Controller, First Responder, and Exit at the upper left corner under *View Controller Scene*, respectively.

Next, let us put a label on the simulated iPhone screen so that it would display "Hello, iOS!" when we click on it.

## 3.2.2    Adding Controls to the Storyboard

The process of building a UI using a storyboard is to drag controls over on to it and then hook them up in a consistent manner with various view controllers. Next, we illustrate how this process works by adding a label control with text "Hello, iOS!" so that when starting up the app, it will display the word "Hello, iOS!"

In order to achieve the objective as stated above, note many items in the Utility area located at the lower right corner of the screen shown in Figure 3.7. You should see the following items there (this is a lengthy list, but as an iOS developer, you should take a comprehensive cursory look at least once so that you would know what controls are available for you to drag to the storyboard, even though you may only need to use a small subset of them):

- ■   View Controller: This kind of controllers support the fundamental view-management model in iPhone OS.
- ■   Table View Controller: This kind of controllers manage a table view.
- ■   Collection View Controller: This kind of controllers manage a collection view.
- ■   Navigation Controller (you may need to scroll it down there in order to see this and other controllers there): This kind of controllers manage navigation through a hierarchy of views.
- ■   Tab Bar Controller: This kind of controllers manage a set of view controllers that represent tab bar items.
- ■   Page View Controller: This kind of controllers present a sequence of view controllers as pages.
- ■   GLKit View Controller: This kind of controllers manage a GLKit view.

- Object: This type provides a template for objects and controllers not directly available in the Interface Builder.
- Label: A control for holding a variably sized amount of static text.
- Button: A control that intercepts touch events and sends an action message to a target object when it's tapped.
- Segmented Control: A control that displays multiple segments, each of which functions as a discrete button.
- Text Field: A control that displays editable text and send an action message to a target object when return is tapped.
- Slider: A control that displays a continuous range of values and allows the selection of a single value.
- Switch: A control that displays an element showing the Boolean state of a value. It allows tapping the control to toggle the value.
- Activity Indicator View: A control that provides feedback on the progress of a task or process of unknown duration.
- Progress View: A control that depicts the progress of a task over time.
- Page Control: A control that displays a dot for each open page in an application and supports sequential navigation through the pages.
- Stepper: A control that provides a user interface for incrementing or decrementing a value.
- Table View: Displays data in a list of plain, sectioned, or grouped rows.
- Table View Cell: A control that defines the attributes and behavior of cells (rows) in a table view.
- Collection View: A control that displays data in a collection of cells.
- Collection View Cell: A control that defines the attributes and behavior of cells in a collection view.
- Collection Reusable View: A control that defines the attributes and behavior of reusable views in a collection view, such as a section header or footer.
- Image View:  A control that displays a single image or an animation described by an array of images.
- Text View: A control that displays multiple lines of editable text and sends an action message to a target object when Return is tapped.
- Web View: A control that displays embedded web content and enables content navigation.
- Map View: Displays maps and provides an embeddable interface to navigate map content.
- Scroll View: A control that provides a mechanism to display content that is larger than the size of the app's window.
- Date Picker: Displays multiple rotating wheels to allow users to select dates and times.
- Picker View: A control that displays a spinning-wheel or slot-machine motif of values.
- Ad BannerView: The ADBannerView class provides a view that displays banner advertisements to the user.
- GLKit View: A control that provides a default implementation of an OpenGL ES-aware view.
- Tap Gesture Recognizer: Provides a recognizer for tap gestures invoked on the view.
- Pinch Gesture Recognizer: A control that provides a recognizer for pinch gestures invoked on the view.

- Rotation Gesture Recognizer: A control that provides a recognizer for rotation gestures invoked on the view.
- Swipe Gesture Recognizer: A control that provides a recognizer for swipe gestures invoked on the view.
- Pan Gesture recognizer: A control that provides a recognizer for panning (dragging) gestures invoked on the view.
- Long Press Gesture Recognizer: A control that provides a recognizer for long press gestures invoked on the view.
- View: A control that represents a rectangular region in which it draws and receives events.
- Container View: A control that defines a region of a view controller that can include a child view controller.
- Navigation Bar: Provides a mechanism for displaying a navigation bar just below the status bar.
- Navigation Item: A control that represents a state of the navigation bar, including a title.
- Search Bar: A control that displays an editable search bar, containing the search icon, that sends an action message to a target object when Return is tapped.
- Search Bar and Search Display Controller: A control that displays an editable search bar connected to a search display controller for managing searching.
- ToolBar: Provides a mechanism for displaying a toolbar at the bottom of the screen.
- Bar Button Item: Represents an item on a UIToolBar or UINavigationItem object.
- Fixed Space Bar Button Item: Represents a fixed space item on a UIToolBar object.
- Flexible Space Bar Button Item: Represents a flexible space item on a UIToolbar object.
- Tab Bar: A control that provides a mechanism for displaying tabs at the bottom of the screen.
- Tab Bar Item: A control that represents an item on a UITabBar object.

If you have followed along to here, you now know what controls are available to drag to the storyboard for your application. Note that there is a search area at the bottom of the Utility area for you to search the control you are interested in. See Figure 3.7 and look at its lower right corner for the search bar with a half-moon icon at its beginning. Type *Label* and hit Return. Clicking on it should bring up a pop-up similar to Figure 3.8 that explains more about the label control.

After reviewing the descriptions about the label control and hitting the *Done* button, drag it to the storyboard by holding down on the lower left corner of your touchpad while dragging it to the storyboard. You should have a label control dragged to the storyboard as shown in Figure 3.8. Then stretch the label's left side towards left until you see the dotted blue borderline appear, and stretch the label's right side towards right until you see the dotted blue borderline appear. Now we can customize this label control as follows:

- **Enter the text**: Locate the text field between the attributes of "Text" and "Color" and change it to "Hello, iOS!" or your own favorite hello message.
- **Center the text**: With the label still selected, click on the "Show the Attributes Inspector" icon located at the upper Inspector bar. Look for the Alignment attribute and select the middle icon to center the text.
- **Change the font**: If you want to change the font, locate the Font attribute and click on the icon with a letter "T" in it. Change Font from System to Custom, select the font and style in their respective drop-down menus, and choose a font size you like. Click Done button to exit.

■  Press Command-S to save it (Xcode actually saves automatically). Press the Run button on the tool bar, and you should see a simulated iPhone with a "Hello, iOS!" message as shown in Figure 3.9. (You can rotate it by pressing Command-<left arrow key> on your keyboard to change from portrait to landscape mode.)

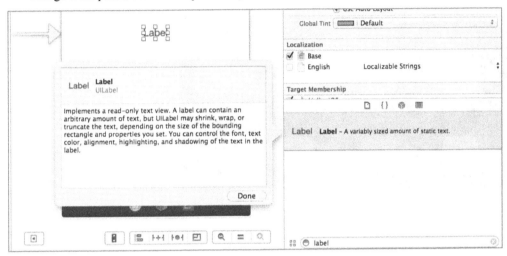

**Figure 3.8** A label control dragged to the storyboard with a pop-up showing a more detailed explanation about the label control

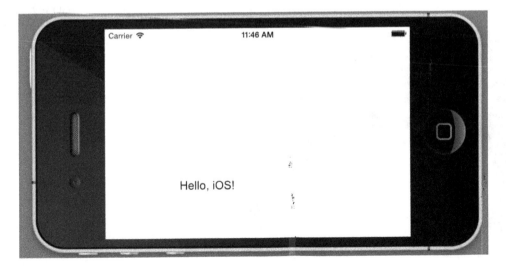

**Figure 3.9** A "Hello, iOS!" message displayed on a simulated iOS screen

You can experiment with it further by doing the following:

- Cycle through the items under View Controller Scene and see how UI responds.
- Change the scheme and re-run it and see what difference each of them makes. For example, when I changed the scheme to iPad Retina and ran the app, I got something similar to Figure 3.10.

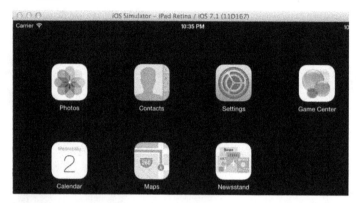

**Figure 3.10** Simulating an iPad Retina

So we don't see a "Hello, iOS!" screen anymore? Actually, if you scroll down to the bottom on your simulated iPad home page, you should see two dots above the Safari browser icon. Click on the second dot and you should see an icon for the "Hello, iOS!" app. Click on it and you should see a screen similar to Figure 3.11. At the lower right bottom corner, you should see a circled "1x" or "2x" icon, which allows you to toggle the size of the app. To quit the app, press Command-Q.

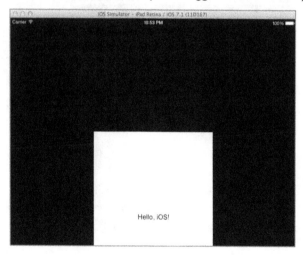

**Figure 3.11** "Hello, iOS!" on a simulated iPad (partial)

Note that we don't seem to see the "Hello, iOS!" message written into any of the files created for the project. If we want to change it to something else, we'll have to change it on the storyboard. In the next chapter, we examine a more complex example, which allows us to interact with some of the implementation files created automatically by Xcode.

Before we conclude this chapter, I'll show you another feature built into Xcode, that is, monitoring and profiling the apps you build.

## 3.3  MONITORING AND PROFILING THE PERFORMANCE OF AN APP

You can monitor and profile your applications to make sure that it will perform and your users will be satisfied. This sample is very primitive, but it is good enough for us to explore the monitoring and profiling features that Xcode provides out-of-the-box. These two features are separate, so we introduce them in two separate sections. To demo these two features, change your scheme to iPhone and start it up. The initial screen may look like Figure 3.12a, and if that's the case, click the second dot above the Safari icon, which should display the "Hello, iOS!" app icon. Click on that icon, which should turn the screen to something similar to Figure 3.12b. To switch back to the Home screen as shown in Figure 3.12a, press the Home button at its bottom.

**Figure 3.12** (a – left) initial Home screen and (b – right) the "Hello, iOS!" app

You might wonder how you can remove the app from the simulated iOS device. The simulated iOS device actually supports removing an app. You just hold down at the left bottom corner of your touchpad for a few seconds until the app icon starts wiggling. Figure 13.3 shows the simulated iPhone screens before (left) and after (right) I held down the left bottom corner of my touchpad. Then click on the "x" icon at the upper left corner of your app icon and a popup window appears with a "Delete" and "Cancel" button for you to select. Select "Delete" and your app should disappear. If you don't want to delete your app, simply click the Home button located at the bottom of your simulated iPhone screen and your app icon should stop wiggling.

**Figure 3.13** The iPhone screens before (left) and after (right) the left bottom corner of the touchpad was held down.

## 3.3.1   Monitoring the Performance of your App

To monitor the performance of your app, first start up your app on the simulated device of your choice. Then locate the "Show the Debug Navigator" icon ≣ on the Navigator bar and click it. Then select the CPU category and you should see a screen similar to Figure 3.14. It is seen that there are two parts: Percentage Utilized by the app and Utilization Comparison with other processes. As you see, the total CPU utilization adds up to 400% on my 13.3" Core i5 based MacBook Pro Retina.

If you click on the Memory category, you should see a screen similar to Figure 3.15. It's similar to CPU utilization charts that it shows both the memory used by the app running and comparison with other processes. It's seen that this app used 9.1 MB.

**Figure 3.14** Monitoring CPU utilizations while a simulated iOS device is running

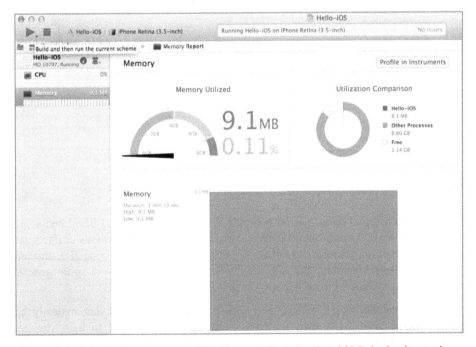

**Figure 3.15** Monitoring memory utilizations while a simulated iOS device is running

Next, let us see how to profile your app using another feature of Xcode called Instruments.

## 3.3.2    Profiling your App

If you look at the upper right corner either in Figure 3.14 or 3.15, you should see a label "Profile in Instruments." Clicking on that label would bring up a screen similar to Figure 13.16. Similar to other profiling tools, the Instruments tool can display call trees associated with the running app. You might want to explore this interesting feature further if you are interested in optimizing the performance of your app running on a simulated iOS device, but it would make more sense to do monitoring and profiling on a physical device than on the simulator.

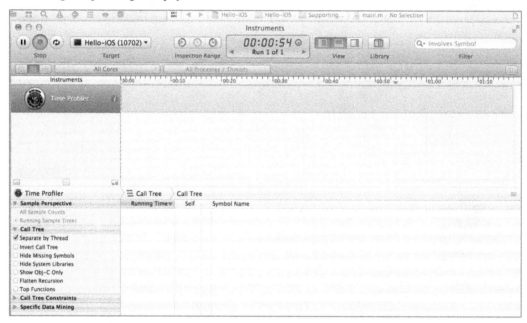

**Figure 13.16** The Instruments panel available on Xcode for profiling iOS apps

## 3.4    SUMMARY

In this chapter, we demonstrated how to build a simple "Hello, iOS!" app and illustrated some basic building blocks of an iOS app in general. We explained in detail how various artifacts are organized in the workspace of a project to help you get familiar with the Xcode IDE further. Being able to code is very important, but it's equally important to understand some general concepts such as products, bundles, linked frameworks and libraries, and so on.

In addition, we examined the source code of the boilerplate files generated automatically by Xcode. Some commonly seen framework functions were covered in detail to help you get prepared for working on some more complicated examples throughout the remainder of the book.

Some programming constructs were explained from the Objective-C's perspective in case you were not very familiar with Objective-C.

We introduced the concept of a storyboard, which is a very powerful, intuitive tool for assisting developers in building user interfaces. We also covered how to test the sample on various iOS devices using the iOS simulator that comes with the Xcode IDE. Finally, we demonstrated how to monitor the resource utilizations of an app under test and even instrument it with the built-in profiler to obtain very useful profiles such as call trees to help us get deeper insights into the performance characteristics of the app under test.

The next chapter focuses on a more complicated example to help push your iOS programming skill to the next level.

# 4 Creating the NoteApp

In the preceding chapter, you learnt how to build and test a simple "Hello, iOS!" app, with many iOS programming concepts introduced. In addition, you learnt how to get around on the Xcode IDE on your OS X. This chapter walks you through a more advanced iOS app to help you solidify what you have learnt so far.

The sample we are going to build is named *NoteApp*, which allows a user to store important notes such as login credentials for the accounts either associated with certain websites or offline systems and applications. I used to use Microsoft OneNote to store such personal data for myself, but it's kind of inconvenient that I had to depend on a Windows PC and the OneNote app to access it.

Without further ado, let's get started with building the NoteApp that can be accessed on an iOS device next.

## 4.1 BOOTSTRAPPING THE NOTEAPP PROJECT

As introduced in Chapter 2, Xcode includes many built-in app templates that we can choose to build common types of iOS apps, such as apps with tab-based navigation, master-detail view apps such as various email apps, games, etc. The benefits with using such templates include automatically generated boilerplate source files and preconfigured interface, and so on. However, for our NoteApp app, we start with an empty application template to help us get deeper into how various important building blocks were created in the first place.

Let's create a new empty iOS application first.

### 4.1.1 Create a New Empty App

Since you have learnt how to create a new iOS project in the previous chapters, I will not include all screenshots for all steps. Just start up your Xcode, click Create a new Xcode project link on the Welcome page, select *iOS/Application* sub-category, then *Empty Application* and then click on *Next*. Enter Product Name, Organization Name, Company Identifier, Class Prefix and Devices as shown in Figure 4.1.

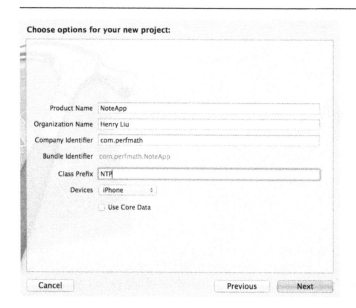

**Figure 4.1** Choose options for your new project

Now choose a folder for this project and click *Create*. In your Navigation area, you should see a structure similar to Figure 4.2, which should look familiar to you, given the "Hello, iOS!" sample we walked through in the preceding chapter. However, to help solidify what you have learnt in the preceding chapter, let us review some of the main elements we learnt previously as follows:

- Class Prefix Name. Xcode uses the class prefix name to name the classes it creates for you. There is a requirement that Objective-C classes must be named uniquely, and the convention is to use unique class name prefixes. Single letter class prefix names are rarely used because of the limited number of single letters available; so usually two-letter class prefix names are reserved by Apple for use in framework classes, while application classes can use three letter or more class prefix names. You might still remember the *NSLog* function we learnt previously, in which case '*NS*' is a two-letter class prefix name.

- Project Files. Compared with the project structure for the "Hello, iOS!" sample shown in Figure 3.1, it's seen that we have all artifacts except the Main.storyboard file and the VewController interface and implementation files, which is because that "Hello, iOS!" sample was created with a single-view app template, while this NoteApp app was created with an empty template . Note the same files created here, such as the AppDelegate interface and implementation files, main.m file, Foundation/CoreGraphics/UIKit/XCTest frameworks, and two Products NoteApp.app and NoteAppTests.xctest.

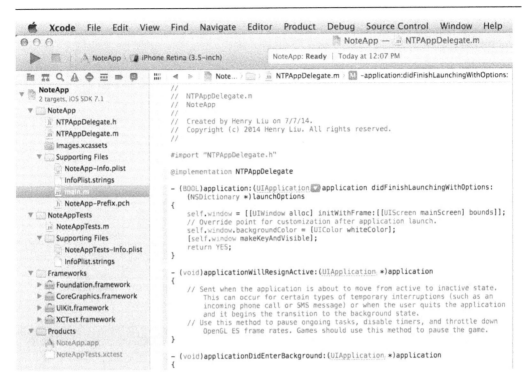

**Figure 4.2** The initial NoteApp created using the Empty Application template on Xcode

In addition, I'd like to introduce a nice feature on Xcode about how you could easily find out more about an interface. Refer to Figure 4.2 and notice the context menu near UIApplication interface. You would get that context menu when you right-click on an interface. Clicking on that menu would bring up a menu similar to Figure 4.3. Notice the *Search With Google* item? Selecting it would lead you to a search result page from Google, similar to Figure 4.4 showing UIApplication Class Reference and UIApplicationDelegate Protocol Reference from Apple's iOS Developer website. This is much more convenient than starting up a separate Google web page, enter the keyword UIApplication and click Search. Next, if you click on the first link shown in Figure 4.4, you would get instant access to the document for that interface as shown in Figure 4.5

```
@implementation NTPAppDelegate

- (BOOL)application:(UIApplication      ....li..ti.. .i.Fi.i.h..u..hi...O.ti..ns:
    (NSDictionary *)launchOptions          Edit All in Scope
{
    self.window = [[UIWindow alloc]                                       .nds]];
    // Override point for customizat     Search With Google
    self.window.backgroundColor = [U     Add to iTunes as a Spoken Track
    [self.window makeKeyAndVisible];
    return YES;
}
```

**Figure 4.3** Context menu associated with an interface

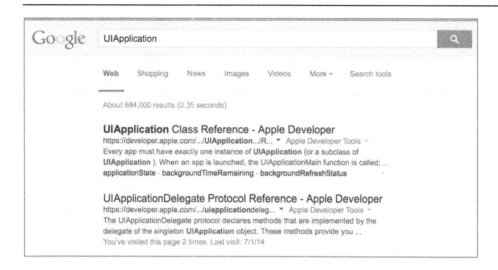

**Figure 4.4** Context-menu-driven search on Google for the UIApplication interface as seen on Xcode

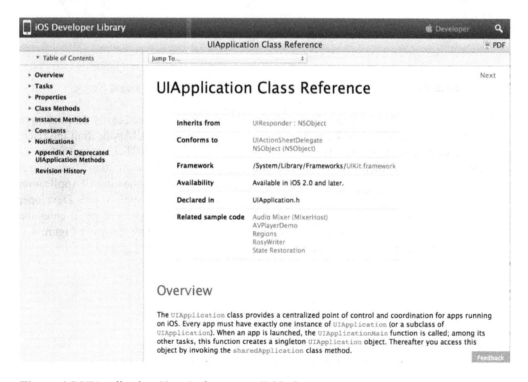

**Figure 4.5** UIApplication Class Reference available from Apple's iOS Developer Library

Besides the new context-menu-driven search feature as introduced above, you should click around on the workspace window for this project and get familiar one more time with various icons about where they would lead you if clicked.

Next, we review how you can test-run the initial NoteApp app on the iOS simulator.

## 4.1.2    Run NoteApp on the iOS Simulator

Although we have not put anything on the NoteApp yet so far, it's a good idea to test-run it once to make sure there are no errors introduced with it yet. This is a simple test as you have learnt from the previous chapter – simply click the Run button at the left-most of the tool bar or press Command-R. You should see a white simulated iPhone screen, which is omitted here to save space. However, I'd like to draw your attention to two areas in the workspace window for this app: the Activity Viewer up on the tool bar and the debug area down at the bottom. To help you identify those two areas, Figure 4.6 shows each area's screenshot, with the upper one being the activity viewer and the lower one being the debug area. Please identify them in your workspace window to get familiar with them.

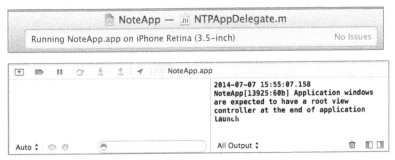

**Figure 4.6** Activity viewer (upper) and debug area (lower)

---

⬛ **Note**: To become a professional iOS app developer, get familiar with various parts of a product workspace window and use them frequently. For example, the icons in the debug area from left to right represent *Hide the Debug area, Toggle global breakpoint state, Pause program execution, Step over, Step into, Step out,* and *Simulate location.* Also, pay attention to the output messages displayed in the debug console.

---

## 4.2    CHECKING THE BOILERPLATE SOURCE CODE

To understand how the NoteApp app is bootstrapped, let us check the boilerplate source files created with the *Empty Application* template. We start with the main.m file, which represents the entry execution point to the app. This file is essentially the same as Listing 3.2 shown in the preceding chapter with one exception that the NSStringFromClass takes the NTPAppDelegate class as its parameter, as shown in Listing 4.1. Note that if you replace the class prefix name of "HLO" for the previous "Hello. iOS!" app with "NTP" for this app, you get the `main.m` file as shown in Listing 4.1 for this app. Once again, this shows the utility of the class prefix name.

**Note:** Single-clicking on a file opens it in the content pane, while double-clicking on it opens it in a separate window.

**Listing 4.1 main.m for the NoteApp app**

```
#import <UIKit/UIKit.h>
#import "NTPAppDelegate.h"

int main(int argc, char * argv[])
{
    @autoreleasepool {
    return UIApplicationMain(argc, argv, nil,
        NSStringFromClass([NTPAppDelegate class]));
    }
}
```

Listing 4.1 doesn't seem to be a lot. However, it reveals a few things that are common for all apps as we explain next.

**Note:** Objective-C has a unique way to invoke a method of a class or instance. It does that by sending a message to the class or instance in the format of
`[ ClassOrInstance method ];`

where *method* is the *message*. If you are familiar with other programming languages, such as Java or C++, this may look strange to you, but it's actually a reflection of the fact that Objective-C is patterned on SmallTalk – the first language that supports Object-Oriented Programming. The other way to express invoking the method of a class or instance is that you consider the class or instance as a receiver and method a message like the following:
`[ receiver message ];`

We'll see many such formats along the way.

## 4.2.1    ARC (Automatic Reference Counting)

The `@autoresourcepool` statement shown in Listing 4.1 specifies that Cocoa's memory reference-counted memory management is supported for your app. Since it's specified at the source code level, it designates that objects instantiated within that block will be automatically managed by keeping tracking of who owns an object. Since this is done at compile time, it's more efficient.

The concept of ARC is different from that of garbage collection. In a reference-counted environment, an `NSAutoreleasePool` object contains objects that have received an `autorelease` message and sends a `release` message to each of those objects when the pool is being drained. Thus, sending `autorelease` instead of `release` to an object extends the lifetime of that object until the pool is drained. Additionally, in a reference-counted environment, Cocoa expects there will be an autorelease pool always available; otherwise, autoreleased objects do not get released and your app leaks memory. However, as long as you use Application Kit with your app, you don't have to worry about it, as the Application Kit creates an autorelease pool by itself on the main thread at the beginning of every cycle of the event loop, and drains it at the end, which releases any autoreleased objects generated while processing an event. However, if your app creates many temporary autoreleased objects within the event loop, it may be beneficial to create "local" autoreleasepools to help minimize the peak memory footprint. For example, you can create a local autoreleasepool within a `for`-loop by using an `@autoreleasepool { ...}` block.

Figure 4.7 explains the concept of an object graph from the memory management point of view. Initially, an instance of Class A could be created with a statement like

```
ClassA *myClassA = [[ClassA alloc] init];
```

Then the retain count for `myClassA` becomes 1. Next, ClassB sends a `retain` message to that object, which increments the retain count to 2. Now, ClassC sends a `copy` message to that object, resulting in a retain count of 1 in the new, lower branch. Next, two separate sequences lead to the original object and the copied object destroyed:

- Upper branch: First ClassA and then ClassB send a release message to the original object, leading to no reference to the original object, which is destroyed.
- Lower branch: ClassC sends a release message to the copied object, decrementing its retain count to zero, which leads to the copied object destroyed.

Now it's important to understand that the concept of an object graph as described above is generic. Objective-C provides the following methods for application memory management:

- Manual Retain-Release (MRR), with which developers explicitly manage memory by specifying retain and/or release messages to objects to help keep tracking the reference count of each object.
- Automatic Reference Counting (ARC) that developers do not need to manually write code to send retain/release messages to objects; instead, such laborious tasks are taken care of by the compiler, which inserts necessary calls to send retain/release messages to various objects. This has significantly simplified memory management and made it much less error-prone.

Although both MRR and ARC help eliminate memory leaks, Apple recommends using ARC over MRR. In fact, ARC is the only memory management mechanism supported since iOS 5 and OS X 10.8.x. You can find more about how memory management has evolved from MRR to ARC from the article *Transitioning to ARC Release Notes* from Apple's *iOS Developer Library*.

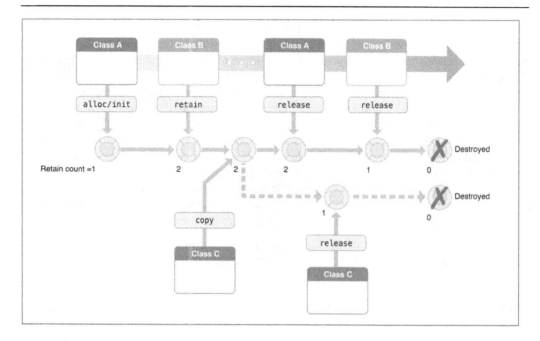

**Figure 4.7** The concept of an object graph

## 4.2.2    Two Initial Components

There are two initial components created in main.m as shown in Listing 4.1: UIApplicationMain and NTPAppDelegate. The UIApplicationMain object is called an *application object*. It is defined as follows:

```
int UIApplicationMain (
   int argc,
   char *argv[],
   NSString *principalClassName,
   NSString *delegateClassName
   );
```

In the above definition, principalClassName is the name of the UIApplication class or subclass, which defaults to UIApplication if a nil is specified; the delegateClassName is the name of the class from which the *application delegate* is instantiated. The UIApplicationMain function call instantiates the application object from the principal class and instantiates the delegate from the given class and sets the delegate for the application. It also sets up the main event loop, including the application's run loop, and begins processing events with the help of the delegate object as discussed next.

Listing 4.2 shows the app delegate interface, NTPAppDelegate. It's essentially the same as Listing 3.4 for the previous "Hello, iOS!" sample except that the class prefix name is different. Note the single property named window, which contains all app content to be drawn, driven by various events as they occur.

**Listing 4.2 NTPAppDelegate.h for the NoteApp app**

```
#import <UIKit/UIKit.h>
@interface NTPAppDelegate : UIResponder <UIApplicationDelegate>

@property (strong, nonatomic) UIWindow *window;
```

How does the application object call the delegate object? That is enabled with the skeleton methods from the delegate's implementation, which is shown in Listing 4.3.When a significant runtime event occurs, the application object calls the corresponding method in the app delegate to execute the proper logic. After launching the application, the application object will call the application:didFinishLaunchingWithOptions: method to execute the code (if any) within the method. You may notice that all methods except the first one in Listing 4.3 contain no code. That's because if a method is empty, then the default behavior takes place. For example, you can delete the three statements related to self.window in the method of didFinishLaunchingWithOptions and leave only the last statement of return YES there. If you are following the instructions given in this chapter instead of importing the downloaded sample for this chapter, delete those three lines of code as described above.

**Listing 4.3 NTPAppDelegate.m for the NoteApp app**

```
#import "NTPAppDelegate.h"

@implementation NTPAppDelegate

- (BOOL)application:(UIApplication *)application
didFinishLaunchingWithOptions:(NSDictionary *)launchOptions
{
    self.window = [[UIWindow alloc] initWithFrame:[[UIScreen mainScreen]
      bounds]];
    // Override point for customization after application launch.
    self.window.backgroundColor = [UIColor whiteColor];
    [self.window makeKeyAndVisible];
    return YES;
}

- (void)applicationWillResignActive:(UIApplication *)application
{
}

- (void)applicationDidEnterBackground:(UIApplication *)application
{
}

- (void)applicationWillEnterForeground:(UIApplication *)application
{
```

```
}

- (void)applicationDidBecomeActive:(UIApplication *)application
{
}

- (void)applicationWillTerminate:(UIApplication *)application
{
}

@end
```

## 4.3  ADDING A STORYBOARD

In the previous chapter, when we created the "Hello, iOS!" sample, a preconfigured storyboard was added to the project automatically. For this NoteApp app, we started with an Empty Application template with no storyboard added automatically.

To add a new storyboard to your product, follow the below procedure:

1    Select File > New > File (or press Command-N). Select iOS > Interface > Storyboard as shown in Figure 4.8. Note other options such as View, Empty, Window and Application, which are all called *Interface Builder document*. Click Next.

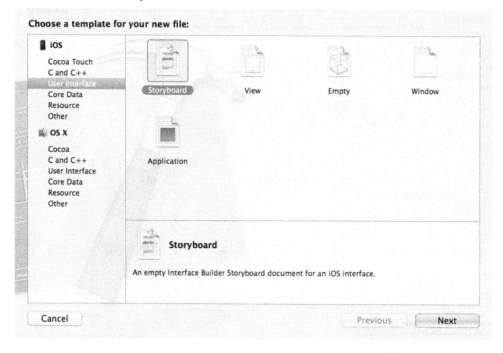

**Figure 4.8** Adding an empty Interface Builder Storyboard document for an iOS interface

2   On the dialog for *Choose options for your new file*, select iPhone for Device Family and click
    Next.
3   In the dialog window as shown in Figure 4.9, enter Main for Save As and accept all other
    default settings such as Where, Group and Targets. Click Create. Now you should see a
    `Main.storyboard` file created under your NoteApp project. If you click on that file, an empty
    content area appears in the center pane with no content yet. Next, I'll show you how to create
    content on that storyboard.

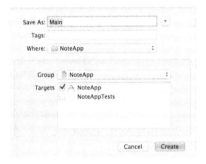

**Figure 4.9** Entries for a storyboard file

## 4.3.1    Setting the Storyboard as the App's Main Interface

The first thing we need to do with this new storyboard is to set it as the NoteApp's main interface.
To do this, follow the below procedure:

1   In the project navigator, select the NoteApp project.
2   At the upper left corner of the content area, toggle the disclosure triangle so that you could
    see Project and Targets entries as shown in Figure 4.10. This area is called *outline*.

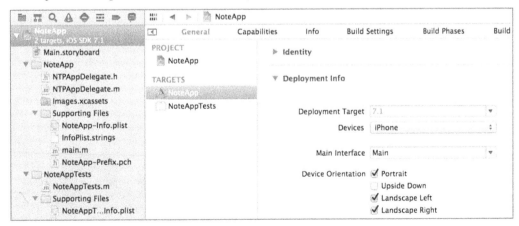

**Figure 4.10** Specifying Main.storyboard as the Main Interface for the NoteApp app

3    Under the General tab, hide Identity by clicking the triangle icon preceding it if it's not hidden.

4    Under Deployment Info, select Main.storyboard as the Main Interface for this app.

Next, let's add a scene to the storyboard we have just created.

## 4.3.2    Adding a Scene to the Storyboard

A storyboard is for storing app content for an app in addition to being a place for user interface design. The app content may consist of visible interface elements that belong in a view, such as buttons, labels, and text fields, as well as invisible elements such as view controllers and gesture recognizers that help define the behavior of the app. Such elements are added by dragging and dropping pre-built elements from the library of objects that Xcode provides.

In this section, we add a view controller and a label on the storyboard to create a simple scene. A view controller manages a view and its subviews. We will describe more about views and view controllers later. For now, we focus more on the Interface Builder and canvas, which are used to build and contain interface elements.

Now if you click on the Main.storyboard file, you should see a split pane in the content area with the left-hand-side outline area labeled "No Scenes," as shown in Figure 4.11. This represents a visual interface editor, which is also called the *Interface Builder*. This is an important tool for building storyboards. The right-had-side area is called a canvas for containing various elements.

Now drag a View Controller from the Object library to the canvas. Then add a label control as illustrated in Chapter 3 with the "Hello, iOS!" sample and change its text to "This is a test!." The content area turned from "No Scenes" as shown in Figure 4.11 into something similar to Figure 4.12, which represents a simple single scene consisting of a single view with a label control, managed by a view controller.

Note the arrow shown in Figure 4.12 that points to the simulated iPhone screen. As the *initial scene indicator*, that arrow means that the scene is loaded first when the app starts.

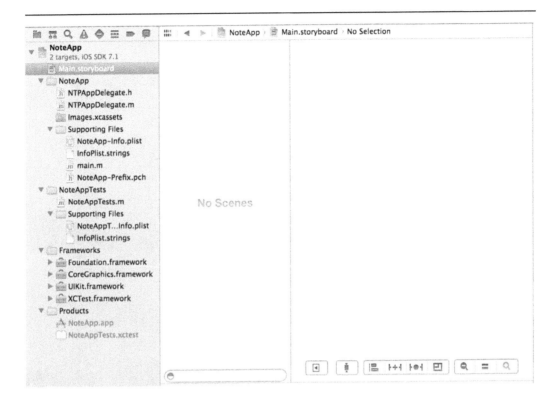

**Figure 4.11** A new storyboard with no scenes

Now you can explore further by completing the following exercise:

- Run this app as is and confirm that the message "This is a test!" shows up as expected. Click the Home button at the bottom so that you could see more items placed on the Home screen of the simulated iPhone device. Press Command-Q to quit the app.
- Click on various items under View Controller Scene, such as View Controller, Top Layout Guide, Bottom Layout Guide, View, Label, First Responder, and Exit, then note how the content changes in the content area.
- Click on View Controller, and then click on each utility editor, such as the File inspector, Quick Help inspector, Identity inspector, Attributes inspector, Size inspector, and Connections inspector, and observe the attributes associated with an inspector when it is clicked.
- Repeat the preceding exercise by clicking on View. This should help you understand further the associations between a view and a view controller.

Next, we illustrate how to add our first note on the NoteApp.

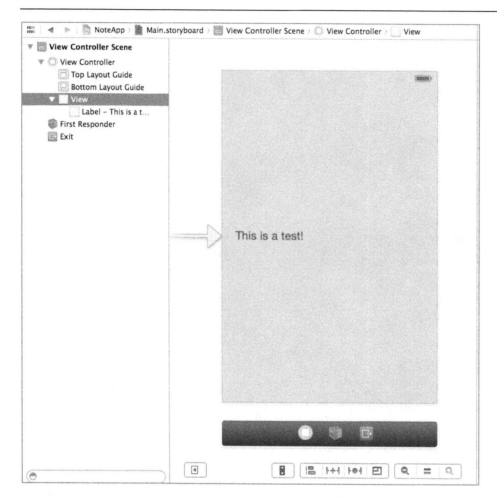

**Figure 4.12** A storyboard with a simple single scene consisting of a view controller and a label control

## 4.4   Adding the First Note Item

In this section, we show how to add the first note item to our NoteApp. In order to do this, we need to delete the label we created in the previous section for testing purposes. To delete that label, click on it to select it; then press the Delete key.

We decide that we use a test view rather than a text field for each note item. To add a text view control, locate the search bar at the bottom in the utility area, enter "text" and press Return. You should see two controls: Text Field and Text View. Here, you see the differences between the two: A Text Field displays editable text and sends an action message to a target object when Return is tapped, while a Text View displays *multiple lines of editable text* and sends an action message to a target when Return is tapped.

Now drag a Text View control to the canvas as you did with the Label control previously. You can move it to near the top of the screen. You can also resize a UI element by dragging its resize handles, which are small white squares that appear on the element's borders. While resizing, use the guidelines to determine when to stop resizing.

Next, let's add a placeholder text for the Text View control we have just added to the screen. While having your Text View control selected, select the Attributes inspector from the inspector selector bar at the upper right corner in the utility area. This is where you can edit the properties of an object on your storyboard. Now enter something like "A new note item here" or something else of your choice in the text field and then click away from it. (It does not support Return, so you have to click somewhere on the storyboard to move out of it.)

You can click the Run button to checkpoint your work so far. If everything went well, you should see a screen similar to Figure 4.13 (a). Once again, if you click the Home button, you should see a screen similar to Figure 4.13 (b). If you click on the dimmed dot next to the bright dot above the Safari icon, it should go back to the standard home screen. To quit the iPhone simulator, press Command-Q.

**Figure 4.13** (a - left) NoteApp capable of displaying one note item; (b-right) The NoteApp icon available in the home screen

However, the NoteApp so far is a bit too primitive to be useful, as it displays only one note item and lacks features for edit/delete an item, etc. We'll make it more complete one step a time in the next few chapters.

## 4.5 SUMMARY

In this chapter, we demonstrated how to create a basic interface using a storyboard. In the next few chapters, you'll learn how to add interactions to the interface and write code to create custom behavior. Along the way, you'll also learn some generic concepts that apply to building all types of interfaces.

# 5 Designing an App

Designing is the first step in the process of creating an app. This chapter helps you understand what issues you need to take into account when you design an app. The next chapter discusses issues associated with implementing an app.

## 5.1 APP DEVELOPMENT PROCESS

In order to be successful in producing an app, you need to follow a standard process that has all factors considered in a streamlined fashion. This section summarizes what app development process you need to follow.

### 5.1.1 Formalizing your Idea

All great things begin with great ideas, and great ideas come from great visions. When you have a great idea out of your great vision, you need to act quickly to formalize your idea, followed by well-planned actions.

When you formalize your idea, here are some of the aspects for you to consider:

■ **Who will use your app**? Your targeted users could be just many individual consumers who may need your app to help them solve some of their problems, or business users such as employees of some organizations. For example, it's very convenient to access your bank online using mobile devices so that you don't have to go to your bank in a physical location to deposit a check, etc. In this case, your users will just be many independent individuals. On the other hand, many organizations allow their employees to access corporate networks and business apps via personal mobile devices, and in this case, your users will be business users.

■ **What main contents will be with your app**? Certainly, when an app is appealing, it might be true that it's mainly because its contents are appealing. For example, if you develop a game that can be played on a mobile device, the theme of the game and associated contents will be the dominating factor about whether your game players will like it or not. As another example, if your app is a messaging app, your content could be textual, or audio/video or mixed. Contents are closely associated with user interfaces, so you may want to consider very carefully about how the contents will be presented to users as well as how users will interact with your app's user interface.

■ **How will your app help your users solve their problems**? In this regard, the number one metric is the convenience, for example, easy to access and use, and so on. Then, your app should perform reasonably well as not all users are equally patient. In addition, your app should be visually appealing as one of the critical factors in determining user experience.

Your great idea for a great app doesn't have to be completely clear or polished as you can keep refining it along the way.

## 5.1.2    Defining a User Interface

As soon as you have formed your idea for your app, the next step is to start sketching a user interface for your app. Your user interface should be made as intuitive as possible so that the user doesn't have to read a lengthy manual in order to be able to use it. Besides, your user interface should be clear, straightforward and well-organized. Keep in mind that your app's user interface is the only media through which your users interact with your app, so you should do whatever it takes to make your users happy rather than being annoyed.

Your user interface helps translate your idea into a design that can be implemented. To ease the task of developing your app's user interface, use storyboards. Storyboards provide a convenient visual environment for you to design and implement your user interface without being bogged down by many unnecessary details. Since a storyboard can mimic what your users will see, you have the convenience of making instantly visible changes to your interface. On the other hand, when you define your user interface with a storyboard, you are essentially working with views, which correspond to some UI classes directly, as you have learnt and will continue to learn.

## 5.1.3    Specifying the Interaction

Users use your app by interacting with your app's user interface. After having completed defining your app's user interface, you need to specify how users will interact with various parts in your user interface. This task is accomplished by writing code to respond to actions that users initiate in your interface.

You might already know that all interactive apps are based on event-driven programming model. More specifically, in event-driven programming model, system requests and user actions/reactions are translated into events, which are handled by pre-built handlers. Whenever a user initiates an action or reacts to the outcome of a previous action, events are triggered internally, which results in the execution of some code. The app's response modifies the content of the interface, which will be a new start point for the user to take his/her next action.

As you have learnt in the previous chapters, view controllers take care of much of the event-handling logic. You'll learn more along the way about coding view controllers, which will be a key part of adding functionality and interactivity to the NoteApp we started earlier.

## 5.1.4    Implementing the Behavior

After having designed your interface and specified the interaction between the user and your app, the next step is to implement the behavior of your app by writing code. In this regard, it's necessary to have a minimal level of knowledge in Objective-C, especially the OOP part of Objective-C, if you're already familiar with C or other widely used languages. If you have never worked with Objective-C, I recommend that you study Appendix B of this book, *An Introduction to Objective-C*, which can help you get up to speed quickly with Objective-C. Instead of just reading it through, I suggest that you run all examples listed there, which will be very helpful for you to understand some important, indispensable concepts, such as:

- **Objects**: The most basic building blocks or elements for building an app. It's fair to say that whenever you code, you deal with objects. Objects have attributes and methods, which correspond to the data and behavior of your app. An app is essentially composed of large number of objects, which collaborate with each other to fulfil some tasks, such as responding to certain user actions, rendering some visual controls in the interface, or persisting data to various data store. Underneath the hook, it's objects such as buttons and labels for visual elements as well as strings and arrays for data objects that make an app live.
- **Classes**: Function as blueprints or casting molds for producing objects. A class specifies common attributes and possible behaviors for all objects it is capable of producing. Developing an app is mainly designing and coding classes, from which various types of objects can be produced to form an interconnected ecosystem according to the specs for an app.
- **Protocols**: Represent common behaviors of the objects that conform to them. A protocol is similar to a messaging channel, through which two objects of different types can exchange information and initiate some of the common behaviors implemented by the protocol-adopting class. You should study the protocol example presented in Appendix B to get a deeper understanding of it, as it's a fairly common concept used for building iOS apps. You will see in Chapter 8 how the concept of protocol is used to enable a user to add/update a note item.

## 5.1.5    Finishing with the Data

After completing designing your interface and implementing your app's behavior, the next step is to create a data model to make your app a real app rather than just a prototype. A data model defines the data that your app can operate upon and operations that your app can operate with. Some data models are simpler than others are. For example, a simple data model could be just as simple as a dictionary of objects, or as complex as an entire database.

A well-designed and implemented data model is crucial to the functionality of your app. To provide easy maintenance, desired scalability, it's necessary to make sure that interface and data are well-separated from each other.

During the initial stage of developing your app, you can use artificial, static data instead of real data so that you can consider as many different test cases as possible. However, after your data model is finalized, you should consider using real data to test your app, as fake data can never be as good as real data.

Whether you code your interface or data model, there are two important principles that you should not break without good justifications:

1  Use design patterns whenever applicable. Design patterns are proven solutions to solving common software problems. They can help you build your app more efficiently and more formal, making maintaining it much less a burden.
2  Use Apple frameworks as much as possible. Apple provides many frameworks for building apps on Apple platforms. It's very necessary to become conversant with those frameworks so that you don't have to build your app from scratch. You'll learn some of them from this book, but no book can cover all frameworks as there are too many of them and each of them is enormous.

Next, we discuss designing a user interface.

## 5.2  DESIGNING A USER INTERFACE

The preceding section described the app development process to give you an idea of what steps you need to take in order to develop a successful app. In this section, we focus on one of the most important steps in developing an app – designing a user interface. As all interactive apps follow the Model-View-Controller (MVC) pattern, we introduce the MVC design pattern in the next subsection.

### 5.2.1  The Model View Controller Design Pattern

The MVC design pattern depicts how the three basic elements of an app, Model, View, and Controller, interact with each other in order to form a closed loop of interactions between the user and the app. As is shown in Figure 5.1, the view part corresponds to the front layer, the controller part corresponds to the middle layer, while the model part corresponds to the back layer. In this section, we elaborate how these parts interact with each other.

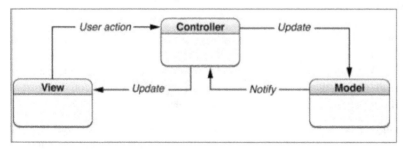

**Figure 5.1** The MVC design pattern.

By following the interaction flows shown in Figure 5.1, we see that the start point is that a user initiates an action from a view, which is directed to the controller. Then, the controller may take one of the two actions or both: updating the model and/or updating the view. If the model is updated, then, the controller is notified, which updates the view. Such interactions are accomplished through many objects at various layers. Thus, objects can be classified according to their roles, such as view objects, controller objects, and model objects.

Those three different types of objects are elaborated further as follows:

- **View Objects**. A view object is a visual control that knows how to draw itself and can respond to user actions. Therefore, view objects are visible to users. A major purpose of view objects is to present data from the app's model objects and provide a mechanism for creating/ modifying/deleting model data. However, view objects and model objects do not interact directly with each other. Instead, they interact with each other through controllers. View objects learn about changes in model data through controller objects and initiate changes to model objects through controllers. For iOS apps, both the UIKit and AppKit frameworks provide collections of view classes, and Interface Builder provides tens of view objects in its library.
- **Controller Objects**. A controller object plays the role of a mediator or intermediary between view objects and model objects. It intercepts and interprets user actions that occurred in the view layer and propagates new or modified data to the model layer. When model data changes, controller objects send such changes to view objects so that view objects can update themselves.
- **Model Objects**. Model objects represent data and offer operations for operating upon model data. Controller objects rely on such operations that model objects provide to initiate changes to data from the view layer to model layer and vice versa.

The above descriptions might sound a bit abstract, but you'll understand better later after you go through the implementation of our NoteApp.

## 5.2.2    The View Hierarchy

Views are organized in hierarchy for two reasons: (1) views are rendered in serial, and (2) views are not isolated from each other, i.e., some views depend on other views and therefore they must follow a pre-specified sequence to render themselves. Therefore, a view could be a subview of its parent view, and a parent view is a container for its child views.

As you may recall from previous chapters, at the top of the view hierarchy is the *window* object, which is a container for all other views. A window object is an instance of the UIWindow class, and its sole purpose is for containing content views, which are added to the window object in order to be rendered. When you use a storyboard, content views are added to the view hierarchy so that you don't have to write code for that specifically. The application object is responsible for loading the storyboard, creating instances of the relevant view controller classes, unarchiving the content view hierarchies for each view controller, and then adding the content view of the initial view controller into the window. Thus, app objects manage view controllers. This kind of framework-level infrastructure is transparent to app developers, which saves developers a lot of time in wiring and orchestrating various objects for the rendering process.

## 5.2.3   Building an Interface Using Views

When you start to use a storyboard to design an interface, you drag views into the storyboard. Therefore, as an app developer, you need to be familiar with what views are available and what their purposes are. Such views are provided by the UIKit framework and organized into categories as follows:

1   **Content Views**: Display a particular type of content. Examples of content views include label, image view, and so on.
2   **Collections Views**: Display collections or groups of views. Examples of collections views include table view, data grid view, collection view, and so on.
3   **Controls Views**: Display information and/or initiate actions. Examples of cControls views include buttons, switch, slider, and so on.
4   **Bars Views**: Enable navigations or perform actions. Examples of bars views include tab bar, tool bar, navigation bar, and so on.
5   **Input Views**: For entering user input. Examples of input views include text field, text view, search bar, and so on.
6   **Containers Views**: For containing other views. Examples of containers views include scroll view, and so on.
7   **Modal Views**: Allow a user to perform some kind of actions by interrupting the regular app flow. Examples of modal views include alert views, action sheets, and so on.

Those views as described above are available through Interface Builder's standard object library. When you design the interface, you can drag and drop an object from the library to the canvas and arrange it the way you want. Then you use inspectors to configure the objects you placed on the canvas. You can see immediately the result, saving the extra work of writing code, building and running your app in order to see the effect.

## 5.2.4   Using Storyboards to Lay out Views

In Chapters 3 and 4, you learnt how to use a storyboard to lay out views on a canvas. You learnt the concept of a scene. However, you might have not realized that the views placed on a scene were automatically added to that scene's view hierarchy, with the view's location within the view hierarchy determined by where the view was placed in the scene. You might still remember that an outline view, appeared on the left side of the canvas, allows you to see a hierarchical representation of the objects in your storyboard.

Of course, the view hierarchy formed in a storyboard scene is actually a "shrinkwrapped" set of Objective-C objects. At runtime, these shrinkwrapped objects are unwrapped and rendered according to the view hierarchy set forth *a priori*.

## 5.2.5   Using Inspectors to Configure Views

After various views are placed in a storyboard scene, there must be a way to configure those views. That function is fulfilled by various inspectors, such as the File inspector, Quick Help inspector, Identity inspector, Attributes inspector, Size inspector, and Connections inspector. Those inspectors have the following purposes:

- File: For specifying general information about the storyboard.
- Quick Help: For providing useful documentation about an object.
- Identity: For specifying a custom class for your object and defining its accessibility attributes.
- Attributes: For customizing visual attributes of an object.
- Size: For specifying the size of an object and Auto Layout properties.
- Connections: For creating connections between the interface and source code.

You will become more familiar with those inspectors as you use them throughout the remainder of this text.

## 5.2.6    Using Auto Layout to Position Views

Xcode provides a very useful auto-layout menu for applying auto-layout to positioning views. The auto-layout options are enabled with a 4-item Auto Layout menu, located at the bottom of the canvas, as shown in Figure 5.2. When you place your mouse pointer over an item, it shows a label for that item, indicating what it might be used for. If you click on an item, it pops up a submenu to allow you to apply auto-layout options. They are labeled *Align/Pin/Resolve Auto Layout Issues/Resizing Behavior* from left to right. The submenu for *Align* is shown in Figure 5.2. You can explore others by clicking on them with our NoteApp created previously open.

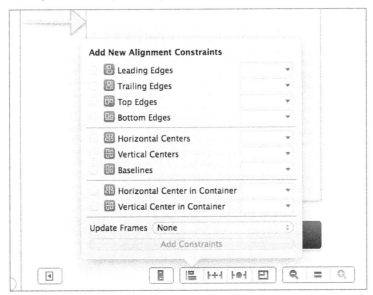

**Figure 5.2** Auto layout menu from the Interface Builder on Xcode

The auto layout feature is very necessary as different types of mobile devices have different sizes, orientations, and so on. Instead of having developers mess with the source code, this feature makes doing layout painlessly.

## 5.3   Defining the Interaction

After a user interface is specified through a storyboard, the next step is to define interactions between the user and the app. Defining the interaction is basically about adding and configuring controllers. As we described in the previous section about the MVC design pattern, controllers acts like a conduit between the view layer and model layer for communicating requests and responses back and forth. The requests may include actions for querying the state of the data or modifying the state of the data, and responses may include requested data or notifications about the changes of the state associated with the data.

This section focuses on how to define the interaction between the view layer and model layer using the Interface Builder to configure various view controllers. We start with view controllers next.

### 5.3.1   View Controllers

After establishing a view hierarchy for your iOS app, you need to enable visual controls to respond to user actions and responses from the model layer. A view controller, which is an instance of UIViewController class, can be used to manage a content view with its hierarchy of subviews, as is shown in Figure 5.3.

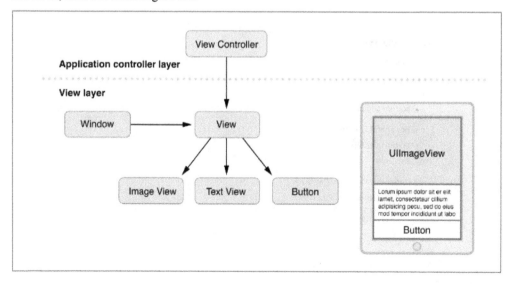

**Figure 5.3** View controllers

A view controller is essentially a mediator that manages the view objects in the view hierarchy and provides views with behavior. Each content view hierarchy requires a view controller, which means writing a custom UIViewController subclass for each content view hierarchy. Therefore, if your app has more than one content view, you need a view controller for each content view.

In addition to coordinating the flow of information between the view layer and model layer, a view controller has the following functions:

- Managing the life cycle of the content views it manages
- Handling orientation changes when a device is rotated
- Responding to user input
- Implementing transitions from one content view to another by removing the views of one view controller and inserting the views of another

The functions of view controllers are implemented by defining connections between the storyboard and source code through actions and outlets as discussed next.

### 5.3.2    Actions

An action is essentially an event handler that is triggered when the events it is registered for are fired in your app. By executing the event handler code, model data may be manipulated or the user interface may be updated.

An action can be coded by creating and implementing a method with an IBAction return type and a dynamically typed sender argument as shown below:

```
-(IBAction) restoreDefaults: (id) sender;
```

The IB class prefix for the IBAction return type designates *Interface Builder*, indicating that the method is an action that you can connect to from your storyboard in Interface Builder. The sender parameter points to the object that triggered the event or the event source. You'll learn more about actions later when we continue to implement our NoteApp.

### 5.3.3    Outlets

Outlets are defined as IBOutlet properties as follows:

```
@property (weak, nonatomic) IBOutlet UITextField *textField;
```

where the IBAction keyword tells Xcode that you can connect to this property from Interface Builder.

An outlet provides a mechanism for referencing objects you added to your storyboard in source code. You create an outlet by Control-dragging a particular object in your storyboard to a view controller file. By doing so, a property as discussed above is created in your source code, allowing to access and manipulate that object from code at runtime. You'll learn more about outlets later when we continue to implement our NoteApp.

## 5.3.4    Controls

A control is a user interface object that users can use to interact with content, enter input, navigate within the app, and perform whatever actions a user is allowed to. It's a mechanism for your code to receive messages from the user interface. When a user interacts with a control, a corresponding control event is generated, which may represent various physical user gestures, such as a tap, a swipe, a pinch, a touch-up or a touch-down action, and so on. Such events are classified into three different categories:

- **Touch and drag events**. This kind of events occurs when a user touches or drags a control. However, how the event is handled could be a bit complicated. For example, when a user touches a finger on a button but prior to lifting the finger, the Touch Down Inside event is triggered; then when the user lifts his finger off the button while still within the bounds of the button's edges, a Touch Up Inside event is triggered. If the user has dragged a finger outside the button before lifting the finger, which effectively cancels the touch, the Touch Up Outside event is triggered. Controls depend on such subtle user gestures to determine which piece of code to execute.
- **Editing events**. This kind of events occurs when a user makes edits in a text field or a text view.
- **Value-changed events**. This kind of events occurs when a user interacts with a control, causing value changes associated with the control.

Therefore, in order to be able to write controller code properly, you need to be familiar with the delicacies of various control events.

## 5.3.5    Navigation Controllers

If your app has more than one content view hierarchy, you need to add a navigating controller to enable transitioning between content view hierarchies. The set of view controllers managed by a navigation controller is called its navigation stack. The navigation stack is maintained as a first-in, last-out , or last-in, first-out collection of custom view controller objects. You have to manually push a view controller onto the stack on the storyboard, but the back button on the navigation bar helps popping off a view controller automatically. However, you have to manually configure your navigation bar.

## 5.3.6    Using Storyboards to Define Navigation

In Chapter 4, we created a single scene of content for our NoteApp using a storyboard. In that case, no navigation is needed. This section discusses how navigation through multiple scenes is supported with the concept of *segue*.

When an app's storyboard contains multiple scenes, each scene represents a view controller and the associated view hierarchy. Scenes are connected by *segues*, which are just a different term for *transitions* between source and destination view controllers. (The definition of the word *segue* as a

noun is that it's *an uninterrupted transition from one piece of music or film scene to another*.)
There are four types of segues one can create:

- **Push Segues**. You use the push segue to add the destination view controller to the navigation stack. Push segues may only be used when the source view controller is connected to a navigation controller.
- **Modal Segues**. First, a *modal* window is essentially like a dialog box that pops up from its main window when certain conditions are met. When a modal window pops up, the user must take an action in order to move forward or return to its main window. Likewise, a modal segue is simply one view controller presenting another view controller *modally*, meaning that a user action is required on the presented controller before returning to the main flow of the app. A modal view controller is not added to the navigation stack; instead, it's a child of the presenting view controller. The presenting view controller is responsible for dismissing the modal view controller it created and presented.
- **Custom Segues**. When necessary, you can define your own segue by subclassing `UIStoryboardSegue`.
- **Unwind Segues**. Unwind segues are used for implementing reverse navigation. An unwind segue moves backwards through one or more segues to return the user to an existing instance of a view controller.

Finally, when you design your interface using a storyboard, it's necessary to designate a view controller as the initial view controller. At runtime, the initial view controller's content view will be rendered the first time when the app is launched. Only from that point on, you can transition to other view controllers' content views.

In the next section, we apply the concepts we have learnt in this chapter so far to continue implementing our NoteApp to see them in action.

## 5.4  LEVERAGING THE POWER OF STORYBOARDS

In this section, we leverage the power of storyboards to continue building our NoteApp app. We'll create some of the key interface flows for the NoteApp app and add behavior to the scene we created in Chapter 4.

Let's begin with adopting auto layout next.

### 5.4.1  Adopting Auto Layout

To continue, open up your NoteApp project from where we left off in Chapter 4. Go to File inspector as shown in Figure 5.4 and note the *Use Auto Layout* box at the bottom. Leave it checked, and run the app in the iOS simulator. You will note that by default the simulated iPhone screen is in the portrait mode. Now, press Command-Left Arrow key sequence to simulate rotating left. You should see that it still works, with a visual appearance similar to Figure 5.5. Then, when you click anywhere in the text field showing "*A new note item here*," the on-screen keyboard should show up as expected.

However, you could see what would happen if Auto Layout were not enabled. To disable Auto Layout, uncheck the Use Auto Layout box and re-run NoteApp in the simulator. Press Command –Left Arrow again, and this time, you would see a blank screen and the text field did not show up. See Figure 5.6 for your reference.

As you see, the Auto Layout feature takes care of repositioning and resizing of the views when the layout changes. Auto layout is about adding constraints as shown in Figure 5.2, which is tedious and not needed for this simple app.

**Figure 5.4** Auto layout selected by default

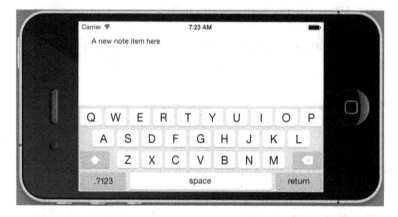

**Figure 5.5** Simulated rotating left to change from *portrait* to *landscape* mode

**Figure 5.6** Effects of no auto layout

## 5.4.2    Creating a Second Scene

Before creating a second scene, I'd like to introduce a nice built-in feature in Xcode that allows us to take a snapshot of the project any time we want. You can select the project and then access that feature by pressing "Ctrl-Command-S" or File > Create Snapshot .... Then, a dialog box similar to Figure 5.7 would show up and you could enter anything you want to help you remember what the snapshot was for. After that, you would have a Restore Snapshot option right below Create Snapshot so that you could pick a snapshot to restore from.

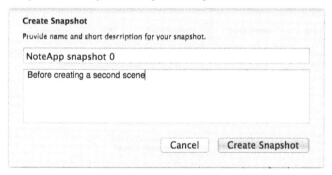

**Figure 5.7** Taking a snapshot before creating a second scene

Up to this point, our NoteApp is very simple that it has only one scene with one text box for entering a note. This section demonstrates how we can add a *table view*, which would allow the app to display a scrolling list of items.

To add a scene with a table view to your storyboard, follow the below procedure:

1    Select Main.storyboard in the project navigator.
2    Open the Object Library in the utility area if it's not open. Alternatively, you could choose View > Utilities > Show Object Library.

3   Drag a Table View Controller object from the object list and drop it to the left of the first scene of the only view controller there. You can click the Zoom in button located at the bottom of the canvas to see better if it's too crowded and you only see a partial view of the two scenes. Figure 5.8 shows the two scenes added on my Xcode IDE.

Now we have two scenes, one for displaying the list of note items and the other for adding a note item. Next, we need to specify that the table view controller scene should be the first scene when the app is launched, as it may not be the most common use case that when the app is launched, a user would want to add a new note item immediately. You use your common sense to decide which scene should be the first scene, and the application needs to know which scene to begin with when the app is launched.

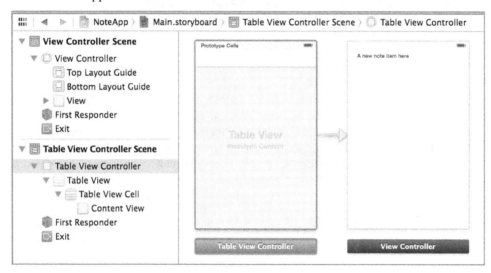

**Figure 5.8** Two scenes for NoteApp

To set the table view controller as the initial scene, follow the below procedure:

1   Make sure the outline is open. If not, click the button in the lower left corner of the canvas to open it.
2   In the outline, select the newly added table view controller.
3   With the table view controller selected, open the Attributes inspector located in the utility area. See Figure 5.9 for the Attributes inspector open on my Xcode IDE.
4   Locate the *Is Initial View Controller* check box and check it. Alternatively, you can drag the initial scene indicator as shown in Figure 5.8 to the table view controller directly on the canvas.

The table view controller is now set as the initial view controller in your storyboard. When the app starts, the table view will be the first scene. Figure 5.10 shows how it looks like in my setup. You can run the app in your iOS simulator and verify that it works as expected.

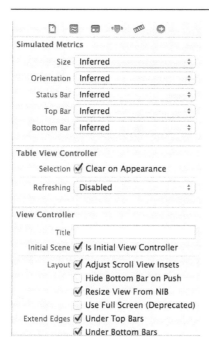

**Figure 5.9** The Attributes inspector for setting the initial view controller

**Figure 5.10** NoteApp with a table view added

### 5.4.3    Displaying Static Content in a Table View

In the preceding section, we demonstrated how to add a table view controller, which resulted in a table view in the first scene. This section shows how to add some note items, each of which has a static text for each item. First, refer to Figure 5.11 for the final result.

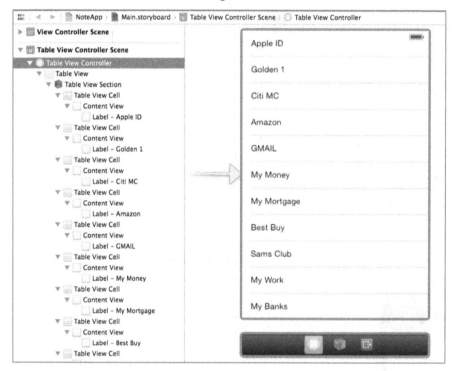

**Figure 5.11** Table view with some static note items added

You can add static content to your table view by following the below procedure:

1    In the outline as shown in Figure 5.11, select Table View in the hierarchy Table View Controller Scene > Table View Controller. (You see that the table view is under the table view controller, as a view controller manages a view.)
2    Open the Attributes inspector in the utility area. (See Figure 5.9 if you forget where the Attributes inspector is located.)
3    In the Attributes inspector, click the dropdown menu next to the Content option and select Static Cells.
4    Now you should see three empty table view cells created by default. Select the top cell.
5    In the Attributes inspector, click the dropdown menu next to Style and select Basic. Now you should see that Xcode has created a default label "Title" in the table cell.
6    Select the label created above.

7    To edit the Title text, double-click on it and change the text to something else, e.g., I changed it to Apple ID, which is one of the note items I'd like to store. In principle, we should add more info, for example, ID, password, URL for accessing the associated website, and createDate, etc., but we do not need to enter so much data right now, as that's static content for test only at this point.

8    Enter some static content for each of the remaining two cells by following the above procedure.

9    Add more cells by copying an existing cell. In order to do that, you need to first select the last cell, then hold down the Alt/Options key while dragging that last cell to the next cell position and finally drop it when you see a plus (+) sign with an arrow over it. Double click on the copied cell text and change it to something else.

Now you can test-run your NoteApp to make sure you don't encounter any errors.

Next, we demonstrate how to make a transition for the first scene to the second scene so that a user can create a new note item.

### 5.4.4    Adding a Segue to Navigate Forward

Transitions between scenes are called *segues*, as we described earlier. However, we have to create a navigation bar first for the user to click to transit from one scene to the next. As we discussed previously, a navigation bar helps manage a navigation stack.

To add a navigation controller to your storyboard, first select the Table View Controller in the outline and then choose Editor > Embed In > Navigation Controller from the menu bar. Figure 5.12 shows the result. As you see, a navigation controller was added prior to the Table View Controller. Note that the navigation controller has been set to be the initial scene. Besides, a *relationship* has been created between the navigation controller and the Table View Controller.

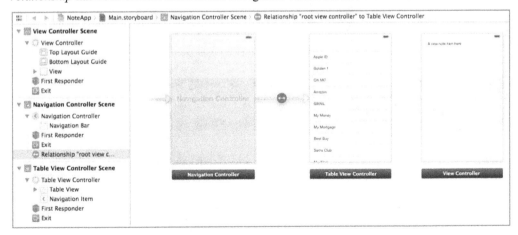

**Figure 5.12** Adding a navigation controller

Note that if you could not see the last scene, you can have more space by hiding the Utilities pane by pressing Option-Command-0 or View > Utilities > Hide Utilities. However, at this point, we are only interested in the relationship between the first two scenes. Therefore, if you click on the connection icon between the navigation controller and table View controller, you should see that it's described as Relationship "root view controller" to Table view Controller – both from the outline in the left and from the information display bar at the top, as shown in Figure 5.12. This implies that the view for the content displayed below the navigation bar will be the table view and that as the root view controller the navigation controller holds all of the content displayed in the app. To be specific, the navigation controller is the container for both the note item list scene (second) and the add-note-item scene (last). Now if you run the app in your iOS simulator, you'll see that you have some extra space at the top above your table view. Refer to Figure 5.13's left screenshot. This is the empty navigation bar. Next, we'll add a title with a button similar to the right screenshot of Figure 5.13 so that a user can click on it to add a new note item.

**Figure 5.13** NoteApp with an empty navigation bar added (left) and after the navigation bar was configured (right)

To configure the navigation bar, follow the below procedure:

1    In the outline or on the canvas, select Navigation Item under Table View Controller Scene > Table View Controller > Table View.
2    In the Attributes inspector, type My Notes in the Title field, and press Enter.

3    Open the Object Library if it's not open.
4    Type "bar button" in the Search box at the bottom and you should see the Bar Button Item, which represents an item on a UIToolbar or UINavigationItem object.
5    Drag the Bar Button Item object to near the right edge of the navigation bar in the table view controller. Drop it there when an icon containing the text "Item" appears.
6    Double click on the Item text there and type the plus sign (+) to make it clear that is for adding a new note item.
7    Run the app in your iOS simulator and you should see an iPhone screen with your NoteApp open similar to the second screenshot shown in Figure 5.13.

In Figure 5.13, you might notice that the navigation bar does not have its own title. Instead, it gets its title from its first child view, which is the table view for your NoteApp's note list.

Now, let's see how we can configure the Add (+) button in the navigation bar so that when a user clicks on it, it will bring up the last add-note-item scene to allow a new note item added to the note list. This can be done as follows:

1    On the canvas, select the Add (+) button.
2    Control-drag from the Add button to the add-note-item view controller, which is the last scene. Now you should see a shortcut menu titled Action Segue in the location where the drag ended, as shown in Figure 5.14.

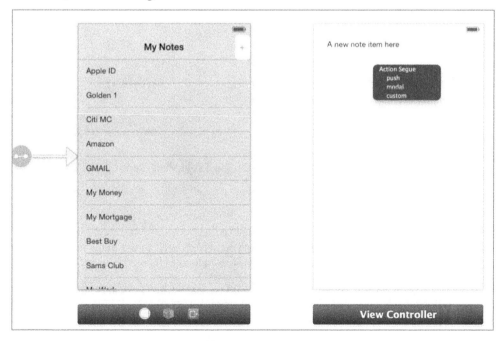

**Figure 5.14** A shortcut menu showing all Action Segues.

3    Select the "push" segue and you should see the push segue between the second and the last scene. Double click on the navigation bar of the last scene, enter "My New Note Item" for the Title and hit Return. Now if you click on the action segue icon, it should look similar to Figure 5.15. Note that the information bar at the top displays that it's a push segue from + to View Controller.

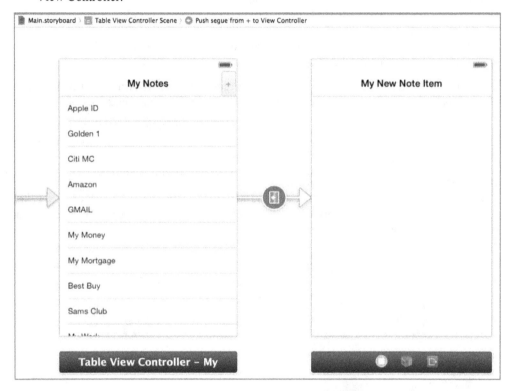

**Figure 5.15** A push action segue that helps transit from the Table View Controller to the View Controller

Now if you run the NoteApp, initially you should see the main view, which is the Table View. When you click on the Add (+) button, it should transit to the Add New Note Item view, with a "< My Notes" label in its navigation bar indicating that you can go back to the main view. Click on the "<" and verify that you can go back to the main view by clicking there.

However, the push segue is not exactly what we want. It would be more appropriate to use a modal segue, which is like a pop-up dialog that when a user completes the action, it would return to its parent view. Next, we describe how we can change the push segue to a modal segue.

To change the segue type, select the segue icon on the canvas and then choose Modal style in the Attributes inspector, as shown in Figure 5.16.

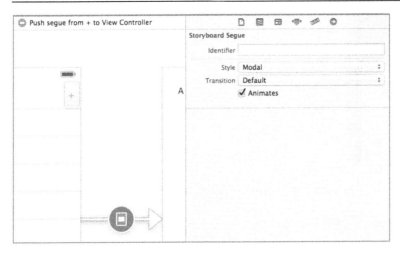

Figure 5.16 Change segue type from push to modal

Since a modal view controller is not added to the navigation stack, it does not get a navigation bar from the table view controller's navigation controller. You can verify that by running the app in your iOS simulator. To solve the issue, we need to add a navigation controller to the add-new-note-item view controller. You can select the view controller on the canvas, and then select Editor > Embed In > Navigation Controller, similar to how we added the navigation controller for the Table View Controller.

Now you can run the app in your simulator again and note the navigation bar added. However, it provides no mechanism for the user to go back to the main view. At this point, we need to add a Cancel button and a Done button to allow the user to cancel the *add-new-note-item* action or complete the *add-new-note-item* action. This can be done by following the below procedure:

1    Select the Navigation Item under View Controller > View in the outline.
2    Drag a Bar Button Item from the Object Library to the far right of the navigation bar in the *add-new-note-item* view controller.
3    In the Attributes inspector, enter Done and hit Return.
4    Drag another Bar Button Item from the Object Library to the far left of the navigation bar in the *add-new-note-item* view controller.
5    In the Attributes inspector, enter Cancel and hit Return.
6    Press Command-R to run a test. Click on the Add (+) button and you should see the *add-new-note-item* view as shown in Figure 5.17. However, if you click on Cancel or Done button, it doesn't do anything yet.

Our next task is to connect the Cancel and Done buttons to their respective actions, which is the subject for the next section.

**Figure 5.17** The add-new-note-item scene with dummy Cancel and Done buttons

## 5.4.5    Creating Custom View Controllers

This section describes how we can turn those two Cancel and Done buttons in the *add-new-note-item* view from dummy into live buttons. You might notice that we have not written any code yet. That's because the table view controller and the view controller are generic view controllers. Most of the time, generic view controllers have very limited uses and we need to create custom view controllers of our own.

First, let's customize the *add-new-note-item* view controller. Our custom view controller for our NoteApp will be called NTPAddNewNoteItemViewController as a subclass of UIViewController. It can be done as follows:

1    Select File > New > File or press Command-N.
2    Select the iOS/Cocoa Touch > Objective-C class and click Next.
3    Enter NTPAddNewNoteItemViewController for Class and select UIViewController for Subclass from the dropdown menu. Leave "Also create XIB file" unchecked and click Next.
4    The save folder and Group/Targets should all be NoteApp by default, which is ok. Click on Create.

Now you should see the NTPAddNewNoteItemViewController.h and NTPAddNewNoteItemViewController.m created under your NoteApp project. Next, follow the below procedure to substitute the generic view controller with the custom view controller NTPAddNewNoteItemViewController we have just created:

1    In the project navigator, select Main.storyboard.
2    Select *Add New Note Item View Controller – My New Note Item* under *Add New Note Item View Controller – My New Note Item Scene*.
3    Open the Identity inspector (the 3rd one counting from left) in the utility area. This inspector allows a developer to make changes to the identity of an object.
4    Select NTPAddNewNoteItemViewController from the dropdown menu next to *Class*. This is the way to specify which view controller to use for a specific scene. In our case, we wanted to assign our custom view controller to the *add new note item* scene that displays a text view for a user to add a new note item.

Now repeat the same procedure as described above to create an NTPMyNotesTableViewController, which subclasses UITableViewController. Also, specify this custom table view controller as the *Custom Class* for *My Notes Table View Controller – My Notes* under *My Notes Table View Controller – My Notes Scene*.

In the next section, we describe how to add custom code to the two customized view controllers created above.

## 5.4.6    Unwinding a Segue to Navigate Back

In addition to push and modal segues, Xcode supports an *unwind segue*, which is specifically designed for performing the action of returning to the previous scene. In our case, we want to add an unwind segue to redirect the execution flow from NTPAddNewNoteItemViewController to NTPMyNotesTableViewController when a user is done with adding a new note item.

To complete the above task, follow the below procedure:

1    In the project navigator, open NTPMyNotesTableViewController.h file by clicking on it.
2    Add the following code below the @interface line:

    - (IBAction)unwindToList : (UIStoryBoardSegue *)segue;

3    In the project navigator, open NTPMyNotesTableViewController.m file by clicking on it.
4    Add the following code below the @implementation line:

```
- (IBAction)unwindToList : (UIStoryBoardSegue *)segue {
{

}
```

As you see, we added an action method to the unwind segue created above. We could have named the method something else other than unwindToList, but the name we chose clearly indicates that the destination is a list view controller.

Next, we need to link the buttons to the unwindToList: method by following the below procedure:

1    Select Main.storyboard in the project navigator.
2    On the canvas, locate the Cancel button from the last scene and Control-drag it to the Exit icon in the *add-new-note-item* dock, as shown in Figure 5.18. Then, lift your finger off your TouchPad.
3    You should see a menu showing *Action Segue > unwindToList* as shown in Figure 5.18. Click unwindToList to select it. This means that when the user clicks the Cancel button, the unwindToList method will be executed.
4    Similarly, Control-drag the Done button to the same Exit icon in the *add-new-note-item* dock.
5    Select the unwindToList: method from the shortcut menu.

Note that the same method of unwindToList: is used for both the Cancel button and the Done button. In the next chapter, we'll illustrate how to implement the unwindToList: method to handle these two different cases.

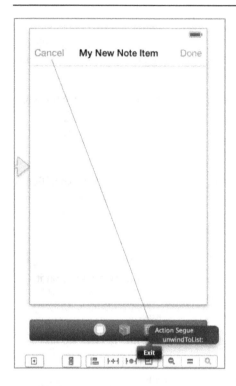

**Figure 5.18** Link the Cancel button to the unwindToList: action

Now we can test out the unwindToList segue by running the app implemented so far. After you start up your NoteApp, click on the Add button to transit to the Add New Note Item view. Then clicking on either Cancel or Done should bring you back to the main view. If nothing happens when you click Cancel or Done button, double check that you did not add the unwindToList: method to NTPAddNewNoteItemViewController accidentally.

However, you may notice that your NoteApp main view is empty without displaying the note items you once added. That's because NTPMyNotesTableViewController.m implementation has two UITableViewDataSource methods, **numberOfSectionsInTableView:** and **numberOfRowsInSection:**, as shown in Listing 5.1, that expect a table view data source for loading data, but we have not configured that data source yet. You can comment out those two methods as shown in Listing 5.1, re-run the app and you should see the static data you once entered. The next chapter walks you through the data part for this app.

**Listing 5.1 Methods in NTPMyNotesTableViewController.m preventing the static text from showing up**

```
/*
#pragma mark - Table view data source
```

```
-  (NSInteger) numberOfSectionsInTableView: (UITableView *) tableView
{
#warning Potentially incomplete method implementation.
    // Return the number of sections.
    return 0;
}

-  (NSInteger) tableView: (UITableView *) tableView
numberOfRowsInSection: (NSInteger) section
{
#warning Incomplete method implementation.
    // Return the number of rows in the section.
    return 0;
}
*/
```

## 5.5 SUMMARY

This chapter focused on introducing the typical app development process, two major parts of which are designing the user interface and defining the interactions among multiple views. We demonstrated how we could get started just by using the Storyboard feature of Xcode without writing much code. The next chapter focuses on the data part of this app.

# 6 Implementing NoteApp

In addition to views and view controllers, designing an effective and efficient data model is also essential to an app. The main concern with a data model is that it should not be closely coupled with views and view controllers. By keeping your data separate from your user interface, you are paving a way for you to implement a universal app that can run both on iPhone and iPad. It also helps make your code more reusable later.

## 6.1 BUILDING A DATA MODEL

Building a data model for your app implies two things: designing your data model and implementing your data model. Let's start with a generic coverage of how to design your data model next.

### 6.1.1 Designing Your Data Model

Designing your data model starts with asking the following questions:

1. **Types of data**. Common types of data may include structured and non-structured data or mixed. Actual data content might be text, images, documents, and so on.
2. **Volumes of data**. The next question is how much data your app expects to deal with. This may determine what technologies you need to use to store your data.
3. **Data Structures**. This may determine whether you need to use framework classes or your own custom classes.
4. **Data access methods**. How your data will be accessed in your app is the last issue you need to deal with. You certainly don't want your user interface to access your data directly. Instead, your view controllers should access your data on behalf of your user interface.

Based on the answers to the above questions, you might consider the following mechanisms for storing data:

1. **NSString.** The NSString class declares a programming interface for an object that manages immutable strings, which cannot be altered once created. It is implemented to hold an array of

Unicode characters. The mutable version of NSString is NSMutableString, which subclasses NSString.

2   **NSArray and/or NSMutableArray.** NSArray and its subclass NSMutableArray manages ordered collections of objects that are generally called *arrays*. The difference between the two is that NSArray holds static arrays, while NSMutableArray holds dynamic arrays. Both of them are from the *Foundation.framework*. These data structures hold data in memory, though.

3   **Files**. You can choose to have your data stored in regular files and managed by an NSFileManager from the *Foundation.framework*. The NSFileManager class enables you to perform many generic filesystem operations transparently against the underlying filesystem. You can also create a unique instance of NSFileManager and use a delegate object to communicate with the file manager.

4   **Core Data framework.** Each data item that your app deals with can be considered a data object, and the Core Data framework enables you to manage a file containing an archive of such objects. The Core Data framework also enables you to archive all your data objects to a file and track changes to the objects to support undo when needed. Besides, the Core Data framework is a universal framework such that it is not limited to database-style apps or document-centric apps or client-server type of apps. It is equally useful as the basis for a vector graphics app such as Sketch or a presentation app such as Keynote.

We illustrate some of the data technologies through our NoteApp sample down the road.

### 6.1.2    Implementing Your Model

Perhaps the most important advice I can give you about implementing your data model is to start with a model that is simple and easy to understand and then refine it over time by taking an iterative approach. However, fundamentally, your data model most likely will be coded in Objective-C. You need to become familiar with Objective-C before writing a fully functional app.

There are many resources for learning Objective-C. You certainly can choose your own approach, but I'd like to recommend that you start with Appendix B, An Introduction to Objective-C, included at the end of this book, and then learn more on an as-needed basis by using the recommended resources given there.

## 6.2  MORE DESIGN PATTERNS

A design pattern is a proven approach to solving a common software development problem. It's an abstract concept, not a concrete implementation, although eventually it has to be implemented for your app once it is chosen. As an iOS developer, it's very important to understand some commonly used fundamental design patterns, especially those used in iOS app development frameworks. The more design patterns you use with your app, the more resuable and extensible and modifiable you app will be.

We once covered the MVC design pattern in the previous chapter. Here, we introduce a few more before we dive into coding right away.

## 6.2.1    Delegation

Delegation is a design pattern in which one object acts on behalf of another object. For example, without complicating it too much, an app may create a proxy object at startup without having to initialize the object that the app may need to use later. This is called lazy binding or late binding that is helpful in saving CPU and memory resources, and thus better performance and smaller footprint or less garbage collections for the app. Later when the app needs to use that object, it initializes that object through the proxy, and the proxy calls that object to perform the task that the app wanted that object to perform.

In the above interaction chain, the proxy is considered the delegating object and the object that performs the actual work is considered a delegate. The proxy keeps sending messages to the delegate to inform the delegate of an event that the delegate object is about to handle or has just handled. The delegate may respond to the message by updating its state or other objects in the app. The main use of delegation is that the behavior of several objects can be customized in one central object. Figure 6.1 illustrates the concept of delegation.

**Figure 6.1** The delegation design pattern

We'll explain more about the delegation pattern when we encounter it later.

## 6.2.2    Target-Action

Target-action is a mechanism for sending information between different parts of an app, thus defining interaction among them. In fact, we have already used the target-action pattern in the preceding chapter. When you tap the Done button in the NTPAddNewNoteViewController, it triggers the unwindToList: action. In this case, the Done button is the message sender, the NTPAddNewNoteViewController is the target object, unwindToList: is the action message, and the user's gesture of tapping the Done button is the event that triggers the event to be sent.

In summary, target-action is a design patter in which one object sends a message to another when a certain event occurs. The action message is a method or selector defined in source code, and the target is the object that receives the message, which is typically a view controller that is capable of performing the action. The object that sends the action message is usually a control, such as a button or text field, that triggers an event in response to user interaction such as a gesture or value change.

We'll explain more about the target-action design pattern when we encounter it later.

## 6.2.3    Key-Value Observing (KVO)

Key-Value Observing (KVO) is a mechanism for an object to be notified directly when a property of another object changes. It is an important mechanism for apps that are built by following the MVC design pattern. For example, you can use it to synchronize the state of model objects with view objects and controller objects. Typically, view objects observe controller objects, and controller objects observe model objects.

However, KVO is significantly different from the publish-subscribe pattern. Instead of a central object that broadcasts notifications to all objects that have registered as observers, KVO notifications go directly to observing objects when changes in property values occur with the observed object.

KVO, along with key-value coding and key-value binding, are instrumental technologies to Cocoa binding, which allow the values in the model are synchronized with view layers of the app without having to write a lot of "glue code." As you have seen from the preceding chapter, the Interface Builder inspectors help establish a mediated channel between a view's property and a data item so that a change in one is reflected in the other.

## 6.3  WARMING UP ON FOUNDATION

As a preparation for writing a custom class in Objective-C next, this section helps you review and learn a bit more about the Foundation framework. This framework provides basic services for writing application code on top of the primitive Objective-C language. We cover two subjects: value classes and collection classes. Value classes are essentially wrappers for primitive data types such as numbers and strings, while collection classes are for storing objects.

Let's begin with Value Classes first next.

### 6.3.1    Value Classes

When you declare a variable, like the following, that is a variable that can be assigned a value of type int.

```
int n;
```

In other words, it's a value, not an object. That difference is important that sometimes you may want more than just a value, or you may want an object so that you can store it in a collection object or pass it like an object to other objects. You may also want to serialize and deserialize it. This's why we need wrapper classes for all primitive data types.

Objective-C supports a value class named NSValue, which is a subclass of NSObject as you might have guessed. An NSValue object is a container for a single C or Objective-C data type. It can hold any of the scalar types such as int, float, char, as well as pointers, structures and object ids. Its purpose is to allow items of such data types to be added to collections such as instances of NSArray and NSDictionary, which require their elements to be objects. NSValue objects are always immutable.

For numerical types, however, most likely, you would use NSNumber, which is a subclass of NSValue. It is a wrapper class for any C scalar (numeric) type. It defines a set of methods specifically for setting and accessing the value as a signed or unsigned char, short, int, long int, long long int, float, double or a BOOL. It defines a compare: method to determine the ordering of two NSNumber objects.

Perhaps a good example can help us learn about some value classes faster. If you want to follow along, create a project named FoundationFramework using the OS X/Other > Empty template, and then add four targets using the OS X/Application > Command Line Tool template, named ValueObjects, Arrays, Mutability and CollectionObjects, respectively. For your reference, Figure 6.2 shows how I created such a project on my MacBook Pro.

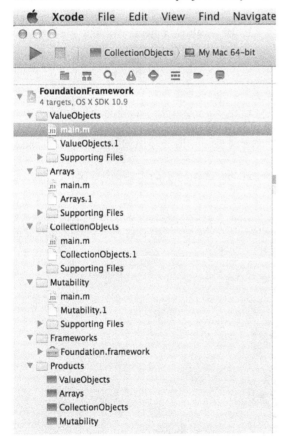

**Figure 6.2** The FoundationFramework project with four targets of ValueObjects, Arrays, Mutability, and CollectionObjects

Now let's start with the main.m file for the ValueObjects target, as shown in Listing 6.1. The first example demonstrates how NSNumber is used. As you see, an int variable named num1 is declared and assigned an initial value 10. Then, an NSNumber object named numObject is created using the numberWithInt: method, followed by an argument, which is the int variable num1 created prior to it. The next statement creates a regular int variable from the value of the numObject. Finally, an if-block compares the value of x and num1 and logs the result using the NSLog function.

The second example shows how you can create an NSNumber object using a shorthand notation by assigning an int value directly (note that the value must be preceded with the @ sign, because the left-hand side is an object rather than a C-type variable.) This eliminates the need to call initializers or class factory methods to create such objects.

The third example demonstrates the value class NSInteger, which is used to describe an integer. This type is a 32-bit integer on a 32-bit platform and a 64-bit integer on a 64-bit platform. Note that we reused the numObject without creating a new one. We also show you how to create an NSInteger object z directly based on another value object without using the numberWithInteger: method.

The last example shows how to create an NSString object using the following three different ways:

1    The first NSString object, string1, is created using a string class method, which takes care of memory allocation, initialization prior to returning the object.
2    The second NSString object, string2, is created using the stringWithFormat: method, followed by an initializer of @", iOS!".
3    The third NSString object, string3, is created by assigning an NSString object @"Have fun!" directly.

If you are new to Objective-C and the Foundation framework, I suggest that you type in the code shown in Listing 6.1 and run it to verify that it works as expected. Or, study the output shown in Listing 6.2 to make sure you understand this example clearly.

**Listing 6.1 main.m for target ValueObjects**

```
#import <Foundation/Foundation.h>

int main(int argc, const char * argv[])
{

    @autoreleasepool {

        // example 1: NSNumber
        int num1= 10;
        NSNumber *numObject = [NSNumber numberWithInt: num1];
        int x = [numObject intValue];

        if ( x == num1) {
           NSLog (@" num1 and x are equal");
        } else {
           NSLog (@" num2 and x are not equal");
        }
```

```
    // example 2: alloc, init and assigning a value all in one
    NSNumber *myIntValue = @99;
    NSLog (@"%i", myIntValue.intValue);

    // example 3: NSInteger
    NSInteger num2 = 20;
    numObject = [NSNumber numberWithInteger: num2];
    int y = [numObject integerValue];

    NSInteger z =[numObject integerValue];

    if ( y == num2) {
        NSLog (@" num2 and y are equal");
    } else {
        NSLog (@" num2 and y are not equal");
    }

    // example 4: NSString
    NSString *string1 = [NSString string];
    string1 = @"Hello";
    NSLog (@"string1: %@", string1);

    NSString *string2 = [NSString stringWithFormat: @", iOS!"];
    NSLog (@"string2: %@", string2);

    NSString *string3 = @"Have fun!";
    NSLog (@"string3: %@", string3);

    }
    return 0;
}
```

**Listing 6.2 Output from running main.m for target ValueObjects**

```
henrys-mbp:ValueObjects henry$ clang -fobjc-arc main.m -o a.out
henrys-mbp:ValueObjects henry$ ./a.out
2014-07-23 22:15:44.300 a.out[50688:507]  num1 and x are equal
2014-07-23 22:15:44.302 a.out[50688:507] 99
2014-07-23 22:15:44.302 a.out[50688:507]  num2 and y are equal
2014-07-23 22:15:44.302 a.out[50688:507] string1: Hello
2014-07-23 22:15:44.303 a.out[50688:507] string2: , iOS!
2014-07-23 22:15:44.303 a.out[50688:507] string3: Have fun!
henrys-mbp:ValueObjects henry$
```

## 6.3.2  Arrays

An array is a container for representing an ordered list of objects. It may not be surprising to you that the Foundation framework provides its own array class –NSArray. The NSArray class can contain different types of objects, as long as they are all Objective-C objects.

Listing 6.3 shows the `main.m` file for the Arrays target. It demonstrates the following about the NSString class:

- **Creating an NSArray object**. First, two NSString objects are created: one by using the `stringWithCString` method with a C-string object as the parameter and the other by directly assigning an NSString object value. Then, an NSArray object was created using the `arrayWithObjects:` method, with the above two NSString objects as parameters. Note that the last item has to be `nil` to signify the end of the NSArray.
- **Accessing array elements using subscription indexing**. The element of an NSArray object can be accessed using subscription indexing just like any other languages. The array index starts with zero, and the number of elements can be obtained by sending a `count` message to the object.
- **Accessing array elements using a defined method**. You can also access the elements of an NSArray object by sending an `objectAtIndex` message, with the index value specified.
- **Sorting an array**. In order to demonstrate sorting an NSArray, we have to create another NSArray for receiving the sorted array, since an NSArray is *immutable*. That's why you see an `unsortedArray` and a `sortedArray` there. The unsortedArray is sorted by sending an `sortedArrayUsingSelector` message to the NSArray object to be sorted using selector `@selector(compare:)`. Finally, the sortedArray is output using the NSLog function to verify that the original array has been indeed sorted. Note the use of a special `for`-loop syntax for cycling through the elements of an array.

You should run this example yourself or study the output shown in Listing 6.4 to make sure that you understand this example clearly.

**Listing 6.3 main.m for target Arrays**

```
#import <Foundation/Foundation.h>

int main(int argc, const char * argv[])
{

    @autoreleasepool {

        // creating an array with different types of objects
        NSNumber *myIntValue = @99;
        NSString *cString = [NSString stringWithCString:"Hello, iOS!"
            encoding:NSUTF8StringEncoding];
        id aStringObject = @"Hello, OS X";
        NSArray *array = [NSArray arrayWithObjects:myIntValue, cString,
            aStringObject, nil];

        int count = [array count];

        // accessing array elements using subscript index
        for (int i = 0; i < count; i++) {
            NSLog (@" i = %i: %@", i, array [i]);
        }
```

```
        // accessing array elements using defined method
        for (int i = 0; i < count; i++) {
            NSLog (@" i = %i: %@", i, [array objectAtIndex:i]);
        }

        // sorting array
        NSArray *unsortedArray = @[cString, aStringObject];
        NSArray *sortedArray = [unsortedArray
            sortedArrayUsingSelector:@selector(compare:)];

        NSLog (@"sorted array:");
        for (id stringObject in sortedArray) {
            NSLog (@"string object: %@", stringObject);
        }
    }
    return 0;
}
```

**Listing 6.4 Output from running main.m for target Arrays**

```
henrys-mbp:Arrays henry$ clang -fobjc-arc main.m -o a.out
henrys-mbp:Arrays henry$ ./a.out
2014-07-23 22:13:06.336 a.out[50667:507]  i = 0: 99
2014-07-23 22:13:06.338 a.out[50667:507]  i = 1: Hello, iOS!
2014-07-23 22:13:06.338 a.out[50667:507]  i = 2: Hello, OS X
2014-07-23 22:13:06.338 a.out[50667:507]  i = 0: 99
2014-07-23 22:13:06.339 a.out[50667:507]  i = 1: Hello, iOS!
2014-07-23 22:13:06.339 a.out[50667:507]  i = 2: Hello, OS X
2014-07-23 22:13:06.339 a.out[50667:507] sorted array:
2014-07-23 22:13:06.340 a.out[50667:507] string object: Hello, OS X
2014-07-23 22:13:06.340 a.out[50667:507] string object: Hello, iOS!
henrys-mbp:Arrays henry$
```

## 6.3.3   Mutability

Mutability refers to the limitation on whether the content of an object can be modified. For example, NSString and NSArray are immutable classes that their contents cannot be altered. Correspondingly, there are NSMutableString and NSMutableArray classes that allow their contents to be modified. For example, you can add, replace, or remove objects with an NSMutableArray.

To illustrate mutability, Listing 6.5 shows main.m for the Arrays target we created in the FoundationFramework Xcode project. As you see, we first created the NSMutableArray named mutableArray using its array class method. Then, three NSString objects were added to the mutableArray by calling the addObject: method. A for-loop is used to output the initial contents of the mutableArray.

In the second part, the object at index 0 was replaced with another object by sending a `replaceObjectAtIndex:` message to the mutableArray. The modified mutableArray was output to verify that it had indeed been modified.

In the third part, the mutableArray was sorted by calling the `sortUsingSelector:` method together with the `@selector(caseInsensitiveCompare:)` applied to each object contained in the mutableArray. Once again, the sorted mutableArray was output for verification purposes.

You should run this example yourself or study the output shown in Listing 6.6 to make sure you understand this example clearly.

**Listing 6.5 main.m for target Mutability**

```
#import <Foundation/Foundation.h>

int main(int argc, const char * argv[])
{

    @autoreleasepool {

        // 1 creating a mutableArray
        NSMutableArray *mutableArray = [NSMutableArray array];
        [mutableArray addObject:@"Orange"];
        [mutableArray addObject:@"Apple"];
        [mutableArray addObject:@"Peach"];

        NSLog (@"\nmutableArray before modifying:");
        for (id obj in mutableArray) {
            NSLog (@"%@", obj);
        }

        // 2 replacing an item in mutableArray
        NSLog (@"\nmutableArray after modifying:");
        [mutableArray replaceObjectAtIndex:0 withObject:@"kiwi"];
        for (id obj in mutableArray) {
            NSLog (@"%@", obj);
        }

        // 3 sorting the mutableArray
        NSLog (@"\nmutableArray after sorting:");
        [mutableArray
            sortUsingSelector:@selector(caseInsensitiveCompare:)];
        for (id obj in mutableArray) {
            NSLog (@"%@", obj);
        }


    }
    return 0;
}
```

**Listing 6.6 Output from running main/m for target Mutability**

```
henrys-mbp:Mutability henry$ clang -fobjc-arc main.m -o a.out
henrys-mbp:Mutability henry$ ./a.out
2014-07-23 22:10:01.052 a.out[50648:507]
mutableArray before modifying:
2014-07-23 22:10:01.054 a.out[50648:507] Orange
2014-07-23 22:10:01.054 a.out[50648:507] Apple
2014-07-23 22:10:01.055 a.out[50648:507] Peach
2014-07-23 22:10:01.055 a.out[50648:507]
mutableArray after modifying:
2014-07-23 22:10:01.055 a.out[50648:507] kiwi
2014-07-23 22:10:01.056 a.out[50648:507] Apple
2014-07-23 22:10:01.056 a.out[50648:507] Peach
2014-07-23 22:10:01.056 a.out[50648:507]
mutableArray after sorting:
2014-07-23 22:10:01.057 a.out[50648:507] Apple
2014-07-23 22:10:01.057 a.out[50648:507] kiwi
2014-07-23 22:10:01.057 a.out[50648:507] Peach
henrys-mbp:Mutability henry$
```

## 6.3.4    Collection Classes

Our last Foundation framework example is about another type of Collection Objects based on NSDictionary. This is a key-value based structure with value for the object and key for identifying the object. You can consider that an NSDictionary is a key-value pair container. Of course, we have NSDictionary class and its mutable counterpart – NSMutableDictionary.

Listing 6.7 shows main.m for target CollectionObjects. The example is programmed with the following parts:

1  **Creating a dictionary with different types of objects**. In this part, we created an NSDictionary with three objects: an NSNumber object, an NSString object, and a generic type object. The method dictionaryWithObjectsAndKeys: was called with three object-key pairs, and the last item was a nil marker signifying the end of the dictionary object.
2  **Enumerating the dictionary**. This part shows how you can enumerate the items of an NSDictionary by using an in-collection driven for-loop. With a given key, the corresponding object is looked up using array subscript index format.
3  **Querying the dictionary**. With a known key, the corresponding object was retrieved using the objectForKey: method.
4  **Removing a dictionary element**. In order to demonstrate this use case, we created an NSMutableDictionary object for the reasons we explained previously. We used the existing NSDictionary object to create the NSMutableDictionary object. Afterwards, the method removeObjectForKey: was called on the NSMutableArray object to remove the object corresponding to the given key. The last statement was to output the removed object, which, of course, no longer exists.

You should run this example yourself or study the output shown in Listing 6.8 to make sure you understand this example clearly.

Of course, the Foundation framework contains a lot more NS-classes than we covered here, which are some very basic classes that you need to become familiar with at a minimum. You'll learn more as you code more throughout the remainder of this book.

**Listing 6.7 main.m for target CollectionObjects**

```
#import <Foundation/Foundation.h>

int main(int argc, const char * argv[])
{

    @autoreleasepool {

        // 1 creating a dictionary with different types of objects
        NSNumber *myIntValue = @99;
        NSString *cString = [NSString stringWithCString:"Hello, iOS!"
            encoding:NSUTF8StringEncoding];
        id aStringObject = @"Hello, OS X";
        NSDictionary *dictionary = [NSDictionary
            dictionaryWithObjectsAndKeys:
                myIntValue, @"myIntValueObj",
                cString, @"cStringObj",
                aStringObject, @"aStringObj",
                nil];

        // 2 enumerating the dictionary
        NSLog(@"There are %ld objects in the dictionary",
            [dictionary count]);
        for (id key in dictionary) {
            NSLog(@"object: %@ - key: %@", dictionary[key], key);
        }

        // 3 querying the dictionary
        NSLog (@"querying the dictionary:");
        id dictionaryElement = [dictionary objectForKey:@"aStringObj"];
        NSLog (@"a dictionary object: %@", dictionaryElement);

        // 4 removing an object and then querying the dictionary
        NSMutableDictionary *mutableDictionary = [NSMutableDictionary
            dictionaryWithDictionary:dictionary];
        NSLog (@"removing an object and then querying the dictionary:");
        [mutableDictionary removeObjectForKey:@"aStringObj"];
        dictionaryElement = [mutableDictionary
            objectForKey:@"aStringObj"];
        NSLog (@"a dictionary object: %@", dictionaryElement);

    }
    return 0;
```

}

**Listing 6.8 Output from running main.m for target CollectionObjects**

```
henrys-mbp:CollectionObjects henry$ clang -fobjc-arc main.m -o a.out
henrys-mbp:CollectionObjects henry$ ./a.out
2014-07-23 22:05:49.094 a.out[50622:507] There are 3 objects in the
dictionary
2014-07-23 22:05:49.096 a.out[50622:507] object: 99 - key: myIntValueObj
2014-07-23 22:05:49.096 a.out[50622:507] object: Hello, iOS! - key:
cStringObj
2014-07-23 22:05:49.096 a.out[50622:507] object: Hello, OS X - key:
aStringObj
2014-07-23 22:05:49.097 a.out[50622:507] querying the dictionary:
2014-07-23 22:05:49.097 a.out[50622:507] a dictionary object: Hello, OS X
2014-07-23 22:05:49.097 a.out[50622:507] removing an object and then
querying the dictionary:
2014-07-23 22:05:49.098 a.out[50622:507] a dictionary object: (null)
henrys-mbp:CollectionObjects henry$
```

# 6.4 WRITING A CUSTOM CLASS

When you have your own idea about how your app should behave or function, especially in handling how your data should be stored, manipulated and displayed, most likely, you need to write your own custom class in Objective-C. This section illustrates how to write an NTPNoteItem custom class, which will help make NoteApp more complete as well. It includes the following steps:

- Designing the NTPNoteItem class for representing a single note item to be added to the NoteApp
- Implementing the NTPNoteItem class
- Adding the NTPNoteItem class to NoteApp

Let's start with designing the NTPNoteItem class first.

## 6.4.1   Designing the NTPNoteItem Class

As you have learnt, an Objective-C class has two parts: the interface file with the .h extension and the implementation file with the .m extension. These two parts are separate with the intention to hide the implementation details from the operations that are exposed to external users.  A huge benefit by separating the interface from the implementation is that implementation can evolve independently as long as the interface remains unchanged.

To get started, open your NoteApp project on your Xcode. Press Command-N to bring up "Choosing a template for your new file," and select iOS/Cocoa Touch > Objective-C class. Click Next. Then specify NTPNoteItem for Class and NSObject for Subclass. Click Next and save it to your NoteApp project.

You now should have two files created as shown in Listings 6.9 and 6.10 for the interface and implementation, respectively. As you see, both of them are empty at this point except that the interface NTPNoteItem is a sublass of NSObject. All objects should either directly subclass NSObject or one of its subclasses to have a minimum behavior or default behavior.

**Listing 6.9 NTPNoteItem.h**

```
#import <Foundation/Foundation.h>
@interface NTPNoteItem : NSObject

@end
```

**Listing 6.10 NTPNoteItem.m**

```
#import "NTPNoteItem.h"
@implementation NTPNoteItem

@end
```

The data you want your class to represent is specified in the interface file as a set of properties or attributes. For this version of the app, a note item should have a name, a user name, a password, a URL, whether it's completed or not and a creationDate. Objective-C has a rule that if a property is put in the interface, it's public in the sense that it can be accessed directly external to the class. If you want to make it private, you need to put it in the implementation file. For example, we want to add a completionDate property and want to make it private, all we need to do is to add a section as follows above the @implementation line:

```
@interface NTPNoteItem ()
@property NSDate *completionDate;
@end
```

The other Objective-C feature is the so-called *property attributes*; for example, you can add a readonly property attribute to the creationDate property to make it unchangeable.

With all things considered, you can fill in the properties for the NTPNoteItem class as shown in Listings 6.11 and 6.12.

**Listing 6.11 NTPNoteItem.h**

```
#import <Foundation/Foundation.h>
@interface NTPNoteItem : NSObject

@property NSString *itemName;
@property NSString *username;
@property NSString *password;
@property NSString *url;
@property BOOL completed;
@property (readonly) NSDate *creationDate;
```

```
@end
```

**Listing 6.12 NTPNoteItem.m**

```
#import "NTPNoteItem.h"

@interface NTPNoteItem ()
@property NSDate *completionDate;
@end

@implementation NTPNoteItem

@end
```

Next, let's consider what methods to add to the NTPNoteItem class.

Methods in general define what operations can be performed on the properties defined or how the class should behave from another perspective. For example, to give a note item (NTPNoteItem) the ability to get marked as complete, you can add a markAsCompleted method to the interface as shown below:

```
-(void) markAsCompleted;
```

In the above definition, the minus sign (-) at the beginning indicates that it's an instance method, which can be called on an object of the class. Another option is the plus sign (+), which is used to signify that the method can only be called by the class itself, making it a *class* method. Examples of class methods include class factory methods and methods that access some shared properties associated with the class. Finally, the (void) part indicates that the method does not return a value.

Of course, we can have methods with parameters. For example, we can redefine the markAsCompleted method so that it will include a parameter to allow the user to toggle between completed and uncompleted. The modified method can be like this:

```
- (void) markAsCompleted : (BOOL) isComplete;
```

One thing to keep in mind is that when mentioning the name of a method with a parameter, the colon sign (:) should be included as well. For example, the above method should be referred to as markAsCompleted: instead of markAsCompleted. Furthermore, we can actually have more than one parameter. For example, we can redefine the markAsCompleted: method with one more parameter named onDate to make it look like:

```
- (void) markAsCompleted : (BOOL) isComplete onDate : (NSDate *)date;
```

Now the method's name is read as markAsCompleted:onDate:. Note that the first and second parameters are separated with a space rather than a comma (,) or something else. The part onDate is optional, and if present, it is considered part of the second parameter. In other words, you could define it like:

```
- (void) markAsCompleted : (BOOL) isComplete : (NSDate *)date;
```

Thus, when the above method is called, it may look like the following:

```
[markAsCompleted : YES onDate : <a_date_object>];
```

## 6.4.2    Implementing Methods

The structure of a class implementation starts with importing necessary interfaces, followed by private properties (if any), and then implementation of each method. For example, Listing 6.13 shows the skeleton of the NTPNoteItem class implementation, with a class extension section for the completionDate property and the implementation for the markAsCompleted method. As you see, we have two methods implemented here: markAsCompleted: and setCompletionDate. The former is a public method as it's declared in the interface file, while the latter is a private method as it's not declared in the interface file but implemented in the implementation file. Private methods are internal to the class itself only, which is a powerful mechanism for adding internal behavior to a class without allowing other objects to access it.

Think about the above implementation again. If we did not make the setCompletionDate method private, any objects outside the NTPNoteItem would be able to set the completionDate to an arbitrary date at will. By carefully designing a class, we could prevent such things from happening.

In terms of the implementation details, note how an important hidden value, self, is used to refer to the current instance object itself. Also, note that the properties are accessed with the dot notation like self.completed, while the method is invoked by sending the message to the instance object itself, which is represented by the keyword self. You'll learn more about such implementation details as we move along.

**Listing 6.13 Implementing the markAsCompleted: method**

```
#import "NTPNoteItem.h"

@interface NTPNoteItem ()

@property NSDate *completionDate;

@end

@implementation NTPNoteItem


- (void) markAsCompleted : (BOOL) isComplete {
    self.completed = isComplete;
    [self setCompletionDate];
}
- (void) setCompletionDate {
    if (self.completed) {
        self.completionDate = [NSDate date];
    } else {
        self.completionDate = nil;
```

```
    }
}
@end
```

## 6.5 ADDING DATA

This section builds on the project you created so far to demonstrate how to add support for dynamic data to the NoteApp by using design patterns, Foundation framework, Objective-C OOP features we covered. The important skills you'll learn include how to create custom data classes, how to take advantage of common Foundation classes, how to implement a delegate and data source protocol, and how to pass data between view controllers.

Let's start with how to create a data class.

### 6.5.1    Creating a Data Class

To get started, open NoteApp in your Xcode. To verify that your NoteApp is in good shape so far, select Product > Build or press Command-B to build your product. You should see a Build Succeeded square appeared and then flashed away, indicating that building your project succeeded.

In the preceding section, we built an NTPNoteItem class to represent a note item. In this section, we illustrate how we can hook it up with the proper view controller so that a user can initiate and add a new note item to the app.

**Load the Initial Data**

First, let's consider how we can load existing note items into the app when the app is launched. In principle, we should store note items in a persisted storage and load it from there. For simplicity, however, let's hard-code some note items in the code so that we don't get into delicacies about how to deal with a file, etc.

Since we have only two controller classes so far, NTPMyNotesTableViewController and NTPAddNewNoteItemViewController, it's natural to think that loading data should be a task that belongs to the NTPMyNotesTableViewController. Then, in which method should we initialize the NSMutableArray that will hold all note items?

Now let's check what methods the NTPMyNotesTableViewController class already has. We see that it has only three methods without counting those we commented out in the previous section:

1    unwindToList:
2    initWithStyle:
3    viewDidLoad

Obviously, the viewDidLoad is the method we should work on, as that's the point right after the view is loaded. The next question is what data structure we should use to hold the note item list. We choose an NSMutableArray for simplicity. It has to be a mutable array so that note items can be added and removed at will by a user.

The next logical question is where we should put the NSMutableArray, in the interface file or implementation file? Since this is an implementation detail issue and external objects don't need to access it directly, we should make it private. Therefore, as we discussed previously, we should put it into the NTPMyNotesTableViewController.m file as follows:

```
@interface NTPMyNotesTableViewController ()
@property NSMutableArray *noteItems;
@end
```

Note that the @interface and @end lines were created by Xcode by default, so you only need to add the @property line.

Next, add the following code to the viewDidLoad method for initializing the NSMutableArray we mentioned above:

```
self.noteItems = [[NSMutableArray alloc] init;
```

You may also note that the viewDidLoad method has the following two statements commented out by default:

```
// self.clearSelectionOnViewWillAppear = NO;
// self.navigationItem.rightBarButtonItem = self.editButtonItem;
```

We have no need to uncomment them so just leave them in.

Should we add code to load data right after the above statement that allocates and initializes the NSMutableArray? You can do that, but it's not good practice. Since it's a modular task, it helps improve code readability if we put it into a separate method. Let's call that method loadInitialData and implement it as follows:

```
- (void) loadInitialData
{
    NTPNoteItem *item1 = [[NTPNoteItem alloc] init];
    item1.itemName = @"Apple ID";
    [self.noteItems addObject:item1];

    NTPNoteItem *item2 = [[NTPNoteItem alloc] init];
    item2.itemName = @"Golden 1";
    [self.noteItems addObject:item2];

    NTPNoteItem *item3 = [[NTPNoteItem alloc] init];
    item3.itemName = @"Citi MC";
    [self.noteItems addObject:item3];

}
```

At this point, you need to add #import "NTPNoteItem.h" to NTPMyNotesTableViewController.m to make the NTPNoteItem class accessible.

**Display the Data**

At this point, if you run the app, you'll notice that the app still loads the original static data as you keyed in in the preceding chapter. To solve the issue, we need to make the

NTPMyNotesTableViewController a data source of the table view. In order to make that happen, you need to do the following three things:

1    Specify how many sections to load for the table view
2    How many rows per section to load in the table
3    Specify whether to use static or dynamic content for a cell.

Next, let us accomplish those three tasks one by one.

We start with specifying the number of sections to load in the table view. This is done by the method numberOfSectionsInTableView:, which is commented out. We can have all note items displayed in a single section, so make that data source method look like the following:

```
- (NSInteger) numberOfSectionsInTableView : (UITableView *)tableView
{
    return 1;
}
```

The next method, tableView:numberOfRowsInSection:, specifies how many rows to display in a given section. Since we have a single section, we want to display all rows. This can be done by applying the count method from NSMutableArray. Locate that method, uncomment it and make it look like the following:

```
- (NSInteger) tableView:(UITableView *) tableView numberOfRowsInSection :
(NSInteger) section
{
    Return [self.noteItems count];
}
```

The last step is to specify that the table view should use prototype cells with dynamic content rather than static content. To make that happen, we have to configure the table view first on the storyboard by following the below procedure:

1    Open the storyboard for this app.
2    Select Table View in the outline under My Notes Table View Controller – My Notes
3    Open the Attributes inspector in the utility area.
4    Change the table view's Content from Static Cells to Dynamic Prototypes.

At this point, you should see Prototype Cells above the first cell as shown in Figure 6.3.

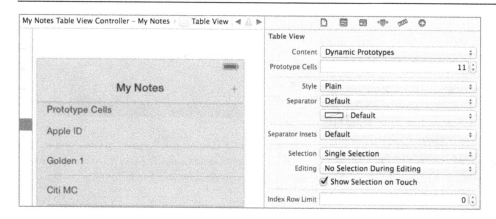

**Figure 6.3** Concept of prototype cells

Prototype cells are configurable cells in terms of text styles, colors, images, and other properties. The data source loads a prototype cell for each row and configures it according to how it is specified. Still, we need to do some extra work: one is to give it an identity and the other is to instruct the data source how to configure the cell for a given row by implementing the tableView's cellForRowAtIndexPath: method. Let's complete these two tasks next.

To configure the prototype cell, follow the below steps:

1    Select the first cell in the table.
2    In the Attributes inspector, locate the Identifier field and type ListPrototypeCell, which is the designated prototype cell name.
3    In the Attributes inspector, locate the Selection field and set it to None. This property is about determining a cell's appearance when a user taps it. Setting the cell selection style to None prevents the cell from being highlighted when a user taps.

The next step is to make some arrangements so that the data source can connect to the configured prototype cell. This is done by the tableView's cellForRowAtIndexPath: method. The table view calls this data source method when it needs to display a given row. If a table view has a small number of rows, this method called on each row to load all rows onscreen. However, for table views that have a large number of rows to display, it would be too slow if all rows were loaded. Instead, only a small fraction of rows should be loaded and the table view only asks for the cells from those rows that are being displayed. The tableView's cellForRowAtIndexPath: method is designed just for that purpose.

Now let's follow the below procedure to implement the logic of fetching a table row and then setting the cell's text label to the item's name:

1    In the project navigator, select NTPMyNotesTableViewController.m.
2    Locate the tableView's cellForRowAtIndexPath: data source method. Uncomment it if it's commented out. The code generated by Xcode is shown below. The first statement of this

data source fetches the cell identified by @"reuseIdentifier". This is where we can hook up the data source with the configured prototype cell.

```
- (UITableViewCell *)tableView:(UITableView *)tableView
    cellForRowAtIndexPath:(NSIndexPath *)indexPath
{
    UITableViewCell *cell = [tableView
        dequeueReusableCellWithIdentifier:@"reuseIdentifier"
            forIndexPath:indexPath];

    // Configure the cell...

    return cell;
}
```

3   Replace the identifier @"reuseIdentifier" with @"ListPrototypeCell" to make it look like:

```
    UITableViewCell *cell = [tableView
      dequeueReusableCellWithIdentifier:@"ListPrototypeCell"
          forIndexPath:indexPath];
```

4   Add the following statements prior to the return statement to get the note item and set its text label:

```
NTPNoteItem *noteItem = [self.noteItems objectAtIndex:indexPath.row];
Cell.textLabel.text = noteItem.itemName;
```

The completed method is shown in Listing 6.14. Now if you run the app in the iOS simulator, it should look similar to Figure 6.4.

**Listing 6.14 Implemented data source method for fetching and configuring a cell**

```
- (UITableViewCell *)tableView:(UITableView *)tableView
    cellForRowAtIndexPath:(NSIndexPath *)indexPath
{
    // fetch the cell
    UITableViewCell *cell = [tableView
      dequeueReusableCellWithIdentifier:@"ListPrototypeCell"
      forIndexPath:indexPath];

    // configure the cell...
    NTPNoteItem *noteItem = [self.noteItems objectAtIndex:indexPath.row];
    cell.textLabel.text = noteItem.itemName;

    return cell;
}
```

**Figure 6.4** NoteApp with dynamic cells

## 6.5.2    Marking Items As Completed

Looking it from another perspective, a view controller is also a delegate of a view. For example, when a user taps a cell in a table view, the table view controller has specific method to respond to that event. Such a method is useful for handling some features of an app. A specific example is that when a user taps an item in NoteApp, the app toggles the item between completed and uncompleted. The method to implement this is the tableView's didSelectRowAtIndexPath: method in NTPMyNotesTableViewController.m. This section shows how this can be done programmatically.

You can follow the below procedure to add the tableView's didSelectRowAtIndexPath: method in NTPMyNotesTableViewController.m:

1    Add the following lines to the end of the file to make it the last method:

```
- (void) tableView:(UITableView *)tableView
    didSelectRowAtIndexPath:(NSIndexPath *)indexPath
{

}
```

2    Since we don't want the cell to stay selected, add the following statement to deselect the cell immediately after selection:

```
[tableView deselectRowAtIndexPath:indexPath animated:NO];
```

3    Add the following statement to find the tapped item:

```
NTPNoteItem *tappedItem = [self.noteItems
   objectAtIndex:indexPath.row];
```

4    Add the following statement to toggle the completion state of the tapped item:

```
tappedItem.completed = !tappedItem.completed;
```

5    Add the following statement to reload the row as it has just been updated:

```
[tableView reloadRowsAtIndexPaths:@[indexPath]
    withRowAnimation:UITableViewRowAnimationNone];
```

Listing 6.15 shows the full implementation of the tableView's didSelectRowAtInexPath: method. You should study this code again so that you will fully understand the implication of every statement therein.

**Listing 6.15 Implementation of the tableView:didSelectRowAtIndexPath: delegate method**

```
- (void) tableView:(UITableView *)tableView
didSelectRowAtIndexPath:(NSIndexPath *)indexPath
{
    [tableView deselectRowAtIndexPath:indexPath animated:NO];
    NTPNoteItem *tappedItem = [self.noteItems
        objectAtIndex:indexPath.row];
    tappedItem.completed = !tappedItem.completed;
    [tableView reloadRowsAtIndexPaths:@[indexPath]
      withRowAnimation:UITableViewRowAnimationNone];
}
```

If you run the app at this point, you will notice that when you tap an item, nothing happens. That's because we have not added code to have a check mark displayed when an item is tapped. Table view cells by design can have a cell accessory displayed on the right side. Although by default there is no accessory, we can add one by adding the following block of code in the tableView's cellForRowAtIndexPath: method:

```
if (noteItem.completed) {
      cell.accessoryType = UITableViewCellAccessoryCheckmark;
   } else {
      cell.accessoryType = UITableViewCellAccessoryNone;
   }
```

Why did we choose the tableView's cellForRowAtIndexPath: method to add the check mark? If you look at the full implementation of that method, you will notice that that's where a table row is fetched and configured, and adding a check mark is a special task of configuring a cell.

If run the app again at this point, you can verify that when an item is tapped (or selected in the iOS simulator), the checkmark appears as expected.

**Figure 6.5** Mark items as completed

## 6.5.3    Add a New Item

This section illustrates how we can add a new note item to NoteApp. When a user taps the plus sign on the far right of the navigation bar, the app should allow a new note item to be added.

From the implementation perspective, just as with the table view, the view controller is the logical place to start with. Essentially, we need to connect the interface to the model by giving the NTPAddNewNoteItemViewController a property to hold the new note item.

Implementing the add-a-new-item functionality can be divided into the following five tasks:

1    Adding an instance of NTPNewNoteItem to the NTPAddNewNoteItemViewController class
2    Connecting the text view to the view controller
3    Connecting the Done button to the view controller
4    Creating a note item after tapping the Done button
5    Storing and displaying the new item

Let's deal with those tasks one by one next.

**Adding an NTPNewNoteItem property to the NTPAddNewNoteItemViewController class**

To add an NTPNewNoteItem property to the NTPAddNewNoteItemViewController class, follow the below procedure:

1    In the project navigator, select NTPAddNewNoteItemViewController.h file.
2    Add an import declaration to NTPNoeItem.h above the @interface line:

```
#import "NTPNoteItem.h"
```

3    Add a noteItem property to the interface between the @interface line the @end line:

```
@property NTPNoteItem *noteItem;
```

**Connecting the text view to the view controller**

To connect the text view to the view controller, follow the below procedure:

1    In the outline, select the Add New Note Item View Controller – My New Note Item.
2    Click the Assistant editor button at the upper right corner of the window's toolbar to open the assistant editor. You should see the NTPAddNewNoteItemViewController.m file opened in an editor area at the bottom, as shown in Figure 6.6. The assistant editor allows you to have two files open at once so that you can perform operations between them, for example, tying a property in the source file with an object in the interface.
3    Select the text view in your storyboard.
4    Control-drag from the text view on your canvas to the assistant edtor area and stop at the line right below the @interface line.
5    In the dialog as shown in Figure 6.7, type textView for the Name attribute, and then click Connect. Xcode adds the necessary code to store a pointer to the text view and configures the storyboard to set up the connection.

**Figure 6.6** Assistant editor displaying the NTPAddNewNoteItemViewController.m file

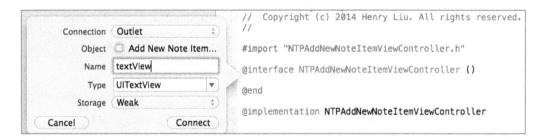

**Figure 6.7** Assistant editor displaying the textView outlet to be created

### Connecting the Done button to the view controller

After connecting the text view to the view controller, we now need to configure the Done button so that when it's tapped, the item will be added to the item list. To do that, we add the Done button as an outlet as follows:

1   Follow the previous step and open the NTPAddNewNoteItemViewController.m file in the Assistant editor, if it's not already open.
2   Select the Done button in the storyboard.
3   Control-drag from the Done button on your canvas to the code displayed in the editor and stop at the line just below the textView property, as shown in Figure 6.8. Enter doneButton for Name and click Connect.

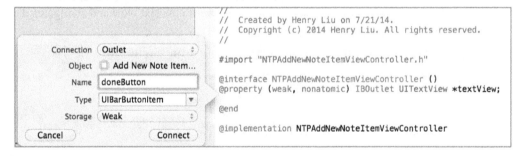

**Figure 6.8** Adding an outlet in Xcode

Note the Done button is configured as an outlet to the view controller. When a user taps the Done button, it initiates an unwind segue back to the note list, as configured in the previous chapter. Before a segue executes, the application object allows the view controller to prepare by calling the prepareForSegue: method. This is the point at which we can check whether the user tapped the Done button, and if so, create a new note item. We perform this step next.

### Creating a note item after tapping the Done button

To create a note item after the Done button is tapped, follow the below procedure:

1    Open the NTPAddNewNoteItemViewController.m file in the Standard editor, if it's not already open.

2    Add the prepareForSegue: method below the @implementation line:

```
- (void) prepareForSegue:(UIStoryboardSegue *) segue sender:(id)
  sender
{
}
```

3    In this method, first, check whether the Done button was tapped. If wasn't, simply return without doing anything.

```
if (sender != self.doneButton) return;
```

4    See whether there is text in the text view:

```
if (self.textView.text.length > 0) {
}
```

5    If there is text, create a new item and give it the name of the text in the text view. Also, set the completed state to NO. If there is no text, there is no need to save the item, so just don't do anything else.

```
self.noteItem = [[NTPNoteItem alloc] init];
self.noteItem.itemName = self.textView.text;
self.noteItem.completed = NO;
```

The prepareForSegue: method should look like the following:

```
- (void) prepareForSegue:(UIStoryboardSegue *) segue sender:(id) sender
{
    if (sender != self.doneButton) return;
    if (self.textView.text.length > 0) {
        self.noteItem = [[NTPNoteItem alloc] init];
        self.noteItem.itemName = self.textView.text;
        self.noteItem.completed = NO;
    }
}
```

**Storing and displaying the new note item**

After a new item is created, it needs to be passed back to NTPMyNotesTableViewController so that it can add the item to the note list. To make that happen, we need to revisit the unwindToList: method created in the previous chapter. This method gets called when the NTPAddNewNoteItemViewController scene closes as the result of a user tapping either the Cancel or the Done button.

To store and display the new note item to the item list, follow the below procedure:

1    Follow the previous step and open the NTPMyNotesTableViewController.m file in the Assistant editor, if it's not already open.

2    Add an import declaration to NTPAddNewNoteItemViewController.h below the current #import line:

```
#import "NTPAddNewNoteItemViewController.h"
```

3    Find the unwindToList: method added in the previous chapter.
4    In that method, retrieve the source view controller from which you're unwinding from, NTPAddNewNoteItemViewController.

```
NTPAddNewNoteItemViewController *source = [segue
   sourceViewController];
```

5    Retrieve the controller's new note item, which is the item created when the Done button was tapped.

```
NTPNoteItem *item = source.noteItem;
```

6    Check whether the item exits. If it's nil, either the Cancel button closed the screen or the text view had no text, so we don't want to save the item. If it does exist, add the item to the noteItems array.

```
if (item != nil) {
        [self.noteItems addObject:item];
}
```

7    Reload the data in the table. As the table view doesn't keep track of its data, it's the responsibility of the data source, namely, the table view controller, to notify the table view that there's new data for it to display.

```
[self.tableView reloadData];
```

The unwindNoteList: method should look like the following now:

```
- (IBAction) unwindToList : (UIStoryboardSegue *) segue
{
    NTPAddNewNoteItemViewController *source = [segue
      sourceViewController];
    NTPNoteItem *item = source.noteItem;
    if (item != nil) {
        [self.noteItems addObject:item];
        [self.tableView reloadData];
    }
}
```

Now run your NoteApp. Click the Add (+) button and create a new item. Verify that you see the new item appears in the list, as shown in Figure 6.9. The NoteApp now takes input from the user, stores it in an object and passes that object between two view controllers. This example shows how you can move data between scenes in a storyboard-based app.

**Figure 6.9** NoteApp with a functioning Add button

## 6.6  SUMMARY

In this chapter, we focused on the data model part of NoteApp. We emphasized the importance of becoming familiar with some basic design patterns and the Foundation framework in order to be able to develop iOS apps effectively and efficiently. We demonstrated how various layers (view, controller and model) work collaboratively to enable user data to be loaded into an app dynamically and updated from time to time.

However, NoteApp at this stage is not a usable app yet. It does not persist data, namely, newly added data will be lost after the user quits the app. In addition, existing note items cannot be revised. The next chapter illustrates how to resolve these issues.

# 7 Data Persistence with Archiving

This section discusses various kinds of data persistence mechanisms that Objective-C and iOS provide. More importantly, we want to explore how we can save note items so that they will be there whenever we launch it. We start with the data persistence mechanisms that Objective-C supports and then illustrate how we can enable it with our NoteApp.

## 7.1 DIRECTORIES

Since iOS is just like any other regular operating systems, it has the capability to provide file system support as well. At the highest level, it supports directories for storing and organizing files. Besides, it also supports iCloud storage that is remote to a device. However, iCloud does not replace local file system, so we focus on local file system first.

However, unlike other file systems, iOS specifies that only two directories are accessible by user's applications: One is the Documents directory and the other is the temporary directory, as is explained next.

### 7.1.1 The App Documents and tmp Directories

The *Documents* and *tmp* directories are where an app is allowed to write to and read from. The iOS manages user files on behalf of the apps that run on iPhone or iPad devices. User apps access these directories using the features provided by Objective-C, such as the NSFileManager, NSFileHandle, NSData classes as so on. Next, we illustrate how these concepts work from Objective-C's perspective.

### 7.1.2 NSFileManager, NSFileHandle and NSData

The Foundation framework supports three basic classes, the NSFileManager, NSFileHandle, and NSData, to facilitate accessing directories and files. They are explained next.

**NSFileManager**

The NSFileManager class is the first class to consider when you need to perform any generic file-system operations. Most file operations can be performed using the shared file manager object. A file manager object usually is your first interaction with the file system. You can use this object not only to create, find, copy, and move files and directories, but also to find information about a file or directory, such as its size, modification date, and BSD permissions. You can also use a file manager object to change the values of many file and directory attributes.

The NSFileManager class supports using the NSString and NSURL classes as ways to specify the location of a file or directory. The support for storing and retrieving a file with the help of an NSURL object makes it possible to integrate with iCloud. Files and directories tagged for iCloud storage are synced to iCloud so that they can be made available to the user's iOS devices and Mac computers. Changes to an item in one location are propagated to all other locations to ensure that the items stay in sync.

**NSFileHandle**

The NSFileHandle class is an object-oriented wrapper for a file descriptor. You can use file handle objects to access data associated with files, sockets, pipes, and devices. For files, you can read, write, and seek within the file, while for sockets, pipes, and devices, you can use a file handle object to monitor the devices and process data asynchronously.

**NSData**

The NSData class and its mutable subclass NSMutableData provide data objects for byte buffers. NSData creates static data objects, whereas NSMutableData creats dynamic objects. They are typically used for data storage and are also used in distributed applications, where data contained in data objects can be moved or copied between applications.

## 7.1.3    Common Directory Operations

Using an NSFileManager object, you can perform the following common directory operations:

■   Identifying a directory
■   Changing directory
■   Creating a new directory
■   Deleting a directory
■   Listing the contents of a directory
■   Getting the attributes of a file or directory

Next, we use an example to illustrate how some of those directory-related operations can be performed through an NSFileManagerObject.

Listing 7.1 shows the main.m file for the Directory target I created in a project named DataPersistence. First, let me help you review the concept of a path. A path specifies the location of a file or directory. On UNIX-like devices, including OS X and iOS, a path is specified with "/" from one level to the next, with the first "/" representing the root directory. A path that starts with

"/" is an absolute path, whereas a path that does not start with a "/" is said to be a relative path – relative to the current working directory.

Now, let's take a look at Listing 7.1. Our first task is to find the Documents directory. As you see, we first declare an NSArray for holding the directory items to be found, and then an NSString for holding the Documents directory. The search is conducted by calling the Foundation function NSSearchPathForDirectoriesInDomains, which has three parameters: NSDocumentationDirectory for directory, NSUserDomainMask for domainMask and YES for expandTilde as a Boolean parameter. These parameters specify what directory to search for, in which domain, and whether it should expand tilde (~).

Next, the first entry found in the Foundation function NSSearchPathForDirectoriesInDomains call is assigned to the docDir variable, which is output to confirm whether it's found or not. I also added a for-loop to see if more than one directory was found. According to the output shown in Listing 7.2, there was only one directory found on my MacBookPro, which was */Users/henry/Library/Documentation*. Notice that with this task, we did not use an NSFileManager. We achieved it just by calling a Foundation function.

The next task is to find the current working directory. In this case, we declared an NSFileManager object, instantiated it with the class factory method defaultManager (which returns the shared file manager object for the process), and retrieved the current working directory by calling the instance method currentDirectoryPath on the fileMgr object. Then, an NSLog function call confirms the current working directory, */Users/henry/Library/Developer/Xcode/DerivedData/ DataPersistence-gkehkzuykqiiuzcndfgmxpgcqvwb/Build/Products/Debug*, which is as shown in Listing 7.2.

The third task is to find the tmp directory. Once again, this was accomplished with a single Foundation function call – NSTemporaryDirectory. The result was */var/folders/m3/wkc8rxb 55255gd8crdbmt4s00000gn/T/*, as is seen in Listing 7.2.

The last task was to list the contents of a directory. It was accomplished by calling the instance method contentsOfDirectoryAtPath with the currentPath obtained from task #2 as the first parameter and a NULL for the second parameter. The two for-loops confirm the entries found in the current working directory, as shown in Listing 7.2.

The next section discusses *Files*.

**Listing 7.1 main.m for Directory target**

```
#import <Foundation/Foundation.h>

int main(int argc, const char * argv[])
{

    @autoreleasepool {

        // 1. find the Documents Directory
```

```
        NSArray *dirPaths;
        NSString *docDir;
        dirPaths = NSSearchPathForDirectoriesInDomains(
           NSDocumentationDirectory, NSUserDomainMask, YES);
        docDir = dirPaths [0];

        NSLog (@"docDir = %@", docDir);
        for (NSString *dir in dirPaths)
           NSLog (@"dir: %@", dir);

        // 2. find the current working directory
        NSFileManager *fileMgr;
        fileMgr = [NSFileManager defaultManager];
        NSString *currentPath = [fileMgr currentDirectoryPath];

        NSLog (@"current dir = %@", currentPath);

        // 3. find the tmp directory
        NSString *tmpDir = NSTemporaryDirectory();

        NSLog (@"tmp dir = %@", tmpDir);

        // 4. list contentes of a dir
        NSArray *fileList;

        //fileMgr = [NSFileManager defaultManager];
        fileList = [fileMgr
             contentsOfDirectoryAtPath:currentPath error:NULL];
        for (NSString *file in fileList)
           NSLog (@"file: %@", file);
        for (int i = 0; i < [fileList count]; i++)
           NSLog (@"file %i: %@", (i + 1), fileList[i]);


    }
    return 0;
}
```

**Listing 7.2 Output of running the Directory target**

```
2014-07-30 10:43:33.936 Directory[1173:303] docsDir =
/Users/henry/Library/Documentation
2014-07-30 10:43:33.937 Directory[1173:303] dir:
/Users/henry/Library/Documentation
2014-07-30 10:43:33.938 Directory[1173:303] current dir =
/Users/henry/Library/Developer/Xcode/DerivedData/DataPersistence-
gkehkzuykqiiuzcndfgmxpgcqvwb/Build/Products/Debug
2014-07-30 10:43:33.938 Directory[1173:303] tmp dir =
/var/folders/m3/wkc8rxb55255gd8crdbmt4s00000gn/T/
2014-07-30 10:43:33.939 Directory[1173:303] file: Date
2014-07-30 10:43:33.939 Directory[1173:303] file: Directory
2014-07-30 10:43:33.940 Directory[1173:303] file: Files
```

```
2014-07-30 10:43:33.940 Directory[1173:303] file 1: Date
2014-07-30 10:43:33.941 Directory[1173:303] file 2: Directory
2014-07-30 10:43:33.941 Directory[1173:303] file 3: Files
Program ended with exit code: 0
```

## 7.2  FILES

Files on an iOS or OS X device can be managed with either an NSFileManager object or an NSFileHandle object. However, they have different purposes. Specifically, the NSFileManager class should be used for the following tasks:

- Checking for the existence of a file
- Checking if a file is readable, writable, executable, or deletable
- Moving/renaming/coping/removing a file
- Comparing the contents of two files
- Creating a symbolic path
- Reading from or writing to a file in its entirety

However, the NSFileManger gives an app no control over how much data to be read from or written to, and from where to be read from or written to, etc. When you need to access a file, read or write, from any location, use the NSFileHandle class for finer granularity in working on a file. This is presented in more details next with an example.

### 7.2.1  Using NSFileHandle for Finer Granularity

In contrast to NSFileManager that provides a shared file manager object, the NSFileHandle class takes ownership of the associated file descriptor, which means that the file handle object is responsible for both creating and closing the object. The example shown in Listing 7.3 illustrates how the NSFileHandle class is typically used.

First, at the beginning of Listing 7.3, two `clock_t` type variables are declared: `start` and `end`. These are helper variables for timing the end-to-end time for this program, so you can ignore them if you are not interested.

Then, as is seen, this example starts with obtaining the shared file object as explained in the preceding example. Then, the entire data from a file at the specified path was read using the instance method `contenstAtPath` into an NSData object, which was written back to another file in its entirety by calling the instance method `createFileAtPath` with the arguments of `contents` and `attributes`. The total time taken by this part was output, as shown in Listing 7.4, which was about 62 milliseconds.

The next part of the example shows how to use the NSFileHandle class to access the same file accessed by the NSFileManager class as discussed above. It goes through the following steps:

- First, an NSFileHandle object was created with the instance method `fileHandleForReadingAtPath` with a parameter specifying the path to the file. Then, an if-statement checks whether the file was not created successfully, and if not, an error message was logged.

- Assuming that the file handle object has been created successfully, the beginning part of the file was read by calling the instance method readDataOfLength:, with a parameter specifying the buffer size. The specified chunk of data was stored in an NSData object.
- The next part shows what you can do with the data read from the file. For our purpose, we wanted to decompose the data line by line, so we created an NSString object for holding the data and then an NSArray object for tokenizing the string using the new line character '\n' by using the NSString's componentsSeparatedByString instance method. Since the input file used contains over 70k lines and 23 lines were fetched with a buffer size of 513 bytes, only the first few tokenized lines were output, as shown in Listing 7.4.

This simple example demonstrates the differences between NSFileManager and NSFileHandle when working on a file. The next section uses an example to illustrate how the NSFileHandle class was used to convert one of my benchmarking programs, *DiskCheck*, from Java and C++ to Objective-C.

**Listing 7.3 main.m for target Files**

```
#import <Foundation/Foundation.h>

int main(int argc, const char * argv[])
{

    @autoreleasepool {
        // for measuring end to end time
        clock_t start, end;
        double elapsed;
        start = clock();

        // 1. get the shared file manager object
        NSFileManager *fileMgr = [NSFileManager defaultManager];

        // 2. read data of a file in its entirety into an NSData object
        NSData *data = [fileMgr contentsAtPath:
         @"/Users/henry/mydev/workspace/ios7/DiskCheck/ioTest1.txt"];

        // 3. write data of a file in its entirety to a file
        [fileMgr createFileAtPath:
           @"/Users/henry/mydev/workspace/ios7/DiskCheck/ioTmp.txt"
        contents:data attributes:nil];

        end = clock();
        elapsed = ((double) (end - start)) / CLOCKS_PER_SEC;
        NSLog(@"Time: %f",elapsed);

        // 4. use NSFileHandle to read a file block by block
           NSFileHandle *file = [NSFileHandle fileHandleForReadingAtPath:
            @"/Users/henry/mydev/workspace/ios7/DiskCheck/ioTest1.txt"];
```

```
    if (file == nil)
        NSLog (@"Cannot open file for read");

    int bufferSize = 513;
    // 5. read the file with a fixed buffer size into an
    // NSData object
    data = [file readDataOfLength: bufferSize];

    // 6. Copy data from an NSData object to an NSString object
    NSString *aStr = [[NSString alloc] initWithData:data
        encoding:NSASCIIStringEncoding];
    NSLog(@"%@",aStr);

    // 7. Tokenize the NSString line by line into an NSArray
    NSArray *tokens = [aStr componentsSeparatedByString: @"\n"];
    int n = (int) [tokens count];
    for (int i = 0; i < n; i++) {
        if (i < 3) NSLog (@"%i: %@", i, tokens[i]);
    }
    NSLog (@"n = %i", n);

    // 8. close the file handle
    [file closeFile];
    }
    return 0;
}
```

**Listing 7.4 Output of running the example shown in Listing 7.3**

```
2014-07-30 11:58:55.408 Files[1554:303] Time: 0.062262
2014-07-30 11:58:55.416 Files[1554:303] SYSTEM_NAME_PREFIX=sys
SYSTEM_START_INDEX=0
SYSTEM_END_INDEX=799
TOP_SERVICE_NAME=StagingServices
SERVICE_NAME_PREFIX=
NUM_OF_LEVELS=4
SUBSERVICES_PER_NODE8
NUM_OF_THREADS=1
ARRAY_SIZE=1
ADD_SERVICES=true
ADD_SYSTEMS=false
DEBUG=true
ALGORITHM=recursive
SERVER_ADDRESS=127.0.0.1
SERVER_PORT=9999
USE_PROXY=true
clearServiceTree=true
HEART_BEAT=100000
recursive ALGORITHM: 31 ms
Recursive call service tree size = 4680
1341255374643,bean,156001000,140400900sun.management.ThreadImpl@314c194d
```

```
13
2014-07-30 11:58:55.416 Files[1554:303] 0: SYSTEM_NAME_PREFIX=sys
2014-07-30 11:58:55.417 Files[1554:303] 1: SYSTEM_START_INDEX=0
2014-07-30 11:58:55.417 Files[1554:303] 2: SYSTEM_END_INDEX=799
2014-07-30 11:58:55.417 Files[1554:303] n = 22
Program ended with exit code: 0
```

### 7.2.2    DiskCheck – a Disk I/O Benchmarking Program

In this section, we take time to illustrate how the NSFileHandle class is used to build a program that has some practical use. The program is named *DiskCheck*, which was developed for benchmarking the I/O capability of a disk drive by reading line by line from a large text file and then writing back line by line to another text file. I wrote this program in Java originally and later converted it to C++ to compare how a disk drive performs in terms of read and write throughput. The problem statement is simple: Given a large text file, how one could write a program in a chosen language to read line by line from the file and write line by line back to another text file, and then report the read and write throughput. It gives some interesting data about the I/O performance of a disk drive versus the version of the program written in different languages, but that's not our focus here. I was interested in how I could re-write the program using Objective-C.

The final version of the program written in Objective-C is shown in Listing 7.5. Although it's lengthy, it shows some interesting techniques about how to solve some commonly-interesting problems in Objective-C. I'll list them one by one next. To help motivate you to follow through, I'd like to mention that we'll apply some of the techniques explained here to multiple versions of our NoteApp with different data persistence mechanisms later.

Let's start with some helper functions first.

**How to return the local time**

We know that there is an NSDate Foundation class that returns the current date and time. However, it uses UTC or GMT by default and it does not report the time local to a specific geography. Many times, we want an app to display the local time, not the UTC or GMT time. This task is implemented in the `getLocalTime` function. Locate this function now in Listing 7.5 and examine it. As you see, it first creates an NSDate object and an NSDateFormatter object. Then, it sets the date formatter by calling the `setDateFormat:` instance method against the `dateFormatter` object with the format @"yyyy-MM-dd' 'HH:mm:ss.SSS'Z'"specified. Note that we could even get the millisecond part with this method. An example output with date format may look like:

```
2014-09-06 10:02:19.174Z
```

Note the last part of 239 ms from the above output. In contrast, the function `currentDateTime()` returns UTC or GMT times.

**How to get start time in seconds**

In addition to getting a time as shown by the preceding example using the getLocalTime function, we might be interested in the absolute number of seconds since a specified reference point –

mostly, January 1$^{st}$, 1970. This is interesting for multiple purposes, and especially, for example, we wanted to get a unique integer number to be used as a postfix to the name of our output text file.

This task was accomplished with the function getStartTimeInSeconds () as shown in Listing 7.5. Locate this function now in Listing 7.5 and examine it. As is seen, it creates an NSDate object and an NSTimeZone object, and then an NSInteger object for holding the number of seconds relative to the GMT time, which was stored in an object named interval. After adding that interval to the GMT interval, we get an integer number that represents the number of seconds since 1970 in our local time. For example, corresponding to the time shown in the preceding example of 2014-09-06 10:02:19.174Z, the function returned a number of 1409997739 as the start time for that run of the program.

**How to create a postfix for naming a file uniquely**

We expect that the output file name will be unique each time we run the program. For this purpose, we need a unique postfix so that we can make it part of the name for the output file. This is accomplished with the getFileNamePostFix function as shown in Listing 7.5. As you see, it simply returns an NSString composed of the number of seconds since 1970 as stated above. Notice the use of the instance method stringWithFormat against the NSString class.

**How to get elapsed time in nanosecond granularity**

We wanted to measure the I/O throughput with a given disk drive, so we needed a timer that is of sufficiently fine granularity. This was accomplished with the function getElapsedTimeInMS, which takes two uint64_t arguments representing start and end of an interval and returns the difference after being converted from nanoseconds to milliseconds. If you jump to the readWriteTest method, you would notice how such variables were declared. Further, you would find that these variables hold the results from calling the function mac_absolute_time () which was defined in the <mach/mach_time.h> header file.

Now, let's take a look at the major part of this program: the main function and the readWriteTest function.

First, the main function requires two input parameters: the input file name and the buffer size for fetching lines block by block. Note that the Foundation framework does not provide a function for reading a file line by line, so I have to fetch block by block and then tokenize for each individual line. There were some specific issues to resolve in Objective-C's context:

- How to extract command-line arguments through the argv [] array to an NSString: This was done using NSString's instance method of stringWithUTF8String: as shown in Listing 7.5.
- How to extract the buffer size parameter as an int value: We took multiple steps to accomplish that. First, we used NSString's intValue instance method to obtain an NSInteger object, and then with that NSInteger object, we obtained an NSNumber object. The int value for representing the buffer size was obtained with the intValue property of the NSNumber object as stated above.

Next, the `readWriteTest` function was called from `main` by passing the `fileName` and `bufferSize` parameters to it. In order to perform read and write operations block by block, we needed the following information:

- Offset: This is the parameter to control from where in the file to read from or write to. The NSFileHandle class has an instance method of `seekToFileOffset:` for pointing to anywhere in a file with the help of the offset parameter.
- Input file size: When using offset to specify the starting point for read/write operations, it's necessary to make sure that the offset falls within the file, not outside the file. The fileSize value was obtained with the NSNumber's instance method of `numberWithUnsignedLongLong:`, together with the NSFileManager's instance methods of `attributesOfItemAtPath` and `fileSize`. You should check the source code in Listing 7.5 to see how it's actually done in Objective-C.

Then, there were a few implementation issues to resolve, including:

- A FileHandleObject can only write to a file that already exists. Therefore, we must create an empty file first before creating an NSFileHandle object for performing write operations. This was accomplished by passing a `contents:nil` parameter to the instance method of `createFileAtPath:` for the NSFileManager object. Check the source code shown in Listing 7.5 under the comment line "`// construct output file handle`" for how this was coded to get a file handle object ready for being used to write data to it.
- How do we determine if end of file (EOF) has reached when reading a file? This was controlled by the condition (`offset < fileSize`) as was shown in the `do-while` loop of the `readWriteTest` function.

Finally, note in the readWriteTest function that the data read in each block is tokenized into an NSArray that contains all lines with a given offset and bufferSize. After a number of lines have been returned, a `for`-loop processes all lines line by line for read and write operations, which is the main logic of this program.

A special note is that when a block of data was obtained with a `readDataOfLength` function call, the last line may only be a partial line. To make sure that the next read returns a block that starts with a complete line, the offset is reset with the following statement, which accounts for the undesirable effect caused by reading block by block rather than line by line:

```
offset += bufferSize - lastLineSize;
```

As a reference, Listing 7.6 shows a typical output obtained with running this program on my MacBookPro. At this point, you should also consult some more results from running this program on my MacBookPro as presented in Preface, illustrating that the Objective-C version outperforms the Java version significantly when both were run on the same machine. This should help give you some confidence that Objective-C potentially can provide far more superior performance than other languages, which is a blessing for all iOS and OS X apps.

This concludes our presentation of this more practical example, which illustrated many aspects about how to use the NSFileManager and NSFileHandle classes for solving file-based data storage problems. The next section introduces how data persistence issue for NoteApp can be solved with different mechanisms from iOS and Objective-C natively.

**Listing 7.5 main.m for the DiskCheck target**

```
//
//  main.m
//  DiskCheck-OBJC (1st param: inputFileName, 2nd param: buffersize in
bytes)
//  bufferSize = 50,000 optimal
//  Created by Henry Liu on 7/29/14.
//
//


#import <Foundation/Foundation.h>
#include <mach/mach_time.h>

// functions must be declared first to avoid error "Conflicting types for
..."
NSString *getFileNamePostFix (); // calls getStartTimeInSeconds for a
postfix
int getElapsedTimeInNS (uint64_t start, uint64_t end); // for timing code
execution using mac_absolute_time
int getStartTimeInSeconds (); // relative to local w/o hard-coding a
timezon
NSString *getLocalTime (); // local with format including ms
NSDate *currentDateTime (); // hard-coded PST

void readWriteTest (NSString *fileName, int bufferSize);

int main(int argc, const char * argv[])
{
   @autoreleasepool {
      NSLog (@"current time: %@", getLocalTime ());

      // extract fileName, bufferSize and call readWriteMethod
      NSString *fileName = [NSString stringWithUTF8String: argv [1]];
      NSString *bufferSizeStr = [NSString stringWithUTF8String:
         argv [2]];
      NSNumber *bufferSize = [NSNumber numberWithInteger:[bufferSizeStr
         intValue]];
       readWriteTest (fileName, bufferSize.intValue);
   }
   return 0;
}

void readWriteTest (NSString *fileName, int bufferSize) {
   // for calculating total execution time
   uint64_t start, end;
   double elapsed;
```

```
// use NSFileHandle to read a file
NSFileHandle *fileHandleIn = [NSFileHandle
   fileHandleForReadingAtPath:fileName];
if (fileHandleIn == nil) {
   NSLog (@"Cannot open file %@ for read", fileName);
   exit (1);
}

// get file size
NSNumber * fileSize = [NSNumber
   numberWithUnsignedLongLong:[[[NSFileManager defaultManager]
   attributesOfItemAtPath:fileName error:nil] fileSize]];
int inputFileSize = [fileSize intValue];

// construct output file handle
NSString *outFileName = [NSString stringWithFormat:@"%@%@%@",
   fileName, @"_", getFileNamePostFix()];
// must create the output file first
[[NSFileManager defaultManager] createFileAtPath:outFileName
   contents:nil attributes:nil];

NSFileHandle *fileHandleOut = [NSFileHandle
   fileHandleForUpdatingAtPath:outFileName];
NSData *outData; // for writeData

//int bufferSize = 50000;
int offset = 0;

//  NSFileManager *fileMgr = [NSFileManager defaultManager];
BOOL eof = false;
uint64_t startRead;
uint64_t endRead;
uint64_t totalReadTime = 0;

uint64_t startWrite;
uint64_t endWrite;
uint64_t totalWriteTime = 0;
int numOfLines = 0;
int writeOffset = 0;

start = mach_absolute_time();
do {
   if (offset < inputFileSize) {
      startRead = mach_absolute_time();
      [fileHandleIn seekToFileOffset: offset];

      NSData *dataBuffer = [fileHandleIn readDataOfLength: bufferSize];
      endRead = mach_absolute_time();
      NSString *block = [[NSString alloc] initWithData:dataBuffer
         encoding:NSASCIIStringEncoding];
      NSArray *lines = [block componentsSeparatedByString: @"\n"];
```

```
      totalReadTime += getElapsedTimeInNS(startRead, endRead);
      int lineCount = (int) [lines count] - 1;

      for (int i = 0; i < lineCount - 1; i++)
      {
         // timing read operations
         startRead = mach_absolute_time();
         NSString* line = lines [i];
         endRead = mach_absolute_time();
         totalReadTime += getElapsedTimeInNS(startRead, endRead);
         numOfLines++;

         // do not use NSMutable data

         outData = [NSMutableData dataWithContentsOfFile: line];
         // timing write operation (seek and write)
         startWrite = mach_absolute_time();
         fileHandleOut seekToFileOffset:writeOffset];
         // do not use writeTofile
         //[line writeToFile:outFileName atomically:YES
            encoding:NSUTF8StringEncoding error:nil];
         [fileHandleOut writeData: outData];
         endWrite = mach_absolute_time();
         writeOffset += outData.length;

         totalWriteTime += getElapsedTimeInNS(startWrite, endWrite);
      }
      int lastLineSize = (int) ((NSString *)lines [lineCount]).length;
      offset += bufferSize - lastLineSize; // subtract lastLineSize
         to discount partial line
   } else {
      eof = true;
   }
} while (!eof);

end = mach_absolute_time();
elapsed = ((double) (end - start)) / 1000000;
// report throughput numbers
NSLog (@"Total Time: %f ms",elapsed);
NSLog (@"test data file size = %f bytes", (double) (inputFileSize));
NSLog (@"Total number of lines: %i", numOfLines);
NSLog (@"total read time = %llu ms", totalReadTime / 1000000);
NSLog (@"read throughput on this drive = %f MB/second", (double)
   (1000.0 * inputFileSize) / totalReadTime);
NSLog (@"total write time = %llu ms", totalWriteTime / 1000000);
NSLog (@"write throughput on this drive = %f MB/second", (double)
 (1000.0 * inputFileSize) / totalWriteTime);
// close file handles
[fileHandleIn closeFile];
[fileHandleOut closeFile];
}
// Get current date/time, format is YYYY-MM-DD.HH:mm:ss GMT
```

```
NSDate *currentDateTime() {
   NSDate *now = [NSDate date];
   NSDate *current = [now dateWithCalendarFormat:@"%Y-%m-%d %H:%M:%S %z"
      timeZone:[NSTimeZone timeZoneWithName:@"PST"]];

   return current;
}
// get current local time with ms
NSString *getLocalTime ()
{
   NSDate *currentDate = [[NSDate alloc] init];
   NSDateFormatter *dateFormatter = [[NSDateFormatter alloc] init];
   [dateFormatter setDateFormat:@"yyyy-MM-dd' 'HH:mm:ss.SSS'Z'"];
   NSString *localDateString = [dateFormatter
      stringFromDate:currentDate];

   return localDateString;
}
int getStartTimeInSeconds () {
   // get current date, timezone and interval from GMT
   NSDate *now = [NSDate date];
   NSTimeZone *zone = [NSTimeZone systemTimeZone]; // local timezone
   NSInteger interval = [zone secondsFromGMTForDate:now];
   //NSDate *startDate = [now addTimeInterval:interval]; //deprecated

   // return start time in seconds - used as a postfix for
      creating a new output file
   int startTime = [now timeIntervalSince1970] + interval; //
   NSLog(@"start time in seconds: %d",startTime);

   return startTime;
}
NSString *getFileNamePostFix () {
   // convert an int to NSString using new literal syntax
   // NSString *fileNamePostFix = [@(getStartTimeInSeconds())
      stringValue];
   NSString *fileNamePostFix = [NSString stringWithFormat:@"%i",
      getStartTimeInSeconds()];
   return fileNamePostFix;
}
```

**Listing 7.6 Output of running main.m shown in Listing 7.5**

```
henrys-mbp:DiskCheck-OBJC henry$ ./a.out ioTest1.txt 50000 > objc-disk-
check-run1.txt
2014-09-06 10:02:19.178 a.out[389:507] current time: 2014-09-06
10:02:19.174Z
2014-09-06 10:02:19.180 a.out[389:507] start time in seconds: 1409997739
2014-09-06 10:02:22.259 a.out[389:507] Total Time: 3079.016733 ms
2014-09-06 10:02:22.260 a.out[389:507] test data file size =
58063070.000000 bytes
```

```
2014-09-06 10:02:22.260 a.out[389:507] Total number of lines: 771320
2014-09-06 10:02:22.260 a.out[389:507] total read time = 79 ms
2014-09-06 10:02:22.261 a.out[389:507] read throughput on this drive =
726.028327 MB/second
2014-09-06 10:02:22.261 a.out[389:507] total write time = 238 ms
2014-09-06 10:02:22.261 a.out[389:507] write throughput on this drive =
243.520446 MB/second
henrys-mbp:DiskCheck-OBJC henry$
```

## 7.3   DATA PERSISTENCE BY ARCHIVING

This section is dedicated to exploring data persistence for our NoteApp. Remember that we had initial data loaded previously in the method of loadInialData in the class implementation file of NTPMyNotesTableViewController.m as follows:

```
- (void) loadInitialData
{

    NTPNoteItem *item1 = [[NTPNoteItem alloc] init];
    item1.itemName = @"Apple ID";
    [self.noteItems addObject:item1];

    NTPNoteItem *item2 = [[NTPNoteItem alloc] init];
    item2.itemName = @"Golden 1";
    [self.noteItems addObject:item2];

    NTPNoteItem *item3 = [[NTPNoteItem alloc] init];
    item3.itemName = @"Citi MC";
    [self.noteItems addObject:item3];


}
```

The above loadInitialData method was called in the viewDidLoad method of the same class of NTPMyNotesTableViewController. This was done at that point as expediency so that we could focus on other implementations, rather than how data should actually be loaded. Apparently, this is not how a real app should load its data. We want the data to be persisted to an offline storage place so that every time when the app is launched, the data should be loaded from there. That would also allow an app to add new data and update existing data.

In this section, we explore multiple options for persisting data for our NoteApp. We start with archiving that is supported by the Foundation framework so that we don't have to start from scratch.

First, follow the below procedure to copy the existing NoteApp to a new project named NoteApp-II:

- Locate your existing NoteApp directory in your file system, right-click on it and select Duplicate.
- Rename the duplicated project to NoteApp-II.
- Right-click on the *NoteApp.xcodeproj* file, select Open With > Xcode, as shown in Figure 7.1.

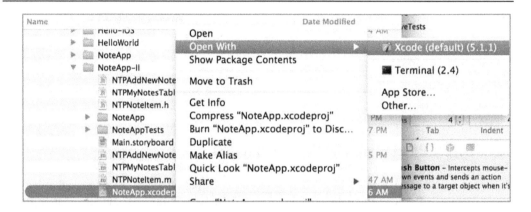

**Figure 7.1** Open the project file for a duplicated Xcode project

- When the duplicated project is open in your Xcode IDE, it's still named NoteApp. Now, click the project name in the left navigation pane, select the Standard Editor > File inspector in the right utility pane, change the name from NoteApp to NoteApp-II under Identity and Type, and press Return.
- Now you should see a popup as shown in Figure 7.2, asking whether you want to rename all classes, etc., as well. Select *"Don't Rename"* and you have completed duplicating your existing NoteApp project.

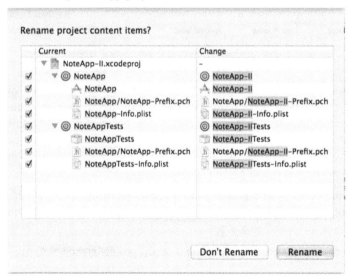

**Figure 7.2** Rename project content items

This is our start point for exploring implementing data persistence with Archiving for our NoteApp. This way, we don't overwrite our existing NoteApp project.

Next, we focus on how to persist data with Archiving for our NoteApp.

Instead of writing code using the Objective-C's file API manually to store the app data to a file and then restore data from it next time when the app is launched, we should use some ready-to-use framework-based mechanisms to accomplish app data persistence. One of such mechanisms is *archiving*, which is a technique involving encoding objects into a format that is writable to an external file. Data stored in a file may be subsequently decoded (or unarchived) and used to automatically rebuild the objects for the app to use after being launched.

One archiving option to accomplish data persistence is to use the Foundation framework's NSKeyedArchiver and NSKeyedUnarchiver classes. In order to understand what these classes do, it's necessary to under three basic concepts of *object graphs*, *archives* and *serializations*, as explained next, according to *Archives and Serializations Programming Guide* from the *iOS Developer Library*.

## 7.3.1    Object Graphs

Object-oriented design creates applications that contain complex webs of interrelated objects. Objects are linked to each other by one object either owning or containing another object or holding a reference to another object to which it sends messages. This web of objects is called an object graph.

In practice, even with very few objects, an application's object graph becomes entangled with cyclic references and multiple links to individual objects. To illustrate the point of complexity involved in an object graph, Figure 7.3 shows a partial object graph for a simple Cocoa application is OS X. Consider the window's view hierarchy portion of the object graph. This hierarchy shows each view containing a list of all of its immediate subviews. However, views have links to each other to describe the responder chain and the keyboard focus loop. Views also link to other objects in the application for target-action messages, contextual menus and much more.

There are situations where we may want to convert an object graph, partial or whole, into a form that can be saved to a file or transmitted to another process or application and then reconstructed. Nib files and property lists are two examples in OS X when object graphs are saved to a file. Nib files are archives that represent the complex relationships within a user interface, such as a window's view hierarchy, whereas property lists are serializations that store simple hierarchical relationship or basic value objects, as discussed next.

## 7.3.2    Archives

An application can use an archive as the storage medium for its data model. Instead of designing and implementing a special file format for your data, you can leverage Cocoa's archiving infrastructure to store the objects directly into an archive. The archive preserves the identity of every object in the graph along with all the relationships it has with all other objects in the graph. When unarchived, the rebuilt object graph would be an exact copy of the original object graph.

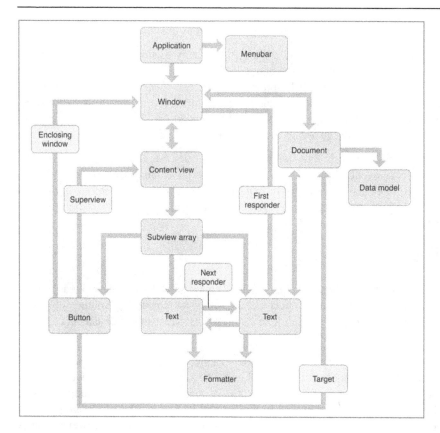

**Figure 7.3** partial object graph of an OS X application

## 7.3.3    Serializations

Serializations stores a simple hierarchy of value objects, such as arrays, strings, dictionaries, and binary data. Serializations only preserve the value of the objects and their position in the hierarchy. Multiple references to the same value object may result in multiple objects when de-serialized.

Property lists are examples of serializations. Application attributes and user preferences are stored as property lists.

## 7.3.4    Root Object and Keyed Archives

A root object is a starting point of an object graph. Its purpose is for avoiding cyclic references, which may result in an infinite processing loop. Keyed archives work on object graphs that have an identifiable root object. They are created by NSKeyedArchiver objects and decoded by NSKeyedUnarchiver, as we will see in the example to be discussed next. Keyed archives differ from sequential archives in that every value encoded in a keyed archive is given a key or name. When decoding the archive, the values can be represented by name, allowing the values to be requested in any order or arbitrarily.

To produce archives with a single object graph, `NSKeyedArchiver` implements two methods: `archiveRootObject:toFile:` and `archivedDataWithRootObject:`. The archives created with `NSKeyedArchiver` can only be unarchived with NSKeyedUnarchiver's methods of `unarchiveObjectWithFile:` and `unarchiveObjectWithData:`. We will see how these two classes are used to implement data persistence for our NoteApp.

### 7.3.5   Data Persistence for NoteApp with Archiving

To implement data persistence for an app, it's important to make the following two decisions carefully:

1   At what point to restore data
2   At what point to save data

It's obvious that data should be restored when the app is loaded. For our NoteApp under development, it would be the `NTPMyNotesTableViewController`'s `viewDidLoad` method. If you still remember, that is where we hard-coded some initial note items as shown by the code snippet given at the beginning of this section. Now we'd like to replace it with `NSKeyedArchiver` class.

Listing 7.7 shows the `viewDidLoad` method that calls the `loadInitialData` method to restore note item data from an archive. First, declare a property named `dataFilePath` for specifying the archive file path in the `NTPMyNotestableViewController`.h file as follows:

```
@property (strong, nonatomic) NSString *dataFilePath;
```

Then, replace the original `loadInitialData` method with the NSKeyedArchiver-based implementation as shown in Listing 7.7. This new implementation works as follows:

- First, the `_dataFilePath` was constructed based on the default Documents directory as explained in Section 7.1. However, that did not work with the iOS simulator and it had to be overwritten with a directory, in this case, /Users/henry/mydev, so that the archive file *noteapp2_data.archive* could be created. (If you decide to try this on your Mac, you need to change this hard-coded path to your own.)
- Next, an NSFileManager shared object was created for checking whether the archive file exists. If it does, an NSMutableArray object named dataArray was declared to receive the archived data. The following statement uses the NSKeyedUnarchiver's `unarchiveObjectWithFile:` method to load the `dataArray` collection object, which self-explains how the archived objects are unarhived with a given archive file:

```
dataArray = [NSKeyedUnarchiver unarchiveObjectWithFile:
        _dataFilePath];
```

Finally, a `for`-loop is used to fill up the `NTPMyNotestableViewController`'s `noteItems` array, which will be used to load the main view of NoteApp. As you see, this is indeed very simple, thanks to the NSKeyedUnarchiver class provided by the Foundation framework.

Note that the `NTPNoteItem` object named `item` must be placed inside the `for`-loop; otherwise, the same last item will be used for filling in all rows in the main table view.

Next, we discuss how to save data with the NSKeyedArchiver class, following Listing 7.7.

**Listing 7.7 The loadInitialData method that uses the NSKeyedUnarchiver class**

```
- (void) viewDidLoad
{
    [super viewDidLoad];

    self.noteItems = [[NSMutableArray alloc] init];
    [self loadInitialData];
    // Uncomment the following line to preserve selection
    // between presentations.
    // self.clearsSelectionOnViewWillAppear = NO;

    // Uncomment the following line to display an Edit button in
    // the navigation bar for this view controller.
    // self.navigationItem.rightBarButtonItem = self.editButtonItem;
}

- (void) loadInitialData
{
    NSString *docsDir;
    NSArray *dirPths;

    dirPths = NSSearchPathForDirectoriesInDomains(
        NSDocumentationDirectory, NSUserDomainMask, YES);
    docsDir = dirPths [0];
    docsDir = @"/Users/henry/mydev";
    _dataFilePath = [[NSString alloc] initWithString:[docsDir
      stringByAppendingPathComponent: @"noteapp2_data.archive"]];

    NSFileManager *fileMgr = [NSFileManager defaultManager];
    if ([fileMgr fileExistsAtPath: _dataFilePath])
    {
        NSLog (@"Load data from file: %@", _dataFilePath);
        NSMutableArray *dataArray;

        dataArray = [NSKeyedUnarchiver unarchiveObjectWithFile:
          _dataFilePath];
        NSLog (@"number of items to load: %i", [dataArray count]);

        //NTPNoteItem *item = [[NTPNoteItem alloc] init];
        for (NSMutableString *itemName in dataArray) {
            NTPNoteItem *item = [[NTPNoteItem alloc] init];
            item.itemName = itemName;
            [self.noteItems addObject:item];
            NSLog (@"added item: %@", item.itemName);
        }
```

```
   } else {
       NSLog (@"File does not exist: %@", _dataFilePath);
   }
}
```

You might think that we could save data in NTPAddNewNoteItemViewController's prepareForSegue:sender method, as that's when the Done button was clicked. However, recall as we discussed earlier that the NSKeyedArchiver class serializes an object graph, which is unlike a traditional database that one could operate on a single item or object with the complex inter-objects relationships maintained internally in the database as constraints. This means that we need to save data in the place where the entire note item list is accessible, which is the NTPMyNoteTableBiewController. In that controller, there is an instance method named unwindToList:segue, which will be triggered whenever the Done button is clicked.

Listing 7.8 shows the unwindToList:segue method, which calls the saveData method for archiving all note items. The first part of the saveData method is identical with that of the loadInitialData method we discussed previously, namely, the _dataFilePath was established first before archiving. In fact, you could comment it out, as it's already established when the app was launched.

Then, an NSMutableArray named itemArray was declared for holding the name of all items, which was done in a for-loop. After that, the NSKeyedArchiver class's archiveRootObject:toFile: method was called to archive the itemArray as shown below:

```
[NSKeyedArchiver archiveRootObject: itemArray toFile: _dataFilePath];
```

That's all it takes to save data using Foundation framework's archiving feature. Figure 7.4 shows how this version of the NoteApp looks like when a few items were added and persisted. You should run your version of the app to make sure it works as expected.

**Listing 7.8 The saveData method that uses the NSKeyedArchiver class**

```
- (IBAction) unwindToList : (UIStoryboardSegue *) segue
{
    NTPAddNewNoteItemViewController *source = [segue
      sourceViewController];
    NTPNoteItem *item = source.noteItem;
    if (item != nil) {
        [self.noteItems addObject:item];
        [self.tableView reloadData];

        // persist data here
        [self saveData];
    }
}
- (void) saveData
{
    NSString *docsDir;
    NSArray *dirPths;
```

```
dirPths = NSSearchPathForDirectoriesInDomains(
    NSDocumentationDirectory, NSUserDomainMask, YES);
docsDir = @"/Users/henry/mydev";
_dataFilePath = [[NSString alloc] initWithString:[docsDir
    stringByAppendingPathComponent: @"noteapp2_data.archive"]];
NSLog (@"save data to: %@", _dataFilePath);

NSMutableArray *itemArray = [[NSMutableArray alloc] init];

for (NTPNoteItem *item in _noteItems) {
    [itemArray addObject:item.itemName];
}
[NSKeyedArchiver archiveRootObject: itemArray toFile: _dataFilePath];
NSLog (@"completed saving data to: %@", _dataFilePath);
}
```

**Figure 7.4** NoteApp-II with data persisted using archiving

## 7.3.6    Performance Considerations

As we all know, serialization and deserialization are very costly in general. Some general performance considerations for archiving and unarchiving data are given below for your reference:

- The less you archive for an object, the less you have to unarchive, and both writing and reading archives are faster.
- It is typically more beneficial for deserialization to be faster than for serialization to be faster, if a trade-off is possible.
- Read only the keys that you need to save the amount of work to be done for deserialization.

This concludes our discussion of data persistence implementation using archiving for our NoteApp. The next section discusses how we can implement data persistence using CoreData.

## 7.4    SUMMARY

In this chapter, we explored how the Foundation framework supports operations on directories and files. We also covered how to solve data persistence with the archiving feature that the Foundation framework provides. The next chapter explores solving the same data persistence issue for NoteApp with the Core Data framework.

# 8 Data Persistence with Core Data

In the previous chapter, we demonstrated how to use NSKeydArchiver and NSKeyedUnarchiver to persist data. In this chapter, we demonstrate how to use the Core Data framework to persist data. The latter is significantly more sophisticated than the former, and preferred for handling larger datasets involved in an app.

## 8.1 SQLITE

Before discussing the Core Data framework, we have to mention another data storage technology – the SQLite. SQLite is an embedded, relational database management system (RDBMS). It's open-sourced and its website is http://www.sqlite.org. Unlike other traditional RDBMS, SQLite has no standalone server process running in the background. Instead, apps use SQLite by statically linking to SQLite's library, which is written in C in the form of C functions and C data structures. As such, app can make direct calls to SQLite's C functions. However, to bridge the disparities between Objective-C and the C-based SQLite library, it's necessary to convert NSString objects to UTF8 format before they can be passed to SQLite's functions as arguments. The rest of it is similar to programming a traditional RDBMS using the SQL language, namely, after opening a database file, you can create tables, insert data , query the data, and so on, by manually writing relevant SQL statements.

However, for those who are app developers, SQLite is a different paradigm and the learning curve is too steep. For this reason, we skip covering SQLite and jump to the Core Data framework, as discussed next.

## 8.2 THE CORE DATA FRAMEWORK

Core Data is an object graph persistence framework provided by Apple for developing and running apps on the Mac OS X and iOS operating systems. It works on the concept of object graphs, which are representations of relational entity-attribute models. Core Data can serialize such models into XML, binary or SQLite stores; and in the case of SQLite store, Core Data interfaces directly with SQLite, taking away the burden of dealing with the SQLite directly from developers.

Figure 8.1 shows the Core Data stack, with apps on the top, and then Managed Object Context, Persistent Store Coordinator, Persistent Store, Data Files, and Managed Object Model. Each component in the stack is elaborated next.

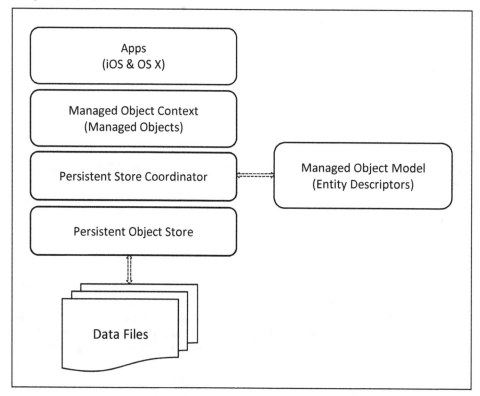

**Figure 8.1** Core Data stack

## 8.2.1    Managed Object Context

By using the Core Data framework, you do not need to interact with the persistent store directly. This is made possible with the concept of managed object context, which takes care of the management tasks against the underlying persistent store on behalf of developers. On the other hand, you can also consider the managed object context layer like a staging area that holds the object graphs temporarily within the context until the context is instructed to save the changes, at which point the changes are flushed down through the stack to the underlying files.

## 8.2.2    Managed Objects

Managed objects are created by the application and correspond to rows or records in a relational database table. All managed objects must be registered within a managed object context. Therefore, to some extent, managed objects are model objects residing in the managed object context layer. You add objects to the object graph and remove objects from the graph using the context. The context tracks the changes you make to the managed objects, and provides undo and redo support as necessary. It also ensures that if you change the relationships between objects, the integrity of the object graph is maintained. If you choose to save the changes you have made, the context ensures that your objects are in a valid state before being written to the persistent store.

### 8.2.3    Persistent Store Coordinator

The persistent store coordinator acts as a mediator between the managed object context layer and the underlying persistent object store. This layer is needed in order to support multiple persistent data stores and multiple managed object contexts, as shown in Figure 8.2. The coordinator ensures that when you fetch or save objects, the appropriate files are accessed.

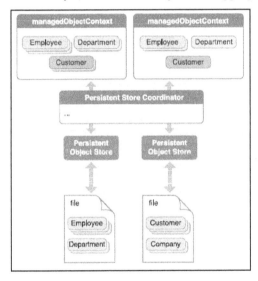

**Figure 8.2** Multiple data stores and multiple contexts coordinated by a managed object coordinator

### 8.2.4    Persistent Object Stores

The persistent object store layer refers to the underlying storage type for storing data. Core Data provides one in-memory store and three types of disk-based persistence store, such as XML, atomic, and SQLite, where the XML type is not available on iOS. The atomic store refers to the binary store type as a built-in store. From the app code perspective, you should not be concerned with implementation details for any particular store type. You should interact with managed objects and the persistence stack. There are, however, behavioral differences between the types of store that you should consider when deciding what type of store to use. Table 8.1 summarizes the differences in terms of speed, object graph and so on.

**Table 8.1 Differences among three types of persistent data store**

| Metric | XML | Atomic | SQLite | In-Memory |
|---|---|---|---|---|
| Speed | Slow | Fast | Fast | Fast |
| Object Graph | Whole | Whole | Partial | Whole |
| Other factors | Externally parsable | | | No backing required |

It's important to keep in mind that Core Data has its own private format in supporting SQLite. You are not allowed to create your own SQLite database using native SQLite API and use it directly with Core Data. If you have an existing SQLite database, you need to import it into Core Data Store and then let Core Data manage it on behalf of you.

## 8.2.5   Managed Object Model

A managed object model is a schema that provides a description of the managed objects or entities in your application. The core concept of the managed object model is entity description, as shown in Figure 8.3, for two entities, Employee and Department. An entity description lists the attributes of an entity as well as its relationships with other entities. Managed object models are typically created using Xcode's Data Model Design (DMD) tool, as you will learn next.

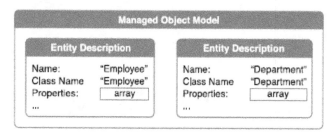

**Figure 8.3** A managed object model with two entities

## 8.3   IMPLEMENTING DATA PERSISTENCE USING CORE DATA

First, we use a standalone project to illustrate how data persistence can be implemented with Core Data without applying it to our NoteApp immediately. After getting a good understanding of how it works, we apply it to our NoteApp in the next section.

The problem statement is that we would like to build a single view interface with a text view box for a user to enter a note, which can then be saved by pressing a *Save* button or searched by pressing a *Find* button. Here is the procedure to accomplish it:

1    **Creating a standalone project**. Our major consideration for this step is that we create a project that has Core Data support included from the beginning. Note, however, that not every project template supports this feature. With Xcode 5, only three project templates support it: the Master-Detail Application, Utility Application and Empty Application. Therefore, in order to have Core Data supported to begin with, use the iOS/Application > Empty Application template to create a new project, as we are not trying to build a master-detail or utility application. For clarity purposes, Figure 8.4 shows the options I chose for this project. You can choose your own product name and class prefix, etc., but make sure you check the Use Core Data box, which is our purpose for this project.

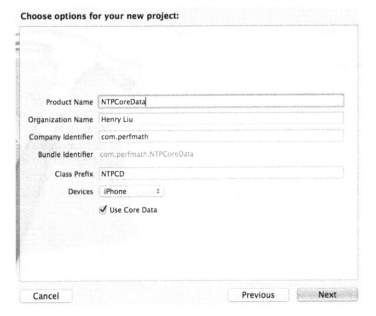

**Figure 8.4** Creating a project with Use of Core Data checked

2    **Creating the entity description**. The next step is to create an entity description for the Core Data framework to work on. This can be done with the built-in Data Model Design (DMD) tool included in Xcode. As you might have noticed, by including Core Data when the project was created, we have an NTPCDAppDelegate class (default interface file and implementation file) and an NTPCoreData.xcdatamodeld file created in the NTPCoreData project folder, among others. The NTPCDAppDelegate class will serve as the delegate between the data model and the user interface, while the NTPCoreData.xcdatamodeld file actually represents the Data Model Design tool we mentioned. So, click on that file in the project navigation pane to bring up the DMD tool. Figure 8.5 shows the entity description created in my environment.

As you see, the entity description is named `Notes` and has only one attribute of `note` of `String` type. It's created by first clicking on the Add Entity button at the bottom, and then adding the note attribute with the String type selected. The entity description was renamed to `Notes` by double-clicking on the default name under the *Entities* tab in the outline pane.

**Figure 8.5** The Notes entity description created with the DMD tool

3 **Adding a storyboard to the project**. Since we chose the *Empty Application* project template, we had no storyboard created from step 1. So now, we need to manually add a storyboard for holding the user interface. To create a storyboard, press *File > New File ...*, select *iOS/User Interface > Storyboard*, and click *Next*. Make sure you select *iPhone* from the *Device Family* menu and click *Next*. Name the storyboard to *Main*, and click *Create* to create it.

4 **Specifying the storyboard to use at deployment**. When a storyboard is created, it doesn't mean that it will be used. You have to specify it. To specify a storyboard to be used for a user interface, click the project in the navigation area, select the *General* tab in the content area, expand the *Deployment Info* tab if not open, and specify the desired storyboard from the drop-down menu next to the *Main Interface* label. Refer to Figure 8.6 for more clarity.

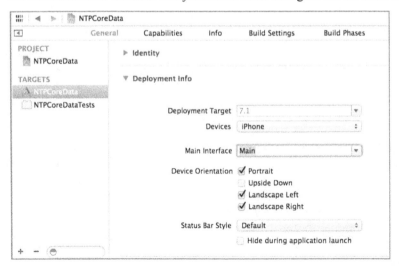

**Figure 8.6** Specifying the Main Interface with the storyboard created

5    **Disabling the window object from the CoreData's delegate class**. Since we are going to use the storyboard for displaying the UI, we do not need to invoke the `window` object for the application. Therefore, locate the body of the `didFinishLaunchingWithOptions:` method in `NTPCoreDataAppDelegate.m`, comment out all statements except the last `return YES` statement.

6    **Adding a view controller**. Since we need a mediator between the data model and the user interface, the next step is to create a view controller. You can add a view controller by first Ctrl-clicking on the *NTPCDCoreData* folder in the navigation pane, and then select *New Files....* Then, select *iOS/Cocoa Touch > Objective-C* class template. Then, enter the Class name and Subclass name as shown in Figure 8.7. Make sure that *the Also create XIB file* is not checked and *iPhone* is selected.

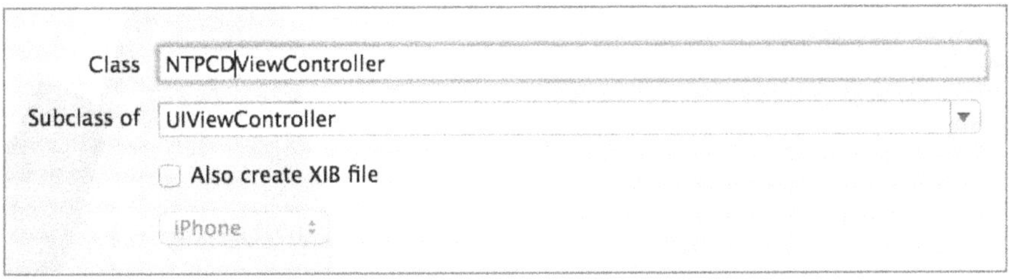

**Figure 8.7** Creating a custom view controller class

7    **Adding a UIViewController instance to the storyboard**. The next step is to add a UIViewController class to the storyboard and associate it with the custom view controller class you've just created. Click on the Main.storyboard file and drag-drop a view controller instance from the Object Library panel onto to the storyboard canvas. You're not done yet. To associate the view controller instance with the custom view controller created above, select the view controller instance in the outline so that the view controller is highlighted in blue in the canvas. Then, select the Identity inspector from the Utility tool bar, and change the *Class* setting from *UIViewController* to *NTPCDViewController* class created above.

8    **Defining the user interface**. As we stated early, we need to put a text view, a *Save* button and a *Find* button in the scene created so far. You should be able to do this yourself with what you have learnt so far, so I would not bore you with specific instructions. Just be reminded that you need to resize the text view box so that it would fit into the iPhone form factor. Also, you can configure the background color of the text view box by setting its background color using the Attributes inspector, as shown in Figure 8.8.

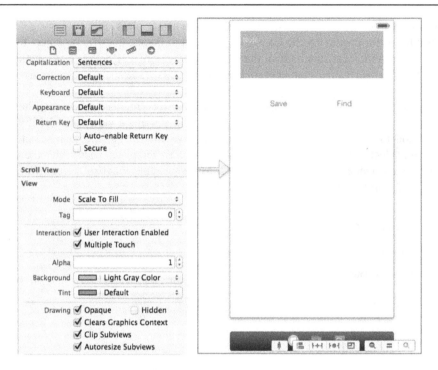

**Figure 8.8** An example of how a UI control can be configured using the Utility tools

9    **Creating outlets and actions**. To tie UI controls to properties and methods of a custom view controller class, you need to create *outlets* and *actions*. That is done by first selecting the UI control, and then selecting the *Assistant Editor* from the editor bar, which should bring up the controller interface file right underneath the storyboard. For this case, do the following:

o    *Creating a text view outlet. Ctrl*-drag from the *text view* control to right below the @interface line of the *NTPCDViewController.h* file, which is displayed in the code editing area. Lift up your finger, and you should see a dialog flanking where you dragged to. Enter *note* for the name, and click *Connect* to create the outlet as shown in Figure 8.9.

o    *Creating a save action.* Now follow the same procedure as stated above to create a *save* action by *Ctrl*-dragging from the *Save* button in the scene to the next *property* position in the *NTPCDViewController.h* file. This time, select *Action* from the *Connection* drop-down menu and name it *saveData*. Refer to Figure 8.10 taken in my environment.

o    *Creating a find action.* Now follow the same procedure as stated above to create a *find* action by *Ctrl*-dragging from the *Find* button in the scene to the next *property* position in the *NTPCDViewController.h* file. Once again, select *Action* from the *Connection* drop-down menu and name it *findNote*.

**Figure 8.9** The *note* outlet that connects the *text view* with the note property of the view controller class

**Figure 8.10** The *saveData* action to be triggered when the *Save* button is pressed

10   **Implementing the *saveData* method**. To be detailed next.
11   **Implementing the *findNote* method**. To be detailed next.

After the UI controls have been tied to the *outlet* properties and *action* methods of the custom view controller class, the last step is to implement those *action* methods. Specifically, you need to implement the saveData and findNote action methods as listed in the *NTPCDViewController.h* file, shown in Listing 8.1.

**Listing 8.1 The NTPCDViewController.h file**

```
#import <UIKit/UIKit.h>
#import "NTPCDAppDelegate.h"

@interface NTPCDViewController : UIViewController
@property (weak, nonatomic) IBOutlet UITextView *note;
- (IBAction)saveData:(id)sender;
- (IBAction)findNote:(id)sender;

@end
```

Listing 8.2 shows how the saveData: method is implemented using Core Data. Reading the code line by line, we see immediately how it is implemented:

1   First, an appDelegate object is created with UIApplication's sharedApplication method and the delegate method thereafter.
2   Then, an NSManagedObjectContext object is created with the appDelegate's managerObjectContext method.

3   An `NSManagedObject` object named `newNote` is created using `NSEntityDescription`'s `insertNewObjectForEnityForName:inManagedObjectContext` method. Notice that the `Notes` entity description we created early in DMD and the `context` object created locally here are passed in as arguments.

4   The `setValue` method of the managed object, `newNote`, is called to set the value for the *note* attribute, using the value from the *text view* control. See Listing 8.1 for the name of the property `note` to understand  why `note.text` represents the text entered in the *text view* box by the user.

5   Finally, the `save:` method of the *context* object is called to save the current content of the *text view* box to the persistent store. If it fails to save, an `NSError` object records the details.

Next, we explain how the `findNote` method is implemented.

**Listing 8.2 The saveData method for the NTPCDViewController.m class**

```
- (IBAction) saveData: (id) sender {
    NTPCDAppDelegate *appDelegate = [[UIApplication sharedApplication]
        delegate];

    NSManagedObjectContext *context = [appDelegate managedObjectContext];
    NSManagedObject *newNote;
    newNote = [NSEntityDescription
        insertNewObjectForEntityForName: @"Notes"
            inManagedObjectContext: context];
    [newNote setValue: _note.text forKey: @"note"];

    NSError *error;
    [context save: &error];
}
```

Listing 8.3 shows the implementation of the `findNote` method. It is explained as follows:

1   The beginning part of creating an `appDelegate` object and a context object is the same as with the `saveData` action, so we would not repeat it further.

2   The unique part of finding an entity is that it requires creating the following three objects first:

o   An `NSEntityDescription` object
o   An `NSFetchRequest` object
o   An `NSPredicate` object

3   Once those three objects as stated above are created as shown in Listing 8.3, the request object's `predicate` property is set, and then context object's `executeFetchRequest:` method is called with the conditioned request object to retrieve the entities that match. The result set is assigned to an `NSArray`. Finally, if some entities are found, either the first entity or all can be accessed using the `valueForKey:` method of the `NSManagedObject` class. Notice that the key is what was specified in DMD, which was also used in the `saveData:` method.

**Listing 8.3 The findNote method for the NTPCDViewController.m class**

```
- (IBAction)findNote:(id)sender {
    NTPCDAppDelegate *appDelegate = [[UIApplication sharedApplication]
        delegate];

    NSManagedObjectContext *context = [appDelegate managedObjectContext];
    NSEntityDescription *entityDesc = [NSEntityDescription
      entityForName:@"Notes" inManagedObjectContext:context];

    NSFetchRequest *request = [[NSFetchRequest alloc] init];
    [request setEntity:entityDesc];

    NSPredicate *pred = [NSPredicate predicateWithFormat:@"(note = %@)",
      _note.text];
    [request setPredicate:pred];

    NSError *error;
    NSArray *objects = [context executeFetchRequest:request
      error:&error];

    NSManagedObject *matches = nil;
    if ([objects count] == 0) {
        NSLog (@"No matches");
    } else {
        matches = objects [0];
        _note.text = [matches valueForKey:@"note"];
        NSLog (@"%lu matches found", (unsigned long) [objects count]);
    }

}
```

You can run this sample in your environment, and the outcome should look similar to Figure 8.11 if you go through the following sequence of activities:

1   Enter something, for example, AppleID, in the text view box, and save it by clicking on the *Save* button.
2   Enter something else and save it again.
3   Now, enter your first entry in the text view box and click *Find* button. You should see a log line in the debug area, showing how many entries have been found.

This concludes our Core Data example. Next, let's see how we can implement data persistence using Core Data for our NoteApp.

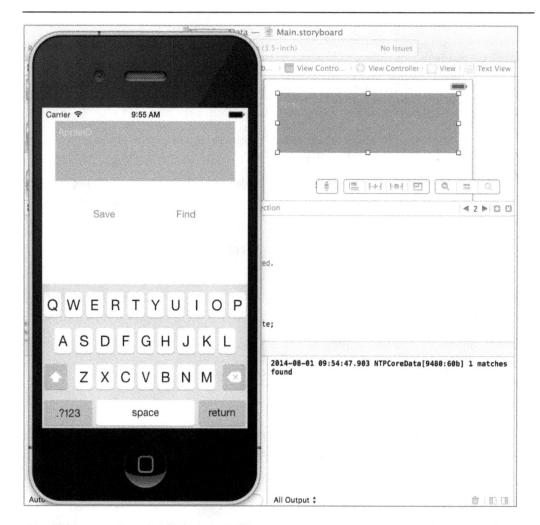

**Figure 8.11** Outcome of running the NTPCoreData example

## 8.4  Implementing Data Persistence using Core Data for NoteApp

Before we start, follow the same procedure as used in Chapter 7 and duplicate our NoteApp-II project to a new project named NoteApp-CD-I, denoting the first version of our NoteApp using Core Data.

At this point, you might want to take a snapshot of your project in case you need to fall back to a specific checkpoint. You can initiate creating a snapshot by pressing *Ctrl-Command-S* or select *File > Creating Snapshot...* Besides, you may want to turn on the "*Show line numbers*" feature as shown in Figure 8.12, just in case you encounter errors during running your app, which in general displays a call stack, for example, as shown in Figure 8.13. (You can bring up the dialog as shown in Figure 8.12 by selecting *Xcode > Preferences* or pressing the key sequence of *Command* and then comma.) After making these preparations, we are ready to explore how we can implement data persistence for our NoteApp with Core Data.

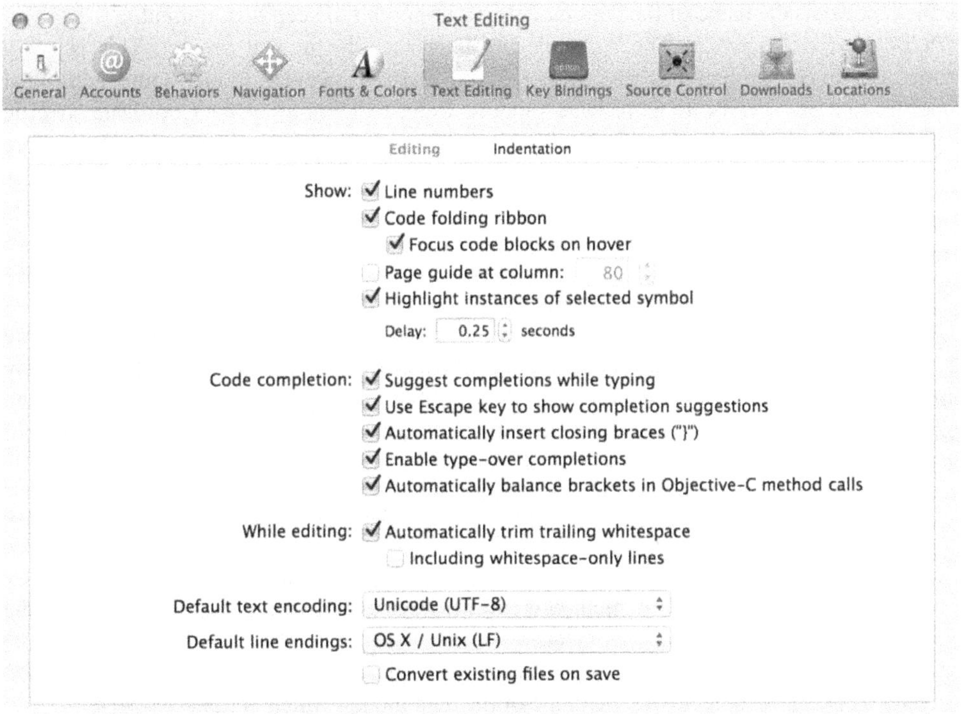

**Figure 8.12** Turning on Xcode's *show line numbers* feature

```
2014-08-01 15:14:18.124 NoteApp[12146:60b] *** Terminating app due to uncaught exception
'NSInvalidArgumentException', reason: '+entityForName: nil is not a legal NSManagedObjectContext parameter
searching for entity name 'Notes''
*** First throw call stack:
(
    0    CoreFoundation                    0x01b591e4 __exceptionPreprocess + 180
    1    libobjc.A.dylib                   0x018d88e5 objc_exception_throw + 44
    2    CoreData                          0x0002aa1b +[NSEntityDescription
entityForName:inManagedObjectContext:] + 251
    3    NoteApp                           0x00003c7d -[NTPMyNotesTableViewController loadInitialData] + 221
    4    NoteApp                           0x00003b98 -[NTPMyNotesTableViewController viewDidLoad] + 184
    5    UIKit                             0x006b733d -[UIViewController loadViewIfRequired] + 696
    6    UIKit                             0x006b75d9 -[UIViewController view] + 35
    7    UIKit                             0x006e2509 -[UINavigationController rotatingSnapshotViewForWindow:] +
52
    8    UIKit                             0x00a29e3c -[UIClientRotationContext
initWithClient:toOrientation:duration:andWindow:] + 420
    9    UIKit                             0x005dec22 -[UIWindow
_setRotatableClient:toOrientation:updateStatusBar:duration:force:isRotating:] + 1495
    10   UIKit                             0x005de646 -[UIWindow
_setRotatableClient:toOrientation:updateStatusBar:duration:force:] + 82
```

**Figure 8.13** An example call stack thrown due to an error uncaught during execution

Let's start with reviewing what files specific to Core Data had been created when you checked the "*Use Core Data*" check box, as shown in Figure 8.4, during creating that NTPCoreData project. If you open up that project in your Xcode, you should see the following three files:

1   *NTPCoreData.xcdatamodeld*: The data model file for that project. Note that the first part of the file represents the name of the data model. It's important to keep this in mind.

2   *NTPCDCoreAppDelegate.h*: The AppDelegate interface file for that project. This is not a surprise, as every project has an appDelegate class. However, it has some additional properties that are specific to Core Data support. Refer to Listing 8.4 for Core Data specific properties added to this interface file by Xcode, which are the major components of the Core Data stack as shown in Figure 8.1:

   o   **managedObjectContext**
   o   **managedObjectModel**
   o   **persistentStoreCoordinator**

3   *NTPCDCoreAppDelegate.m*: The AppDelegate implementation file for that project. Listing 8.5 shows the parts that are specific to Core Data, with irrelevant methods and many comment lines removed to save space. First, notice the synthesized properties at the beginning of the implementation. Then, note the following methods that are specific to Core Data:

   o   applicationWillTerminate:. This method has a statement [self saveContext] to save the context before terminating.
   o   saveContext. This is the method called by the previous method.
   o   managedObjectContext. This method creates the managedObjectContext object and the persistentStoreCoordinator object.
   o   managedObjectModel: This method creates the managedObjectModel object. It also creates a modelURL object with the name of the data model, which is NTPCoreData.
   o   persistentStoreCoordinator: This method returns the persistentStoreCoordinator object with a storeURL object that has the store name of "NTPCoreData.sqlite" in it.
   o   applicationDocumentsDirectory: This method returns the path for the Documents directory.

**Listing 8.4 The default AppDelegate interface file for an Xcode-generated project with "Use Core Data" checked**

```
#import <UIKit/UIKit.h>

@interface NTPCDAppDelegate : UIResponder <UIApplicationDelegate>

@property (strong, nonatomic) UIWindow *window;

@property (readonly, strong, nonatomic) NSManagedObjectContext
*managedObjectContext;
@property (readonly, strong, nonatomic) NSManagedObjectModel
*managedObjectModel;
```

```
@property (readonly, strong, nonatomic) NSPersistentStoreCoordinator
*persistentStoreCoordinator;

- (void)saveContext;
- (NSURL *)applicationDocumentsDirectory;

@end
```

**Listing 8.5 The default AppDelegate implementation file for an Xcode-generated project with "Use Core Data" checked**

```
#import "NTPCDAppDelegate.h"

@implementation NTPCDAppDelegate

@synthesize managedObjectContext = _managedObjectContext;
@synthesize managedObjectModel = _managedObjectModel;
@synthesize persistentStoreCoordinator = _persistentStoreCoordinator;

// This part is removed to save space. The remaining part is
// specific to Core Data
- (void)applicationWillTerminate:(UIApplication *)application
{
    [self saveContext];
}

- (void)saveContext
{
    NSError *error = nil;
    NSManagedObjectContext *managedObjectContext =
      self.managedObjectContext;
    if (managedObjectContext != nil) {
        if ([managedObjectContext hasChanges] && ![managedObjectContext
            save:&error]) {
            NSLog(@"Unresolved error %@, %@", error, [error userInfo]);
            abort();
        }
    }
}

#pragma mark - Core Data stack

- (NSManagedObjectContext *)managedObjectContext
{
    if (_managedObjectContext != nil) {
        return _managedObjectContext;
    }

    NSPersistentStoreCoordinator *coordinator = [self
      persistentStoreCoordinator];
    if (coordinator != nil) {
```

```
        _managedObjectContext = [[NSManagedObjectContext alloc] init];
        [_managedObjectContext etPersistentStoreCoordinator:coordinator];
    }
    return _managedObjectContext;
}

- (NSManagedObjectModel *)managedObjectModel
{
    if (_managedObjectModel != nil) {
        return _managedObjectModel;
    }
    NSURL *modelURL = [[NSBundle mainBundle] RLForResource:@"NTPCoreData"
      withExtension:@"momd"];
    _managedObjectModel = [[NSManagedObjectModel alloc]
      initWithContentsOfURL:modelURL];
    return _managedObjectModel;
}

- (NSPersistentStoreCoordinator *)persistentStoreCoordinator
{
    if (_persistentStoreCoordinator != nil) {
        return _persistentStoreCoordinator;
    }

    NSURL *storeURL = [[self applicationDocumentsDirectory]
      URLByAppendingPathComponent:@"NTPCoreData.sqlite"];

    NSError *error = nil;
    _persistentStoreCoordinator = [[NSPersistentStoreCoordinator alloc]
      initWithManagedObjectModel:[self managedObjectModel]];
    if (![_persistentStoreCoordinator
      addPersistentStoreWithType:NSSQLiteStoreType configuration:nil
      URL:storeURL options:nil error:&error]) {

        NSLog(@"Unresolved error %@, %@", error, [error userInfo]);
        abort();
    }

    return _persistentStoreCoordinator;
}

#pragma mark - Application's Documents directory

- (NSURL *)applicationDocumentsDirectory
{
    return [[[NSFileManager defaultManager]
URLsForDirectory:NSDocumentDirectory inDomains:NSUserDomainMask]
lastObject];
}

@end
```

Now let's add Core Data support manually to our NoteApp-CD-I project by following the below procedure:

1   **Adding a data model**. Go by pressing Command-N or selecting File > New Files.... Select iOS/Core Data > Data Model template. Name the data model NTPCDM, or something of your own. After this step, you should see an *NTPCDM.xcodemodeld* file under your project.

2   **Creating an entity description.** Follow the same  procedure as used for the previous NTPCoreData project. The entity description and the only attribute should be named Notes and note, respectively.

3   **Adding Core Data specific properties to NTPAppDelegate.h file.** Refer to Listing 8.4.

4   **Adding Core Data specific methods to NTPAppDelegate.m file.** Refer to Listing 8.5. Remember to replace the data model name and data model file name from *NTPCoreData* and *NTPCoreData.sqlite* to *NTPCDM* and *NTPCDM.sqlite*, respectively.

5   **Replacing the saveData method in the NTPMyNotesTableViewController.m file**. See Listing 8.6 for the contents of the replacement. This method will be called when a user clicks the Done button, which triggers the unwindToList: method, which is also shown in Listing 8.6. However, unlike the archiving method, we need to pass an NTPNoteItem object in as we only need to deal with the new note item rather than the entire object graph.

6   **Replacing the loadInitialData method in the NTPMyNotesTableViewController.m file**. See Listing 8.7 for the contents of the replacement. This method will be called when the app is launched. It will load all note items as specified by the predicate @"(note != %@)", nil.. The last for-loop does the actual loading work.

7   **Importing the Core Data framework**. At this point, you might see many errors marked in red. That's because you have not imported the relevant Core Data header files yet. To finish it up, perform the following two tasks:

   o   Open up the NoteApp-Prefix.pch file located in the *Supporting Files* folder and add #import <CoreData/CoreData.h> as shown in Listing 8.8.

   o   Add CoreData.framework to the *Link Binary With Libraries* section in your project's *Build Phases* setting, as you did before with your previous project.

**Listing 8.6 saveData method implemented with Core Data**

```
- (IBAction) unwindToList : (UIStoryboardSegue *) segue
{
    NTPAddNewNoteItemViewController *source = [segue
        sourceViewController];
    NTPNoteItem *item = source.noteItem;
    if (item != nil) {
        [self.noteItems addObject:item];
        [self.tableView reloadData];

        // persist data here
        [self saveData:item ];
    }
}
- (void) saveData: (NTPNoteItem *)item
```

```
{
    NTPCDAppDelegate *appDelegate = [[UIApplication sharedApplication]
      delegate];

    NSManagedObjectContext *context = [appDelegate managedObjectContext];
    NSManagedObject *newNote;
    newNote = [NSEntityDescription
      insertNewObjectForEntityForName:@"Notes"
        inManagedObjectContext:context];
    [newNote setValue: item.itemName forKey: @"note"];

    NSError *error;
    [context save: &error];
    NSLog (@"context saved");
}
```

**Listing 8.7 loadInitialData method implemented with Core Data**

```
- (void) loadInitialData
{
    // load initial data using Core Data
    NTPCDAppDelegate *appDelegate = [[UIApplication sharedApplication]
      delegate];

    NSManagedObjectContext *context = [appDelegate managedObjectContext];
    NSEntityDescription *entityDesc = [NSEntityDescription
      entityForName:@"Notes" inManagedObjectContext:context];

    NSFetchRequest *request = [[NSFetchRequest alloc] init];
    [request setEntity:entityDesc];

    NSPredicate *pred = [NSPredicate predicateWithFormat:@"(note != %@)",
      nil];
    [request setPredicate:pred];
    NSManagedObject *matches = nil;

    NSError *error;
    NSArray *objects = [context executeFetchRequest:request
      error:&error];
    if ([objects count] == 0) {
       NSLog (@"No matches");
    } else {
       NSLog (@"%lu matches found", (unsigned long) [objects count]);
    }
    for (NSManagedObject *item in objects) {
       NTPNoteItem *newItem = [[NTPNoteItem alloc] init];
       newItem.itemName = [item valueForKey:@"note"];
       [self.noteItems addObject:newItem];
       NSLog (@"added item: %@", newItem.itemName);
    }
}
```

**Listing 8.8 Adding <CoreData/CoreData.h> to the projects precompiled header file – NoteApp-prefix.pch**

```
#ifdef __OBJC__
    #import <UIKit/UIKit.h>
    #import <Foundation/Foundation.h>
    #import <CoreData/CoreData.h>
#endif
```

To verify your implementation, run the app in iOS simulator. Add a few items, quit it, and relaunch it to verify that the app works as expected. You can also rotate it by pressing Command – <left arrow>key sequence to make sure it still works. For your reference, Figure 8.14 shows how it looks in my environment.

**Figure 8.14** NoteApp-CD-I

## 8.5   MORE FEATURES FOR NOTEAPP

We have built a working NoteApp with data persistence using Core Data in the previous section. In this section, we explore some more features for NoteApp to make it more practical. Specifically, we explore two more features: (1) Make the table view scrollable, and (2) make it possible for a user to delete a note item.

We start with how to make NoteApp's table view scrollable first next.

### 8.5.1   Scrolling in a table view

In fact, the UITableView class has already made a table view scrollable by default. If you open up the System Preferences > TrackPad > Point & Click dialog, as shown in Figure 8.15, notice that there is a Three finger drag setting that is unchecked by default. Now, check it and exit the dialog.

**Figure 8. 15** Enabling three-finger drag for scrolling a table view

Now, open your NoteApp, click somewhere in the table view to set the focus, and apply three fingers on your TouchPad by moving up and down. You should see that the rows of the table view move up and down as well. This is what we would expect when scrolling a view.

## 8.5.2    Deleting a note item

For this exercise, let's first duplicate our previous project, NoteApp-CD-I, to NoteApp-CD-II by following the procedure described previously.

By default, table views are read only, which means that users are prevented from deleting table view items or rows. To enable editing a table view, we need to make some changes. The first change we need to make is to expose the Edit button, which is controlled buy one statement as follows in the viewDidLoad method of the NTPMyNotesTableViewController.m file:

```
// Uncomment the following line to display an Edit button
// in the navigation bar for this view controller.
   // self.navigationItem.rightBarButtonItem = self.editButtonItem;
```

Since we already have an Add button there for adding a new note, uncomment the above line and change right to left as follows:

```
self.navigationItem.leftBarButtonItem = self.editButtonItem;
```

After making this change, you should see an Edit button at left in the navigation bar. Clicking on it should make all visible rows deletable. If you click on the delete icon located at the beginning of a row, the Delete button will be exposed, as shown in Figure 8.16. However, if you press the Delete button, it will not respond, which is because we have not actually implemented anything to make that happen yet. Next, we describe what it takes to make that happen.

**Figure 8. 16** Delete icon (left) and Delete (right) button for each row of a table view after the Edit button is enabled

Now, do this experiment: Uncomment the two methods as shown in Listing 8.98 in the NTPMyNotesTableViewController.m file. Note that the first method, canEditRowAtIndexPath, makes an individual row deletable by returning a Boolean value YES. To confirm this, you can do a three-finger swipe towards left on a row, which would bring up a single row for deleting as shown in Figure 8.17. However, pressing that Delete button would result in an uncaught exception complaining that it's an *Invalid update*, as shown in Figure 8.18. That is, once again, because we have not instructed the app how to delete a note item yet. We complete it next.

**Figure 8.17** Delete a single made possible with a three-finger swipe toward left

```
⊡  ▶  I▶  ⟳  ⬇  ⬆  ◢   NoteApp ⟩ ⛨ Thread 1 ⟩ ▦ 14 main
2014-08-02 16:03:34.589 NoteApp[19447:60b] *** Assertion failure in -[UITableView
_endCellAnimationsWithContext:], /SourceCache/UIKit_Sim/UIKit-2935.137/UITableView.m:1368
2014-08-02 16:03:34.592 NoteApp[19447:60b] *** Terminating app due to uncaught exception
'NSInternalInconsistencyException', reason: 'Invalid update: invalid number of rows in section 0.  The number of
rows contained in an existing section after the update (11) must be equal to the number of rows contained in that
section before the update (11), plus or minus the number of rows inserted or deleted from that section (0
inserted, 1 deleted) and plus or minus the number of rows moved into or out of that section (0 moved in, 0 moved
out).'
*** First throw call stack:
(
    0   CoreFoundation                      0x01b581e4 __exceptionPreprocess + 180
    1   libobjc.A.dylib                     0x018d78e5 objc_exception_throw + 44
    2   CoreFoundation                      0x01b58048 +[NSException raise:format:arguments:] + 136
    3   Foundation                          0x014b74de -[NSAssertionHandler
handleFailureInMethod:object:file:lineNumber:description:] + 116
```

**Figure 8.18** Uncaught exception thrown with deleting a row

**Listing 8.9 Methods to uncomment in a table view controller to support editing**

```
// Override to support conditional editing of the table view.
- (BOOL)tableView:(UITableView *)tableView
    canEditRowAtIndexPath:(NSIndexPath *)indexPath
{
    // Return NO if you do not want the specified item to be editable.
    return YES;
```

```
}

// Override to support editing the table view.
- (void)tableView:(UITableView *)tableView
  commitEditingStyle:(UITableViewCellEditingStyle)editingStyle
    forRowAtIndexPath:(NSIndexPath *)indexPath
{
    if (editingStyle == UITableViewCellEditingStyleDelete) {
        // Delete the row from the data source
        [tableView deleteRowsAtIndexPaths:@[indexPath]
      withRowAnimation:UITableViewRowAnimationFade];
    } else if (editingStyle == UITableViewCellEditingStyleInsert) {
        // Create a new instance of the appropriate class, insert it
        // into the array, and add a new row to the table view
    }
}
```

Listing 8.10 shows the deletion logic for this exercise. We actually need to delete a row twice, first in memory and then in the Core Data database to persist it. If we just delete it in memory, the deleted item will show up when the app is launched again. The Core Data deletion part is done with the following statement, eventually:

```
[context deleteObject:objects[0]];
```

Since we already covered how Core Data works in the previous section, we would not spend time explaining the entire deletion logic line by line here. Instead, we explore another interesting feature – moving a row up or down in the table view.

**Listing 8.10 The commitEditingStyle:forRowAtIndexPath method for deleting a row**

```
- (void)tableView:(UITableView *)tableView
  commitEditingStyle:(UITableViewCellEditingStyle)editingStyle
    forRowAtIndexPath:(NSIndexPath *)indexPath
{
    if (editingStyle == UITableViewCellEditingStyleDelete) {

        // save the item before deleting from memory
        NTPNoteItem *item = [self.noteItems objectAtIndex:indexPath.row];
        [self.noteItems removeObjectAtIndex:indexPath.row];

        // Delete the row from the data source
        NTPAppDelegate *appdelegate = [[UIApplication sharedApplication]
          delegate];
        NSManagedObjectContext *context =
          appdelegate.managedObjectContext;
        NSEntityDescription *entityDesc = [NSEntityDescription
          entityForName:@"Notes" inManagedObjectContext:context];

        NSFetchRequest *request = [[NSFetchRequest alloc] init];
        [request setEntity:entityDesc];
```

```
    NSPredicate *pred = [NSPredicate predicateWithFormat:@"(note =
        %@)", item.itemName];
    [request setPredicate:pred];

    NSError *error;
    NSArray *objects = [context executeFetchRequest:request
        error:&error];
    [context deleteObject:objects[0]];

    [context save:&error];

    // Animate the deletion
    [tableView deleteRowsAtIndexPaths:@[indexPath]
        withRowAnimation:UITableViewRowAnimationFade];

    } else if (editingStyle == UITableViewCellEditingStyleInsert) {
        // Create a new instance of the appropriate class, insert
        // it into the array, and add a new row to the table view
    }
}
```

## 8.5.3    Moving a note item up or down

If you look at the NTPMyNotesTableViewController.m file, you would notice that two methods relating to move were commented out by default. Just uncomment those two methods as shown in Listing 8.11, run the app, click on Edit and then a delete icon, you would see a screen as shown in Figure 8.19. Notice that we have a new icon at the far right end or each row, which is a handle for moving a row to a new position. This may not be a must-have feature, but as an example, it just shows what you can do with styling cells of a table view.

**Listing 8.11 methods to uncomment in a table view controller to support moving a row**

```
// Override to support rearranging the table view.
- (void)tableView:(UITableView *)tableView
    moveRowAtIndexPath:(NSIndexPath *)fromIndexPath
        toIndexPath:(NSIndexPath *)toIndexPath
{
}

// Override to support conditional rearranging of the table view.
- (BOOL)tableView:(UITableView *)tableView
    canMoveRowAtIndexPath:(NSIndexPath *)indexPath
{
    // Return NO if you do not want the item to be re-orderable.
    return YES;
}
```

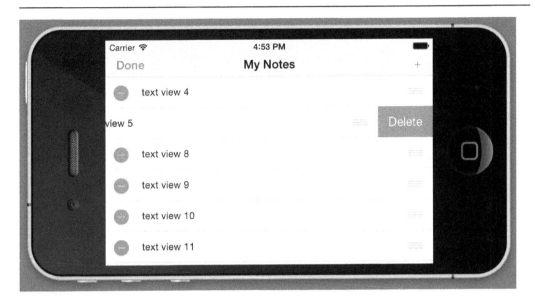

**Figure 8.19** The move handle enabled for moving a row up or down

## 8.6 SUMMARY

In this chapter, we have given a more thorough coverage of how the Core Data framework works. We illustrated how to implement data persistence using the Core Data framework with our NoteApp. At the end of the chapter, we demonstrated how to make a table view scrollable, how to delete a row, and how to move a row up or down.

The next chapter introduces you to implementing NoteApp for iPad and iPhone devices by using the master-detail app structure and Core Data framework. It's a good opportunity not only for you to check what you've learnt so far, but also for you to learn some new skills, such as how to use Objective-C's delegate protocol feature to pass data from one view controller to another.

# 9 Implementing NoteApp for iPad and iPhone Devices

The previous chapters focused on a specific version of NoteApp targeting iPhone as a tableview based app. If we ran it on the iOS Simulator for iPad, it would look similar to Figure 9.1. Although it works, perhaps we want to make it look a bit fancier, because an iPad has a much larger form factor than an iPhone does. In fact, Apple recommends using a split view and a popover for developing apps that run on iPad devices. Accordingly, this chapter focuses on developing a version of NoteApp specifically for running on iPad devices first and then for iPhone devices. You'll see what it takes to make our NoteApp run on both iPad and iPhone devices using a new master-detail structure. This is also a good opportunity for you to learn some delicacies associated with developing an app that runs both on iPhone and iPad devices.

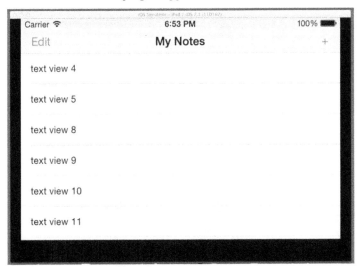

**Figure 9.1** Running the NoteApp on iOS Simulator for iPad

## 9.1    MASTER-DETAIL APPS

You might be familiar with master-detail apps that divide a user interface into a master view and a detail view, where the master view is more like an index and the detail view shows actual contents for a given index. An email app is a typical example of a master-detail app, where the left pane shows email items and the right pane displays the content when a particular email item is selected. This type of apps fits iPad devices particularly well due to an iPad's larger form factor.

### 9.1.1    Xcode-Generated Skeleton Master-Detail App

To help you quickly get a perception about what a master-detail app looks like, let's create one by using the default master-detail project template from Xcode. This can be easily done by following the below procedure:

1    Start up your Xcode and Select Create a new Xcode project
2    Select iOS/Application > Master-Detail Application and then click Next
3    Enter a product name (e.g., Master-Detail), a Class Prefix (e.g., MD), iPad for Devices, and then lick Next
4    Save your project by clicking on Create

You should now have a master-detail skeleton project created, with a user interface similar to Figure 9.2. (The original font for each label was too small and relabeled for better visibility.)

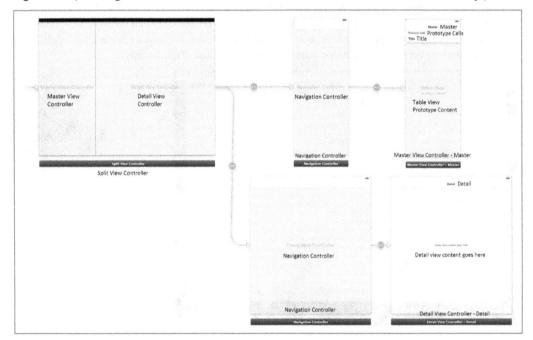

**Figure 9.2** The user interface of a master-detail app created by Xcode

Figure 9.3 shows the files created by the Master-Detail project template, along with the outline for the user interface, which was not included with the screenshot shown in Figure 9.2 due to space limitation. From the programming perspective, Xcode created three classes with the default master-Detail app template: an AppDelegate class, a MasterViewController class, and a DetailViewController class. From the user interface perspective, Xcode generated five scenes: a Split View Controller Scene as the initial scene, two navigation controller scenes, one for each of the Master Scene and Detail Scene, respectively, and a Master Scene and a Detail Scene. In addition to the standard view controller, first responder and exit components, the root scene has two relationships, one to each of the two navigation controllers for Master and Detail, respectively, while each of the two navigation controllers has a relationship corresponding to the master and detail view controllers, respectively. This is the big picture of how a skeleton master-detail app user interface looks like.

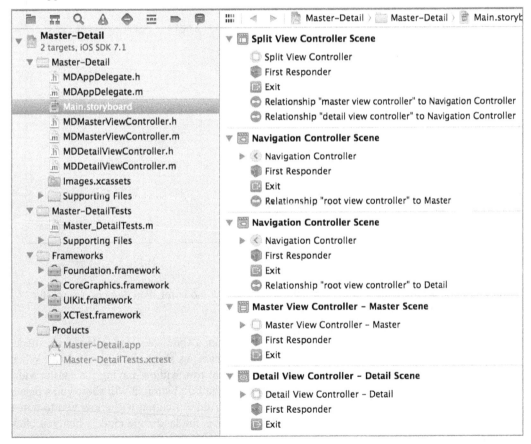

**Figure 9.3** The project structure of a master-detail app created by Xcode automatically

Although we have not implemented any app logic yet, you can actually run the skeleton master-detail app for iPad. Figure 9.4 shows how the default master-detail app looks on a simulated iPad in portrait mode. At the startup, you'll see a Master button located at the left end at the top, as shown in Figure 9.4 (a). (If you cannot see it, you can scroll up to make it visible.) When you click on it, you will see a split view between the master and detail, as shown in Figure 9.4 (b). When you click on the Edit button, it will show you a delete icon at the beginning of each row, while clicking on the Add (+) button will allow you to add a new row. (Note that the default behavior with the Add button is to create a timestamp, which is, of course, modifiable.) The master view shown in Figure 9.4 (b) is called a *popover*. Clicking anywhere in the detail view will take you back to the initial view with the popover disappeared.

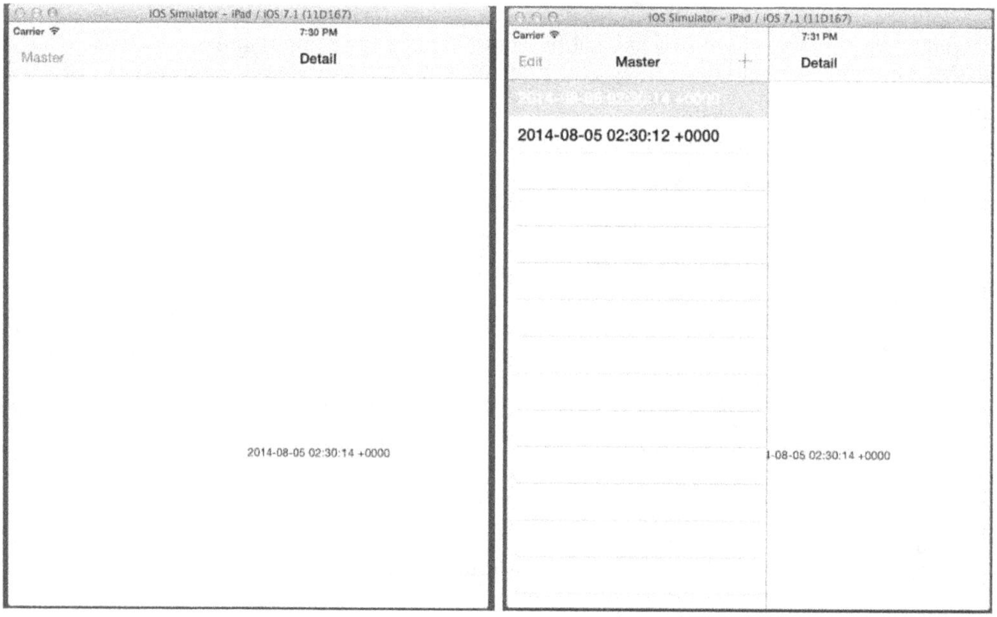

(a)                                              (b)

**Figure 9.4** The default master-detail app running in *portrait* mode for iPad devices: (a) master view; (b) popover

Figure 9.5 shows how the default master-detail app looks on a simulated iPad in landscape mode. At the startup, you see a Master view located in the left pane, as shown in Figure 9.5 (a). When you click on an item, you will see the detail view for that row without having the master view disappear, as shown in Figure 9.5 (b). When you click on the Edit button, it will show you a delete icon at the beginning of each row, while clicking on the Add (+) button will allow you to add a new row. Unlike in the portrait mode, there is no popover in the landscape mode when you click anywhere in the detail view.

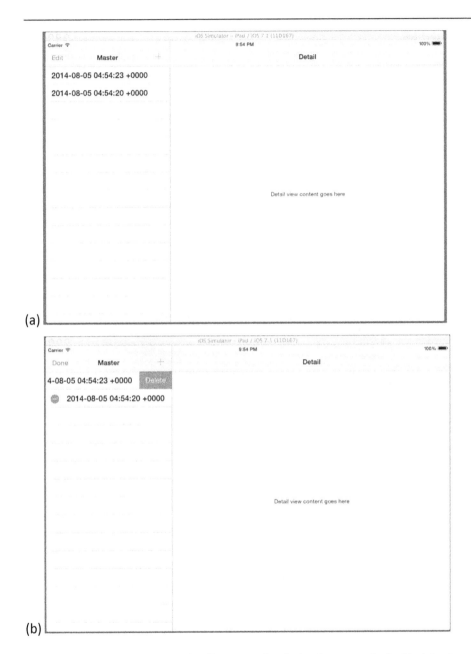

**Figure 9.5** The default master-detail app running in *landscape* mode for iPad devices: (a) initial view; and (b) after the Edit button is clicked

## 9.1.2    The *Universal* App Type

You might notice that when the previous master-detail project was created, there were three types of devices to choose from: *iPad*, *iPhone* and *Universal*. The Universal type is meant for both iPad and iPhone. You might wonder how the project would look like if the Universal type was chosen when a master-detail app was created. Actually, Xcode would generate two storyboards when the *Universal* type were chosen for Devices. Figure 9.6 shows the overall project structure and storyboard outline for iPhone storyboard, while Figure 9.7 shows the user interface associated with the storyboard for iPhone devices.

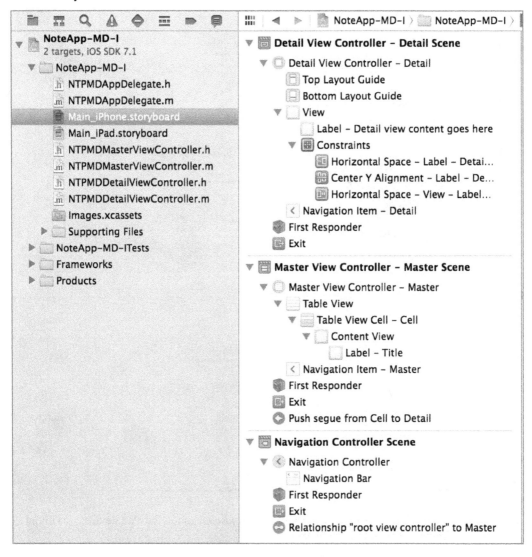

**Figure 9.6** Overall project structure and the outline for the iPhone storyboard created by Xcode for Universal type of devices with the master-detail project template

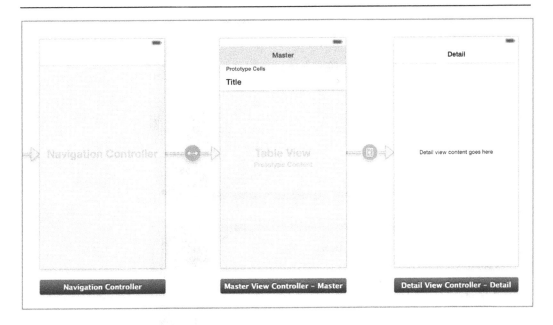

**Figure 9.7** User interface for iPhones created by Xcode for Universal type of devices with the master-detail project template

As you see, Xcode creates a different user interface for iPhone than for iPad when the *Universal* type for devices was chosen with the master-detail project template. Compare Figure 9.2 with Figure 9.7, we see that the user interface for iPhone does not have those two intermediate navigation controllers as can be found with the iPad version of the user interface. Besides, you can run the default iPhone master-detail view app and you should see the following differences:

■ **The Master view**: Has an Edit button on the left and an Add (+) button on the right of the navigation bar located at the top, as shown in Figure 9.8 (a). (Note that the default behavior with the Add button is to create a timestamp, which is, of course, modifiable.)

■ **The Detail view**: Replaces the master view when the user clicks on the ">" sign located at the end of each row, as shown in Figure 9.8 (b). You go back to the Master view by clicking on the < *Master* button located at the beginning of the top navigation bar.

■ **The Edit view**: Shows up when the user clicks on the Edit button in the master view, as shown in Figure 9.8 (c). Furthermore, if you click on the delete icon, it will allow you to delete a row. Clicking on the Done button will put the user back to the main view.

As you see, the user interface looks different between the iPhone version and the iPad version. In practice, the iPhone version and the iPad version for an app should be developed separately, although some code could be shared. Next, we explain how an iPad version of our NoteApp could be implemented.

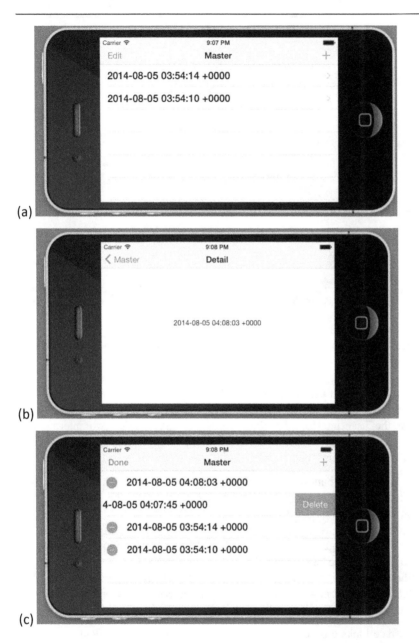

**Figure 9.8** Default user interface generated by Xcode for a master-detail app on iPhone: (a) main view; (b) detail view; and (c) edit view

## 9.2   THE START POINT FOR IMPLEMENTING NOTEAPP AS A MASTER-DETAIL APP FOR IPAD

To start with, let's create a new project for implementing our NoteApp as a master-detail app for iPad.

## 9.2.1    Creating the Master-Detail project

At this point, you should already be familiar with the process of creating a new project with a specific project template. The specs are given below for you to follow:

- Project template: iOS/Application > Master-Detail Application
- Project options: as shown in Figure 9.9.

The overall structure of the project created by following the above specs is shown in Figure 9.10.

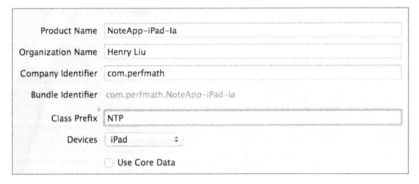

**Figure 9.9** The NoteApp-iPad-Ia project created by Xcode using the iOS Master-Detail Application template

**Figure 9.10** The NoteApp-iPad-Ia project created by Xcode using the iOS Master-Detail Application template

## 9.2.2    Modifying the MasterVewController class

Now, let's make some customizations as described below:

1   Change the default name of the Master view. Locate the Master view on the storyboard, double-click on the Title, change it to My Favorite Websites, and press Return. Refer to Figure 9.11 for how it's done in my environment.
2   Locate the NTPMasterViewController.h file and add two properties as shown in Listing 9.1.
3   Locate the viewDidLoad method in the NTPMasterViewController.m file, comment out the existing code and replace it with the code as shown in Listing 9.2.
4   Modify the numberOfRowsInSection method in the NTPMasterViewController.m file so that it returns _siteNames.count, as shown in Listing 9.3.
5   Modify the cellForRowAtIndexPath: method in the NTPMasterViewController.m file so that it sets the cell.textLabel.text property for each table row cell, as shown in Listing 9.4.
6   Locate the didSelectRowAtIndexPath: method in the NTPMasterViewController.m file and make it look as shown in Listing 9.5. As you see, we have commented out the original boilerplate code put there by default by Xcode, and replaced it with our own. The new logic is obvious: It first constructs a URL String object based on the siteUrls property from the master view controller, and then an NSURL object is constructed accordingly. Next, an NSURLRequest object is constructed based on the NSURL object created in the preceding step. The last two statements set the scalePageToFit property for the detail view controller to YES and execute the loadRequest method for the webView assigned to the detail view controller.

At this point, you can check your modifications by running the app on a simulated iPad Retina device. Figure 9.12 shows how it looks running in my environment in *landscape* mode.

**Figure 9.11** Change the name of the Master view

**Listing 9.1 Modified the NTPMasterViewController.h file**

```
#import <UIKit/UIKit.h>

@class NTPDetailViewController;

@interface NTPMasterViewController : UITableViewController
@property (nonatomic, retain) NSArray *siteNames;
@property (nonatomic, retain) NSArray *siteUrls;
```

```
@property (strong, nonatomic) NTPDetailViewController
*detailViewController;

@end
```

**Listing 9.2 Modified the viewDidLoad method in the NTPMasterViewController.m file**

```
- (void)viewDidLoad
{
    [super viewDidLoad];
    _siteNames = [[NSArray alloc] initWithObjects:@"Apple",
        @"Google", @"PerfMath",  nil];
    _siteUrls = [[NSArray alloc] initWithObjects:@"http://www.apple.com",
        @"http://www.google.com", @"http://www.perfmath.com", nil];
    self.detailViewController = (NTPDetailViewController *)
[[self.splitViewController.viewControllers lastObject]
topViewController];
}
```

**Listing 9.3 Modified the numberOfRowsInSection: method in the NTPMasterViewController.m file**

```
- (NSInteger)tableView:(UITableView *)tableView
    numberOfRowsInSection:(NSInteger)section
{
    return _siteNames.count;
}
```

**Listing 9.4 Modified the cellForRowAtIndexPath: method in the NTPMasterViewController.m file**

```
- (UITableViewCell *)tableView:(UITableView *)tableView
    cellForRowAtIndexPath:(NSIndexPath *)indexPath
{
    UITableViewCell *cell = [tableView
      dequeueReusableCellWithIdentifier:@"Cell" forIndexPath:indexPath];

    //NSDate *object = _objects[indexPath.row];
    //cell.textLabel.text = [object description];
    cell.textLabel.text = _siteNames[indexPath.row];
    return cell;
}
```

**Listing 9.5 The modified didSelectRowAtIndexPath: method in the NTPMasterViewController.m file**

```
- (void)tableView:(UITableView *)tableView
didSelectRowAtIndexPath:(NSIndexPath *)indexPath
{
```

```
    //NSDate *object = _objects[indexPath.row];
    //self.detailViewController.detailItem = object;
    NSString *urlString = [_siteUrls objectAtIndex:indexPath.row];
    NSURL * url = [NSURL URLWithString:urlString];
    NSURLRequest *request= [NSURLRequest requestWithURL:url];
    self.detailViewController.webView.scalesPageToFit = YES;
    [self.detailViewController.webView loadRequest:request];
}
```

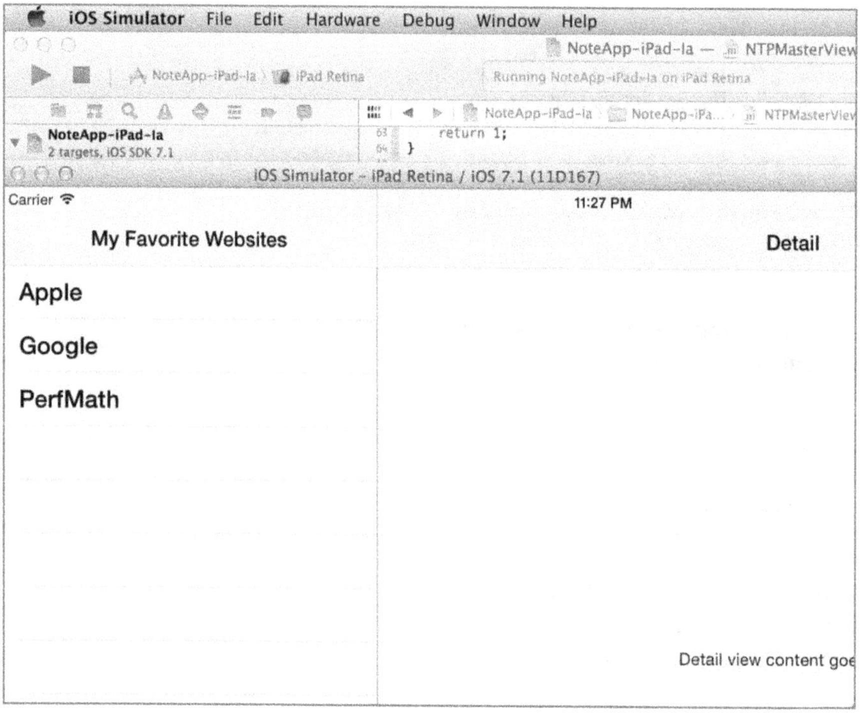

**Figure 9.12** Running the app with modified NTPMasterViewController class

## 9.2.3    Modifying the NTPDetailViewController Class

Follow the below procedure to modify the NTPDetailViewController class:

1    Click on the View Controller scene, double click on *Detail view content goes here* and delete it. (Note you may need to make the scene to its default size in order to make this change. You may not make a change in a zoom-out size).

2    Drag and drop a WebView control from the Object Library and resize it to its largest possible size using all four edge guidelines (upper / lower / left / right).

3    Create an outlet named *webView* from the NTPDetailViewController to the NTPDetailViewController.h file, as shown in Figure 9.13.

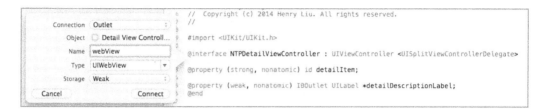

**Figure 9.13** The webView outlet

The final part is to enable popover when the app is run in portrait mode on an iPad device. This part has already been hooked up automatically by Xcode when the project was created. Popover is accomplished with two methods in the NTPDetailViewController.m file: the willHideViewController: method and the willShowViewController: method. The willHideViewController: method gets called when the iPad device is rotated to portrait orientation, which sets the title to "Master" by default, but was changed to "My Favorite Websites" to make it consistent with our example. It then calls the setLeftBarButtonItem: method with a message of animated:YES to enable editing. It finally sets the popover controller for the master view controller. The willShowViewController: method gets called when the view is shown again in the split view, which invalidates the button and popover controller, as is already denoted there.

**Listing 9.6 The willHideViewController: method and  willShowViewController: method in the NTPDetailViewController.m file**

```
#pragma mark - Split view

- (void)splitViewController:(UISplitViewController *)splitController
willHideViewController:(UIViewController *)viewController
withBarButtonItem:(UIBarButtonItem *)barButtonItem
forPopoverController:(UIPopoverController *)popoverController
{
    barButtonItem.title = NSLocalizedString(@"My Favorite Websites",
      @"My Favorite Websites");
    [self.navigationItem setLeftBarButtonItem:barButtonItem
      animated:YES];
    self.masterPopoverController = popoverController;
}


- (void)splitViewController:(UISplitViewController *)splitController
willShowViewController:(UIViewController *)viewController
invalidatingBarButtonItem:(UIBarButtonItem *)barButtonItem
{
    // Called when the view is shown again in the split view,
      // invalidating the button and popover controller.
    [self.navigationItem setLeftBarButtonItem:nil animated:YES];
    self.masterPopoverController = nil;
}
```

You can run the app to check that it works as expected. Figure 9.14 shows how it looks when it's run in landscape mode with the Apple's website name clicked in the Master view. Your output may look different, depending on what Apple would put up there at the time when you run it.

**Figure 9.14** Running the sample NoteApp-iPad-Ia on a simulated iPad Retina device in landscape mode with Apple's website selected in the master view

However, when you start up the app in portrait mode initially, your experience would be different that you would first see a blank screen, as shown in Figure 9.15 (a), and then the master view, as shown in Figure 9.15 (b), and the detail view when you click on a website, for example, Apple, in the case shown there. Notice that the detail view would be covered partially by the master view popover. Rotate it to landscape will make it a full split view as shown in Figure 9.14.

(a)

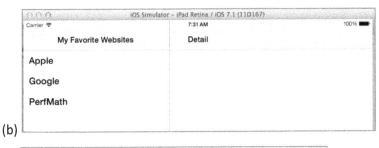

**Figure 9.15** Running NoteApp-iPad-Ia on a simulated iPad Retina device in portrait mode with Apple's website selected in the master view

## 9.3   IMPLEMENTING NOTEAPP AS A MASTER-DETAIL APP FOR IPAD

Now let's implement NoteApp as a Master-Detail App for iPad, based on the previous example. The steps we will take include:

1    Remove hard-coded table rows in the master view and replace them with those stored in a SQLite database made available through Core Data
2    Associate items in the master view with their contents to be displayed in the detail view.
3    Enable adding/updating/deleting note items

Before getting started, duplicate the current project and rename it to NoteApp-iPad-Ib. Figure 9.16 shows the duplicated project in my environment. Optionally, you can rename the scheme by going to *Manage Schemes…* and duplicate/rename the original scheme for a new scheme and delete the original scheme, as shown in Figure 9.17.

**Figure 9.16** Project NoteApp-iPad-Ib duplicated from NoteApp-iPad-Ia

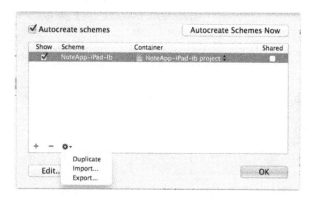

**Figure 9.17** Rename a scheme

Next, we take a step-by-step approach to making our NoteApp a fully functional app for iPad devices. We start with the data model first.

## 9.3.1    Creating the Data Model

Follow the procedure illustrated in Chapter 8 and add a data model to the current version of the NoteApp project. Figure 9.18 shows the data model created in my environment. Note that the name of the entity description is *Notes*, which has two attributes of type *String*, itemName and content. The itemName attribute will be displayed in the master view, while the content represented by the content attribute will be displayed in the detail view.

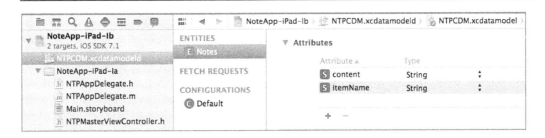

**Figure 9.18** Data Model for the NoteApp-iPad-Ib project

The next step is to add Core Data support for the project.

## 9.3.2    Adding Core Data Support in the NTPAppDelegate Class

We once went through this in Chapter 8, so get it done by following the below procedure:

1    Add core data specific properties to your NTPAppDelegate.h file. Refer to Listing 8.4.
2    Add core data specific methods to your NTPAppDelegate.m file. Refer to Listing 8.5.
3    Import the Core Data framework by adding it to the project's .pch support file.
4    Add CoreData.framework to the project's Link Binary With Libraries section in your project's Build Phases setting, as shown in Listing 8.8.

The next step is to add `loadInitialData` and `saveData` methods to support persistence based on Core Data.

## 9.3.3    Adding loadInitialData and saveData: methods

Since the data model has been changed with a different entity description that has two instead of one attribute, the `loadInitialData` and `saveData`: methods will be different from Listings 8.6 and 8.7, respectively. Listings 9.7 and 9.8 show how these two methods should look now. Notice the use of the two attributes, `itemName` and `content` in these two methods.

You may still remember that in that project illustrated in Chapter 7, we had an unwindToList segue associated with the doneButton in the NTPAddNewNoteItemViewController class to help transition back to the NTPMyNotesTableViewController class. For this project, we will not use such a segue any more, as the structure of the project has changed. We will discuss more about where the `loadInitialData` and `saveData`: get called later in more proper context.

Next, we describe adding an NTPNoteItem class.

**Listing 9.7 The loadInitialData method in the NTPMasterViewController.m file**

```
- (void) loadInitialData
{
    // load initial data using core Data
    NTPAppDelegate *appDelegate = [[UIApplication sharedApplication]
```

```
    delegate];

    NSManagedObjectContext *context = [appDelegate managedObjectContext];
    NSEntityDescription *entityDesc = [NSEntityDescription
     entityForName:@"Notes" inManagedObjectContext:context];

    NSFetchRequest *request = [[NSFetchRequest alloc] init];
    [request setEntity:entityDesc];

    NSPredicate *pred = [NSPredicate
     predicateWithFormat:@"(itemName != %@)", nil];
    [request setPredicate:pred];

    NSError *error;
    NSArray *objects = [context executeFetchRequest:request
     error:&error];
    if ([objects count] == 0) {
        NSLog (@"No matches");
    } else {
        NSLog (@"%lu matches found", (unsigned long) [objects count]);
    }
    _itemNames = [[NSMutableArray alloc] init];
    _itemContents = [[NSMutableArray alloc] init];
    for (NSManagedObject *item in objects) {
        NTPNoteItem *newItem = [[NTPNoteItem alloc] init];
        newItem.itemName = [item valueForKey:@"itemName"];
        newItem.content = [item valueForKey:@"content"];
        [self.noteItems addObject:newItem];
        NSLog (@"added item: %@", newItem.itemName);
        [self.itemNames addObject:newItem.itemName];
        [self.itemContents addObject:newItem.content];
    }
}
```

**Listing 9.8 The saveData method in the NTPMasterViewController.m file**

```
- (void) saveData: (NTPNoteItem *)item
{
    NTPAppDelegate *appDelegate = [[UIApplication sharedApplication]
        delegate];

    NSManagedObjectContext *context = [appDelegate managedObjectContext];
    NSManagedObject *newNote;
    newNote = [NSEntityDescription
        insertNewObjectForEntityForName:@"Notes"
            inManagedObjectContext:context];
    [newNote setValue: item.itemName forKey: @"itemName"];
    [newNote setValue: item.content forKey: @"content"];

    NSError *error;
    [context save: &error];
```

```
    NSLog (@"context saved");
}
```

## 9.3.4    Adding an NTPNoteItem Class

To work with the new data model that has two attributes of `itemName` and `content` as described before, we need to add a new NTPNoteItem class. This is a simple task and we would not describe the procedure in detail, as you should have become familiar with this by now.

Listings 9.9 and 9.10 shows the NTPNoteItem.h and NTPNoteItem.m file for this project. Make sure you add this class to your project before moving to the next step.

**Listing 9.9 The NTPNoteItem.h file**

```
#import <Foundation/Foundation.h>

@interface NTPNoteItem : NSObject
@property NSString *itemName;
@property NSString *content;
@end
```

**Listing 9.10 The NTPNoteItem.m file**

```
#import "NTPNoteItem.h"

@implementation NTPNoteItem

@end
```

The next step is to modify the NTPMasterViewController class to replace `siteNames` and `siteUrls` NSMutableArray objects with `itemNames` and `itemContents` NSMutableArrays.

## 9.3.5    Replacing siteNames and siteUrls with itemNames and itemContents

In the preceding project, we used `siteNames` and `siteUrls` NSMutableArray objects to hold site names for the master table view and detail view, respectively. For the present project, we need to replace those collection objects with their counterparts for this object: `itemNames` and `itemContents` NSMutableArrays objects. Listing 9.11 shows the modified NTPMasterViewController.h file, with the two NSMutableArray objects replaced. Listing 9.12 shows the beginning part of the modified NTPMasterViewController.m file, with the `noteItems` NSMutableArray object added. Other changes will be introduced as we move along.

**Listing 9.11 The NTPMasterViewController.h file**

```
#import <UIKit/UIKit.h>
#import "NTPDetailViewController.h"
```

```
@class NTPDetailViewController;

@interface NTPMasterViewController : UITableViewController
@property (nonatomic, retain) NSMutableArray *itemNames;
@property (nonatomic, retain) NSMutableArray *itemContents;

@property (strong, nonatomic) NTPDetailViewController
*detailViewController;

@end
```

**Listing 9.12 The beginning part of the NTPMasterViewController.m file**

```
#import "NTPMasterViewController.h"
#import "NTPDetailViewController.h"
#import "NTPAppDelegate.h"
#import "NTPNoteItem.h"

@interface NTPMasterViewController () {
    NSMutableArray *_objects;
}
@property NSMutableArray *noteItems;
@end

@implementation NTPMasterViewController
......
```

The next step is to modify the viewDidLoad and didSelectRowAtIndex: methods in the NTPMasterViewController.m file.

## 9.3.6    Modifying the viewDidLoad and didSelectRowAtIndex: methods in the NTPMasterViewController.m file

If you refer back to Figure 9.14, you would notice that there were no Edit and Add (+) buttons in the Master view's navigation bar. That's because the relevant code was commented out in the viewDidLoad method of the NTPMasterViewController.m file. In addition, we need to load initial data from the SQLite database using the Core Data framework. With all these requirements taken into account, the modified viewDidLoad method for the NTPMasterViewController.m file is shown in Listing 9.13. As you see, this method adds the leftBarButtonItem for the Edit button and the rightBarButtonItem for the Add button first. It then sets the detailViewController object to set the stage for interacting with the detailViewController. Finally, it creates the noteItems NSMutableArray object and invokes the loadInitialData method to load initial data.

**Listing 9.13 The modified viewDidLoad method for the NTPMasterViewController.m file.**

```
- (void)viewDidLoad
{
```

```
    [super viewDidLoad];
  // Do any additional setup after loading the view, typically
  // from a nib.

    self.navigationItem.leftBarButtonItem = self.editButtonItem;

    UIBarButtonItem *addButton = [[UIBarButtonItem alloc]
      initWithBarButtonSystemItem:UIBarButtonSystemItemAdd
        target:self action:@selector(insertNewObject:)];
    self.navigationItem.rightBarButtonItem = addButton;
    self.detailViewController = (NTPDetailViewController*)
     [[self.splitViewController.viewControllers lastObject]
     topViewController];

    self.noteItems = [[NSMutableArray alloc] init];
    [self loadInitialData];
}
```

Listing 9.14 shows the modified didSelectRowAtIndexPath: method of the NTPMasterViewController.m file. It's responsible for populating the textField and textView contents in the detail view. Since we have not come to the point of discussing the NTPDetailViewController class yet, you may see errors now, but don't worry and we'll fix all issues and errors as we move along.

**Listing    9.14    The    modified    didSelectRowAtIndexPath:    method    for    the NTPMasterViewController.m file**

```
- (void)tableView:(UITableView *)tableView
didSelectRowAtIndexPath:(NSIndexPath *)indexPath
{
    NSString *itemName = [_itemNames objectAtIndex:indexPath.row];
    NSString *content = [_itemContents objectAtIndex:indexPath.row];
    NSLog (@"fill the detail view with %@", content);
    self.detailViewController.textField.text = itemName;
    self.detailViewController.textView.text = content;
}
```

There are other two trivial updates, as shown in Listing 9.15, for the numberOfRowsInSection: and cellForRowAtIndexPath: methods of the NTPMasterViewController class. Just go ahead and make these changes in your NTPMasterViewController.m file now. The numberOfRowsInSection: method returns the number of items in the master table view, while the cellForRowAtIndexPath: method sets the text of the cell in the master table view.

It's time to discuss the NTPDetailViewController class next.

**Listing 9.15 The numberOfRowsInSection: and cellForRowAtIndexPath: methods**

```
- (NSInteger)tableView:(UITableView *)tableView
  numberOfRowsInSection:(NSInteger)section
{
    return _itemNames.count;
```

```
}

- (UITableViewCell *)tableView:(UITableView *)tableView
  cellForRowAtIndexPath:(NSIndexPath *)indexPath
{

    UITableViewCell *cell = [tableView
      dequeueReusableCellWithIdentifier:@"Cell" forIndexPath:indexPath];
    cell.textLabel.text = _itemNames[indexPath.row];
    return cell;
}
```

### 9.3.7    Adding a Save Bar Button to the Navigation Bar of the Detail View

Note in Figure 9.14 that there has not been a Save button in the detail view's navigation bar yet. We would like to add a Save button to support adding a new note item and updating an existing note item. There is significant amount of work to do to achieve that, so let's get it done step-by-step next.

We start with adding a Save button in the detail view's navigation bar first. Drag and drop a Bar Button object from the Object Library and change its Title to Save. This is straightforward, so I would not bore you to show a screenshot.

Next, we need to add one label and one text field for holding the itemName attribute and a text view for holding the content for a given item name.

### 9.3.8    The Detail View User Interface

To help save time, Figure 9.19 shows the detail view user interface created in my environment. Note the Save button, the Item ID label, the text field next to the Item ID label, and the text view beneath the Item ID label and the text field. Add these visual controls to your detail view and make appropriate changes so that they would look similar to Figure 9.19.

Next, we describe creating outlets and actions to connect some of these controls to the NTPDetailViewController class.

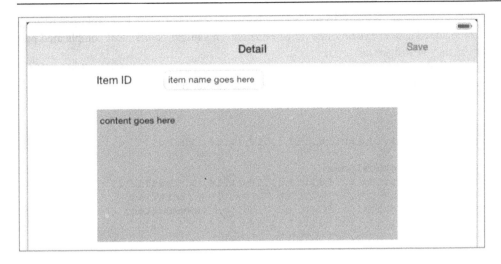

**Figure 9.19** The detail view user interface

## 9.3.9    Adding Outlets and Actions to the NTPDetailViewController Class

Perhaps this is a good point for us to examine the NTPDetailViewController.h file created in my environment. Listing 9.16 shows the partially-finished NTPDetailViewController.h file created in my environment. Note the outlets of textFileld, textView and saveButton. You can create them easily by Ctrl-dragging from a specific control to the NTPDetailViewController.h file with the Assistant inspector open, as we have done many times in the previous chapters.

In addition to those outlets, we also need to create an action named saveData so that when a user clicks on the Save button, either newly created note item or updated note item in the detail view can be persisted. So, create this action as well by following the similar procedure for creating an outlet.

At last, note the property named currentRowIndex. This is placed there to help the NTPMasterViewController to decide whether it should treat the item present in the detail view as a new item and add it or as an existing view to be updated. This is the simplest way for helping making such a decision, which is necessary for the adding/updating a note item functionality. So, go ahead and add it to your NTPDetailViewController.h file. Because of this property, you need to add a statement in the didSelectRowIndexPath: method of the NTPMasterViewController.m file as follows to set the index of the currently selected row:

```
self.detailViewController.currentRowIndex = indexPath.row;
```

This property will be set to -1 when the Add (+) button is clicked by a user to initiate adding a new note item from the master table view. We will get back to this when we discuss adding a new note item later.

Next, we discuss adding a protocol to the NTPDetailViewController class to enable persisting a new item to be added and an existing item to be updated. This might be the most complicated part of this project, as you will see next.

**Listing 9.16 The partially-finished NTPDetailViewController.h file**

```
#import <UIKit/UIKit.h>

@interface NTPDetailViewController : UIViewController

@property int currentRowIndex;
@property (weak, nonatomic) IBOutlet UITextField *textField;
@property (weak, nonatomic) IBOutlet UITextView *textView;
@property (weak, nonatomic) IBOutlet UIButton *saveButton;

@property (strong, nonatomic) id detailItem;
- (IBAction)saveData:(id)sender;

@property (weak, nonatomic) IBOutlet UILabel *detailDescriptionLabel;

@end
```

## 9.3.10   Adding an NTPDetailViewControllerDelegate Protocol to the NTPDetailViewController Class

A delegate in Objective-C is similar to a callback function in C. In some cases, it's much cleaner than using a segue for passing information between view controllers. In this section, we demonstrate how to use a delegate protocol added to the NTPDetailViewController class to pass the note item present in the detail view to the master view so that the master view can add or save it.

The procedure for adding a custom delegate protocol to a view controller is described as follows:

1   Modifying the view controller interface file. This is the first step we have to take in order to add a delegate protocol to a view controller class. As you see in Listing 9.17, I have highlighted all modifications relating to adding the NTPDetailViewControllerDelegate to the NTPDetailViewController.h file for better clarity. It can be summarized as follows:

   o   The @protocol definition. This part declares the delegate protocol. Note the saveItemRequest: method, which is the delegate method we set up.
   o   The @class NTPDetailViewController; line following the delegate protocol definition informs the compiler the view controller with which the defined protocol should be associated.
   o   The last part defines a delegate property for other objects to get hold of the delegate object.

2   Make the following changes to the NTPDetailViewController.m file:

   o   Add the following statement after the @implementation line:

```
@synthesize delegate;
```

o   Implement the saveData method as shown in Listing 9.18. As you see, when another view controller is triggered to execute the saveData method, the _detailItem is passed to it via the saveItemRequest: delegate method as follows:

```
[self.delegate saveItemRequest:_detailItem];
```

Before leaving the NTPDetailViewController class for the NTPMasterViewController class, add the following statement to NTPDetailViewController's viewDidLoad method to handle the case that a user may directly press the Add button in the master view right after starting up the app:

```
self.currentRowIndex = -1;
```

We move back to the NTPMasterViewController to see how the master view controller can save a new or existing item with the help of the NTPDetailViewControllerDelegate protocol.

**Listing 9.17 The comple NTPDetailViewController.h file with a delegate protocol added**

```
#import <UIKit/UIKit.h>

@protocol NTPDetailViewControllerDelegate <NSObject>
-(void)saveItemRequest:(id)itemToSave; // delegate method
@end
@class NTPDetailViewController;

@interface NTPDetailViewController : UIViewController
<UISplitViewControllerDelegate>
@property (nonatomic, strong) id <NTPDetailViewControllerDelegate>
delegate;

@property int currentRowIndex;
@property (weak, nonatomic) IBOutlet UITextField *textField;
@property (weak, nonatomic) IBOutlet UITextView *textView;
@property (weak, nonatomic) IBOutlet UIButton *saveButton;

@property (strong, nonatomic) id detailItem;
- (IBAction)saveData:(id)sender;

@property (weak, nonatomic) IBOutlet UILabel *detailDescriptionLabel;

@end
```

**Listing 9.18 The saveData method added to the NTPDetailViewController.h file**

```
- (IBAction)saveData:(id)sender {
    self.textField.text = _textField.text;
    self.textView.text = _textView.text;
    NTPNoteItem *item;
    item = [[NTPNoteItem alloc] init];
    item.itemName = _textField.text;
```

```
    item.content = _textView.text;
    _detailItem = item;

    [self.delegate saveItemRequest:_detailItem];

}
```

## 9.3.11   Making NTPMasterViewController Adopt the NTPDetailViewControllerDelegate Protocol

In this section, let's look at how the NTPMasterViewController class can adopt the NTPDetailViewControllerDelegate protocol to get the values associated with the itemName text field and content text view present in the detail view prior to a user clicking on the Save button.

We start with Listing 9.19, which shows the complete NTPDetailViewController.h file. As you see, the < **NTPDetailViewControllerDelegate**> protocol is attached to the @interface line, which is all it takes to declare that it adopts that protocol. It's one part of the protocol mechanism for hooking up the class that defines the protocol and the class that adopts the protocol.

**Listing 9.19 The complete NTPDetailViewController.h file**

```
#import <UIKit/UIKit.h>
#import "NTPDetailViewController.h"

@class NTPDetailViewController;

@interface NTPMasterViewController : UITableViewController
<NTPDetailViewControllerDelegate>

@property (nonatomic, retain) NSMutableArray *itemNames;
@property (nonatomic, retain) NSMutableArray *itemContents;

@property (strong, nonatomic) NTPDetailViewController
*detailViewController;

@end
```

The next part is seen in the NTPMasterViewController class implementation file, as shown in Listing 9.20. Recall from Listing 9.17 that the NTPDetailViewController class defines the saveItemRequest: method, which is invoked in its saveData method to pass the itemToSave object. However, the NTPDetailViewController class does not implement the saveItemRequest: delegate method. The implementation of a delegate method is left for the protocol adopting class. When a user clicks on the Save button in the detail view, the saveData: method in the NTPDetailViewController object is called, which triggers the saveItemRequest message to inform the adopter or adopters of the protocol that the Save action has been requested and the item to save is passed along.

On the side of the protocol adopter or adopters, the delegate method gets executed, as shown in Listing 9.20. Because the data has been passed over, an adopter of the protocol simply retrieves the data passed to it, and then processes the data. In our case, the NTPMasterViewController class either adds a new item or updates the existing item, depending on whether it's an *add* request or *update* request controlled by the parameter currentRowIndex, which is assigned a value of -1 if it were an add request. This is how a delegate protocol works with this real example, which shows how powerful and convenient the Objective-C delegate protocol feature is.

**Listing 9.20 The saveItemRequest: method in the NTPMasterViewController.m file**

```
-(void) saveItemRequest: (id) itemToSave {
    NTPNoteItem *item = [[NTPNoteItem alloc] init];
    item = itemToSave;
    int index = self.detailViewController.currentRowIndex;
    NSLog (@"save item from detail view: %@ %@ %i", item.itemName,
        item.content, index);
    if (self.detailViewController.currentRowIndex < 0) {
        [self.noteItems addObject:item];
        // add item
        NSLog (@"added item: %@", item.itemName);
        [self.itemNames addObject:item.itemName];
        [self.itemContents addObject:item.content];
        // persist to CD
        [self saveData: item];
    } else {
        [self.noteItems replaceObjectAtIndex:index withObject:item];
        [self.itemNames replaceObjectAtIndex:index
            withObject:item.itemName];
        [self.itemContents replaceObjectAtIndex:index
           withObject:item.content];
    }

    [(UITableView*)self.view reloadData];
}
```

## 9.3.12   Inserting a New Note Item

Recall that in the master view navigation bar, there is an Add (+) button, which helps convey a user's intention to add a new note item. When a user clicks on that button, the insertNewObject: method of the NTPMasterViewController class gets called, which is shown in Listing 9.21. Note that this method just sets some default values for the text field and text view in the detail view, and also sets the currentRowIndex value to -1 to help distinguish between adding a new item and updating an existing note item as we discussed above. When a user clicks the Save button in the detail view, the execution control returns to the master view controller as we discussed above. This completes the task of adding or updating a note item.

**Listing 9.21 The insertObject: method in the NTPMasterViewController.m file**

```
- (void)insertNewObject:(id)sender
{
    self.detailViewController.textField.text = @"Add item name here";
    self.detailViewController.textView.text = @"Add item content here
       (when done, click Save)";
    self.detailViewController.currentRowIndex = -1;
}
```

## 9.3.13   Deleting a Note Item

Finally, let us explore how an item is deleted in the master view. The delete operation is implemented in the commitEditingStyle: method as shown in Listing 9.22. A delete operation is triggered when a user swipes across a row from right to left for a single row deletion or when a user clicks on the Edit button in the master view's navigation bar, which will make all items subject to deleting. No matter how a delete intention is conveyed, it's the same method as shown in Listing 9.22 that gets called.

With regard to how a delete operation is carried out, it has to be two parts: one part for the real-time update of the master view, and one part for persisting to the database so that the deleted item will not show up next time when the app is relaunched. The actual logic for the delete operation is obvious and you should read through the code as shown in Listing 9.22 to make sure that you understand it clearly.

**Listing 9.22 The commitEditingStyle: method in the NTPMasterViewController.m file**

```
- (void)tableView:(UITableView *)tableView
commitEditingStyle:(UITableViewCellEditingStyle)editingStyle
forRowAtIndexPath:(NSIndexPath *)indexPath
{
    if (editingStyle == UITableViewCellEditingStyleDelete) {
        // save the item before deleting from memory
        NSLog (@"delete at index %i", indexPath.row);

        NTPNoteItem *item = [self.noteItems objectAtIndex:indexPath.row];

        [self.noteItems removeObjectAtIndex:indexPath.row];
        [self.itemNames removeObjectAtIndex:indexPath.row];
        [self.itemContents removeObjectAtIndex:indexPath.row];


        // Delete the row from the data source
        NTPAppDelegate *appdelegate = [[UIApplication sharedApplication]
            delegate];
        NSManagedObjectContext *context =
        appdelegate.managedObjectContext;
        NSEntityDescription *entityDesc = [NSEntityDescription
            entityForName:@"Notes" inManagedObjectContext:context];

        NSFetchRequest *request = [[NSFetchRequest alloc] init];
```

```
[request setEntity:entityDesc];

NSLog (@"Search for %@", item.itemName);
NSPredicate *pred = [NSPredicate predicateWithFormat:@"(itemName
    = %@)", item.itemName];
[request setPredicate:pred];

NSError *error;
NSArray *objects = [context executeFetchRequest:request
    error:&error];
NSLog (@"found %i items", [objects count]);
for (NSManagedObject *item in objects) {
    NTPNoteItem *newItem = [[NTPNoteItem alloc] init];
    newItem.itemName = [item valueForKey:@"itemName"];
    //[self.noteItems addObject:newItem];
    NSLog (@"found item: %@", newItem.itemName);
}

[context deleteObject:objects[0]];

[context save:&error];

// Animate the deletion
[tableView deleteRowsAtIndexPaths:@[indexPath]
    withRowAnimation:UITableViewRowAnimationFade];
} else if (editingStyle == UITableViewCellEditingStyleInsert) {
    // Create a new instance of the appropriate class, insert it
    // into the array, and add a new row to the table view.
}
}
}
```

## 9.3.14 Testing the New Version of NoteApp

At this point, the implementation for NoteApp targeting iPad devices is complete. Since it's a lengthy process, I am not sure if I introduced all implementation details in the previous sections. If not by any chance, it might be a good opportunity for you to trouble-shoot or refer to my project that you can download from this book's website. Trouble-shooting is another way to learn, often times.

In this section, I share with you some of the test cases I tried to verify that all operations work as expected. It's impossible to write perfect code without going through a rigorous testing process, no matter how simple an app is.

Here are a few test cases to try out at a bare minimum:

1   Adding a new item. Start up your NoteApp on your iOS simulator and it should look similar to Figure 9.20. (You might need to scroll down if you don't see the top part of it.)
2   Click on My Notes in the navigation bar of the master view to reveal the Edit and Add (+) buttons. It should look similar to Figure 9.21. (Note that I have some existing items already so

it may look different than yours.) If you click anywhere in the detail view, the master popover would retreat and disappear.

3    Now, click on the Add button, change to the detail view, make some changes in the Item ID text field and the text view box, and click on Save in the upper right corner. Now, bring up the master view popover and you should see the new item you've just added. The added item always goes to the last position of the master view item list. For your reference, Figure 9.22 shows the new item I added while performing this test.

4    Now, let's test updating an existing item. Click on an existing item in the master view and change to the detail view. Make some changes and click on Save. Switch back to the master view and verify the updates you've made. Figure 9.23 shows the operation I carried out in my environment.

5    Testing delete operations. When you click on the Edit button, you bring up a view for deleting any items, as shown in Figure 9.24. Pick one, delete it, and change back to the master view by clicking on the Done button to verify that the item has indeed been deleted. Figure 9.25 verifies that the item shown in Figure 9.24 has indeed been deleted.

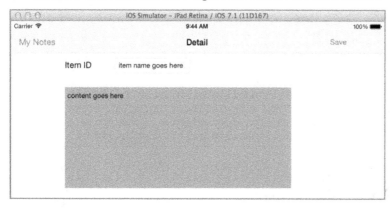

**Figure 9.20** Initial screen of the NoteApp for iPad devices in portrait mode

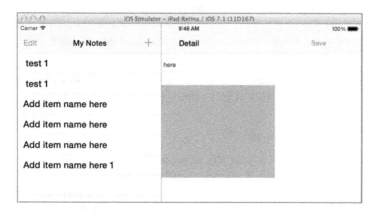

**Figure 9.21**The screen with popover for the master view

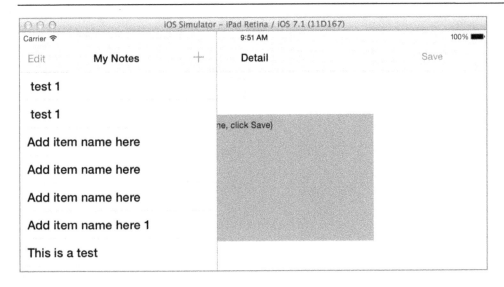

**Figure 9.22** The screen showing a new item added

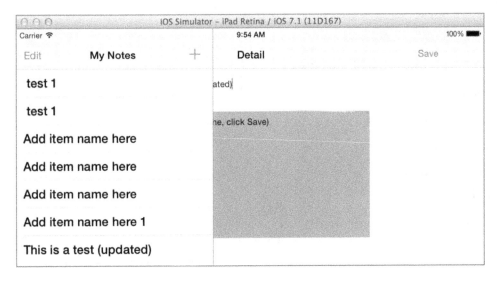

**Figure 9.23** The screen showing an existing item has been updated

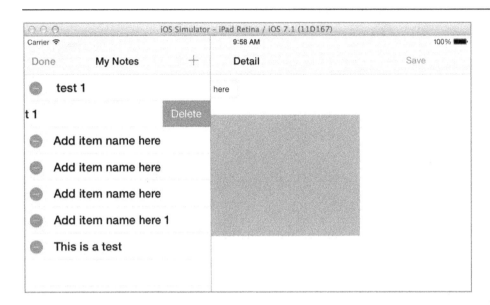

**Figure 9.24** The screen showing the delete function initiated by clicking on the Edit button

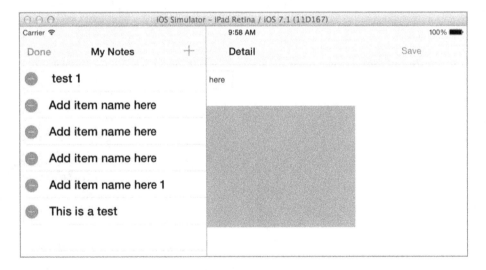

**Figure 9.25** The screen showing one of the "test 1" items has been deleted

## 9.4   IMPLEMENTING NOTEAPP FOR IPHONE DEVICES

We demonstrated how to implement the iPad version of NoteApp using the master-detail view structure and Core Data. The next step is to do the same for the iPhone version. To help you learn more effectively, I leave this as a challenging project for you to try out yourself, using what you have learnt so far. It should be very doable if you have followed along throughout all examples presented in this book.

To provide you with some assistance, Figure 9.26 shows the project options I used for creating the NoteApp-iPhone-I project. The remaining four figures are:

- Figure 9.27 (a): The initial screen when the app is launched
- Figure 9.27 (b): The screen after clicking on the Edit button
- Figure 9.28 (a): The screen after clicking on the Add (+) button
- Figure 9.28 (b): The screen after clicking on an existing item

Listings 9.23 – 9.26 show the header and implementation files for the master view controller and detail view controller classes. I suggest that you try it out on your own without peeking at my implementation. After finishing your own implementation, you can then compare your implementation with my implementation. If you forget how to carry out certain tasks, refer back to the previous chapters. This is a better way for you to learn than having me walk you through this project again in detail. It's not required to learn anything new – every detail has been covered if you did not jump to here. Good luck!

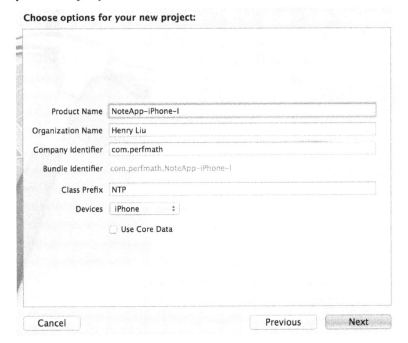

**Figure 9.26** Options for creating the NoteApp-iPhone-I project

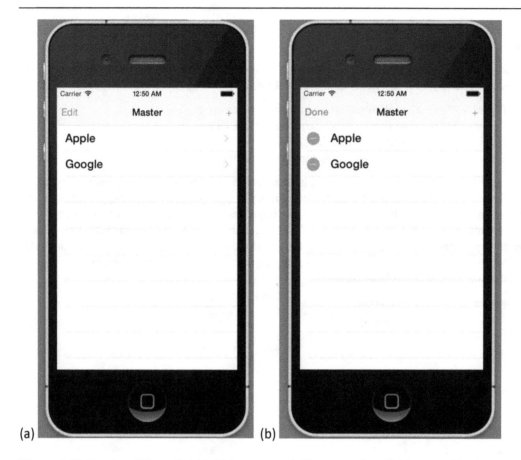

(a)                                    (b)

**Figure 9.27** NoteApp-iPhone-I: (a) initial screen, and (b) screen after clicking on Edit

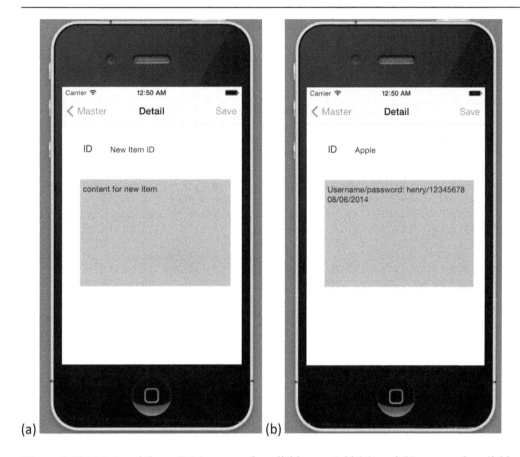

(a)                                  (b)

**Figure 9.28** NoteApp-iPhone-I: (a) screen after clicking on Add (+), and (b) screen after clicking on an existing item

**Listing 9.23 NTPMasterViewController.h**

```
#import <UIKit/UIKit.h>
#import "NTPDetailViewController.h"
@class NTPDetailViewController;

@interface NTPMasterViewController : UITableViewController
@property (weak, nonatomic) IBOutlet UIBarButtonItem *createButton;
@property (nonatomic, retain) NSMutableArray *itemNames;
@property (nonatomic, retain) NSMutableArray *itemContents;

- (IBAction) unwindToMasterView:(UIStoryboardSegue *)segue;
@end
```

**Listing 9.24 NTPMasterViewController.m**

```objc
#import "NTPMasterViewController.h"
#import "NTPDetailViewController.h"
#import "NTPNoteItem.h"
#import "NTPAppDelegate.h"

@interface NTPMasterViewController () {
    NSMutableArray *_objects;
}
@property NSMutableArray *noteItems;
@end

@implementation NTPMasterViewController
- (IBAction) unwindToMasterView:(UIStoryboardSegue *)segue {
    NSLog (@"Got back from detail view controller");
    NTPDetailViewController *source = [segue sourceViewController];
    NTPNoteItem *item = source.noteItem;

    if (item != nil) {
    int index = source.currentRowIndex;
    NSLog (@"save item from detail view: %@ %@ %i", item.itemName,
item.content, index);
    if (source.currentRowIndex < 0) {
        [self.noteItems addObject:item];
        // add item
        NSLog (@"added item: %@", item.itemName);
        [self.itemNames addObject:item.itemName];
        [self.itemContents addObject:item.content];
        // persist to CD
        //[self saveData: item];
    } else {
        [self.noteItems replaceObjectAtIndex:index withObject:item];
        [self.itemNames replaceObjectAtIndex:index
withObject:item.itemName];
        [self.itemContents replaceObjectAtIndex:index
withObject:item.content];
    }
        [self saveData: item];
  [(UITableView*)self.view reloadData];
        //[self.noteItems addObject:item];
        NSLog (@"added item: %@", item.itemName);
    } else {
        NSLog (@"No item returned");
    }

}
- (void)awakeFromNib
{
    [super awakeFromNib];
}

- (void)viewDidLoad
{
```

```
    [super viewDidLoad];
  // Do any additional setup after loading the view, typically from a
nib.
    self.navigationItem.leftBarButtonItem = self.editButtonItem;
/*
    UIBarButtonItem *addButton = [[UIBarButtonItem alloc]
initWithBarButtonSystemItem:UIBarButtonSystemItemAdd target:self
action:@selector(insertNewObject:)];
    self.navigationItem.rightBarButtonItem = addButton;
 */
    self.noteItems = [[NSMutableArray alloc] init];
    [self loadInitialData];
}
- (void) loadInitialData
{
    // load initial data using core Data
    NTPAppDelegate *appDelegate = [[UIApplication sharedApplication]
delegate];

    NSManagedObjectContext *context = [appDelegate managedObjectContext];
    NSEntityDescription *entityDesc = [NSEntityDescription
entityForName:@"Notes" inManagedObjectContext:context];

    NSFetchRequest *request = [[NSFetchRequest alloc] init];
    [request setEntity:entityDesc];

    NSPredicate *pred = [NSPredicate predicateWithFormat:@"(itemName !=
%@)", nil];
    [request setPredicate:pred];

    NSError *error;
    NSArray *objects = [context executeFetchRequest:request
error:&error];
    if ([objects count] == 0) {
        NSLog (@"No matches");
    } else {
        NSLog (@"%lu matches found", (unsigned long) [objects count]);
    }
    _itemNames = [[NSMutableArray alloc] init];
    _itemContents = [[NSMutableArray alloc] init];
    for (NSManagedObject *item in objects) {
        NTPNoteItem *newItem = [[NTPNoteItem alloc] init];
        newItem.itemName = [item valueForKey:@"itemName"];
        newItem.content = [item valueForKey:@"content"];
        [self.noteItems addObject:newItem];
        NSLog (@"added item: %@ %@", newItem.itemName, newItem.content);
        [self.itemNames addObject:newItem.itemName];
        [self.itemContents addObject:newItem.content];
    }
}

- (void) saveData: (NTPNoteItem *)item
```

```
{
    NTPAppDelegate *appDelegate = [[UIApplication sharedApplication]
delegate];

    NSManagedObjectContext *context = [appDelegate managedObjectContext];
    NSManagedObject *newNote;
    newNote = [NSEntityDescription
insertNewObjectForEntityForName:@"Notes" inManagedObjectContext:context];
    [newNote setValue: item.itemName forKey: @"itemName"];
    [newNote setValue: item.content forKey: @"content"];

    NSError *error;
    [context save: &error];
    NSLog (@"context saved");
}

- (void)didReceiveMemoryWarning
{
    [super didReceiveMemoryWarning];
    // Dispose of any resources that can be recreated.
}

- (void)insertNewObject:(id)sender
{
    if (!_objects) {
        _objects = [[NSMutableArray alloc] init];
    }
    [_objects insertObject:[NSDate date] atIndex:0];
    NSIndexPath *indexPath = [NSIndexPath indexPathForRow:0 inSection:0];
    [self.tableView insertRowsAtIndexPaths:@[indexPath]
withRowAnimation:UITableViewRowAnimationAutomatic];
}

#pragma mark - Table View

- (NSInteger)numberOfSectionsInTableView:(UITableView *)tableView
{
    return 1;
}

- (NSInteger)tableView:(UITableView *)tableView
numberOfRowsInSection:(NSInteger)section
{
    //return _objects.count;
    return [self.noteItems count];
}

- (UITableViewCell *)tableView:(UITableView *)tableView
cellForRowAtIndexPath:(NSIndexPath *)indexPath
{
```

```
    UITableViewCell *cell = [tableView
dequeueReusableCellWithIdentifier:@"ListPrototypeCell"
forIndexPath:indexPath];

    //NSDate *object = _objects[indexPath.row];
    //cell.textLabel.text = [object description];
    NTPNoteItem * item = [self.noteItems objectAtIndex:indexPath.row];
    cell.textLabel.text = item.itemName;
    return cell;
}

- (BOOL)tableView:(UITableView *)tableView
canEditRowAtIndexPath:(NSIndexPath *)indexPath
{
    // Return NO if you do not want the specified item to be editable.
    return YES;
}

- (void)tableView:(UITableView *)tableView
commitEditingStyle:(UITableViewCellEditingStyle)editingStyle
forRowAtIndexPath:(NSIndexPath *)indexPath
{
    if (editingStyle == UITableViewCellEditingStyleDelete) {
        NSLog (@"delete at index %i", indexPath.row);

        NTPNoteItem *item = [self.noteItems objectAtIndex:indexPath.row];

        [self.noteItems removeObjectAtIndex:indexPath.row];
        [self.itemNames removeObjectAtIndex:indexPath.row];
        [self.itemContents removeObjectAtIndex:indexPath.row];


        // Delete the row from the data source
        NTPAppDelegate *appdelegate = [[UIApplication sharedApplication]
delegate];
        NSManagedObjectContext *context =
appdelegate.managedObjectContext;
        NSEntityDescription *entityDesc = [NSEntityDescription
entityForName:@"Notes" inManagedObjectContext:context];

        NSFetchRequest *request = [[NSFetchRequest alloc] init];
        [request setEntity:entityDesc];

        NSLog (@"Search for %@", item.itemName);
        NSPredicate *pred = [NSPredicate predicateWithFormat:@"(itemName
= %@)", item.itemName];
        [request setPredicate:pred];

        NSError *error;
        NSArray *objects = [context executeFetchRequest:request
error:&error];
        NSLog (@"found %i items", [objects count]);
```

```
    for (NSManagedObject *item in objects) {
        NTPNoteItem *newItem = [[NTPNoteItem alloc] init];
        newItem.itemName = [item valueForKey:@"itemName"];
        //[self.noteItems addObject:newItem];
        NSLog (@"found item: %@", newItem.itemName);
    }

    [context deleteObject:objects[0]];

    [context save:&error];

    // Animate the deletion
    [tableView deleteRowsAtIndexPaths:@[indexPath]
withRowAnimation:UITableViewRowAnimationFade];

    /*
    [_objects removeObjectAtIndex:indexPath.row];
    [tableView deleteRowsAtIndexPaths:@[indexPath]
withRowAnimation:UITableViewRowAnimationFade];
     */
    } else if (editingStyle == UITableViewCellEditingStyleInsert) {
        // Create a new instance of the appropriate class, insert it into
the array, and add a new row to the table view.
    }
}

- (void)prepareForSegue:(UIStoryboardSegue *)segue sender:(id)sender
{
    if ([[segue identifier] isEqualToString:@"showDetail"]) {
        NSIndexPath *indexPath = [self.tableView
indexPathForSelectedRow];
        NTPNoteItem *item = [[NTPNoteItem alloc] init];
        item.itemName = self.itemNames [indexPath.row];
        item.content = self.itemContents [indexPath.row];
        [[segue destinationViewController] setDetailItem:item];
        [[segue destinationViewController]
setCurrentRowIndex:indexPath.row];
    } else if ([[segue identifier] isEqualToString:@"addItem"]) {
        NTPNoteItem *item = [[NTPNoteItem alloc] init];
        item.itemName = @"New Item ID";
        item.content = @"content for new item";
        [[segue destinationViewController] setDetailItem:item];
        [[segue destinationViewController] setCurrentRowIndex:-1];
    }
}

@end
```

**Listing 9.25 NTPDetailViewController.h**

```
#import <UIKit/UIKit.h>
```

```
#import "NTPNoteItem.h"

@interface NTPDetailViewController : UIViewController
@property int currentRowIndex;

@property (weak, nonatomic) IBOutlet UITextField *textField;
@property (weak, nonatomic) IBOutlet UITextView *textView;
@property (weak, nonatomic) IBOutlet UIBarButtonItem *saveButton;
@property  NTPNoteItem *noteItem;
@property (strong, nonatomic) id detailItem;

@property (weak, nonatomic) IBOutlet UILabel *detailDescriptionLabel;
@end
```

**Listing 9.26 NTPDetailViewController.m**

```
#import "NTPDetailViewController.h"

@interface NTPDetailViewController ()
- (void)configureView;
@end

@implementation NTPDetailViewController
@synthesize textView = _textView;
@synthesize textField = _textField;
@synthesize noteItem;

#pragma mark - Managing the detail item

- (void)setDetailItem:(id)newDetailItem
{
    if (_detailItem != newDetailItem) {
        _detailItem = newDetailItem;

        // Update the view.
        [self configureView];
    }
}

- (void)configureView
{
    // Update the user interface for the detail item.

    if (self.detailItem) {
        self.detailDescriptionLabel.text = [self.detailItem description];
        NTPNoteItem *item = [[NTPNoteItem alloc] init];
        item = _detailItem;
        self.textView.text = item.content;
        self.textField.text = item.itemName;
    }
}
```

```objc
- (void)viewDidLoad
{
    [super viewDidLoad];
    // Do any additional setup after loading the view, typically from a
nib.
    [self configureView];
    //self.currentRowIndex = -1;
}

- (void)didReceiveMemoryWarning
{
    [super didReceiveMemoryWarning];
    // Dispose of any resources that can be recreated.
}

- (void) prepareForSegue:(UIStoryboardSegue *)segue sender:(id)sender
{
    if (sender != self.saveButton) return;
    if (self.textField.text.length > 0) {
        NSLog (@"text field length is not zero");
        self.noteItem = [[NTPNoteItem alloc] init];
        self.noteItem.itemName = self.textField.text;
        self.noteItem.content = self.textView.text;
        NSLog (@" itemName = %@ 2 %@", self.noteItem.itemName,
self.textField.text);
    } else {
        NSLog (@"text field length is zero");
    }
}

- (IBAction)saveButton:(id)sender {
}
@end
```

## 9.5 Summary

Built on the projects and samples introduced in all previous chapters, this chapter focused on implementing the NoteApp for iPad and iPhone devices to make it a fully functioning app. We adopted two different approaches to enabling adding/updating note items: protocol/delegate for the iPad version and segue for the iPhone version. These are good examples to demonstrate how to pass data between view controllers. I hope you can study these examples carefully and use them effectively in your own projects.

The book ends here for this version of it, but your learning shouldn't. I hope that this book has helped you establish a good foundation from multiple perspectives, such as Objective-C, iOS programming basic concepts and building blocks, user interface design and implementation, and data persistence with the Archiving and Core Data frameworks, and so on. With time, I'll continue to add more iOS programming features on the same context of the NoteApp, and whatever new chapters I write will be made freely downloadable from the book's website – www.perfmath.com. Finally, if you have time and are willing to do it, please send me your comments, which will be valuable for future readers and future versions of this book.

Thank you!

# Appendix A Getting around on MAC OS X

In this appendix, we summarize some of the convenient tricks to help you learn how to get around on Max OS X more easily. We can always click around to do various things, but remembering some keyboard shortcuts can help ease our navigation on a Mac OS X machine significantly. I'll start with some useful keyboard shortcuts next.

## A.1 SOME KEYBOARD SHORTCUTS ON MAC OS X

A KB (knowledge base) article posted at http://support.apple.com/kb/ht1343 summarizes all OS X keyboard shortcuts, which are divided into the following categories:

- Startup shortcuts
- Sleep and shutdown shortcuts
- Finder keyboard shortcuts
- Application and other OS X shortcuts
- Universal Access – voice over keyboard shortcuts
- Full keyboard access
- Universal Access – mouse keys

Our purpose here is not to repeat all those shortcuts. Instead, I'd like to share some that I wish I took time and learnt before rather than clicking around clumsily as I had been. However, before getting started, familiarize yourself with the modifier key symbols as shown in Figure A.1, as some of them exist only on Mac OS X and are not available on other OS platforms.

| ⌘ | Command key |
|---|---|
| ^ | Control key |
| ⌥ | Option key |
| ⇧ | Shift Key |
| ⇪ | Caps Lock |
| fn | Function Key |

**Figure A.1** Modifier key symbols on OS X menus

Note a few differences:

- The **Command** key: This key is unique on OS X. Sometimes, it plays the role of the Control key found on Windows. For example, on Windows you use Ctrl-C/Ctrl-V to copy/paste, but on OS X, you use Command-C/Command-V to copy/paste.

- The **Option** key: This key is named "Alt" key on Windows. Note its strange symbol that I've never seen on other platforms.

- The **fn** key: On Windows, F1 – F12 keys are labeled directly on the keys, but on OS X, these keys play dual-roles and you need to press this key while pressing any of those Fn keys.

The main point is that navigation experience is different on OS X from on Windows, so whether you're new to OS X or not, I suggest that you learn a small subset of keyboard shortcuts on OS X to facilitate you with your use of OS X. For your reference, here is a list of shortcuts for performing some routine tasks based on my own experience (note that some shortcuts can toggle between its two *opposite* states):

1  **Accessing all apps**: Press the F4 key without pressing the fn key. This is equivalent to clicking the *LaunchPad* icon located on the Dock.
2  **Accessing your Desktop**: Press the Command-F3 key combination without pressing the fn key. This is useful when you have many windows or apps open and you don't want to manually close every one of them to get access to your desktop.
3  **Accessing your home folder**: Press Command-Shift-H key combination to open up your home folder.
4  **Minimizing a window**: Press Command-M key combination.
5  **Minimizing all windows**: Press Command-Option-M key combination.
6  **Opening Utilities folder**: Press Command-Shift-U key combination.
7  **Cycling through apps forward**: Hold Command-Tab key, cycle through by pressing/lifting the Tab key and hit Enter to select the app of interest. This is equivalent to Alt-Tab key combination on Windows.
8  **Selecting a list of files**: Click the first file, hold down Shift and select the last file.
9  **Deleting a selected item**: Press Command-Delete key combination.
10  **Emptying trash**: Press Command-Shift-Delete key combination.
11  **Hiding or showing all open windows**: Press fn-F11 key combination.

12   **Capturing a selection to a file**: Press Command-Shift-4, select the region of interest and then release. The screenshot will be saved to your desktop by default.

13   **Quitting an app**: Press Command-Q.

## A.2 HOW DO I FIND MORE KEYBOARD SHORTCUTS ON MAC OS X

Note that we are not interested in remembering all or too many keyboard shortcuts. Actually, you can learn more shortcuts by looking at the shortcuts that show up when you click a selected item. For example, I had a folder named *objective-c* on my desktop. I selected it with a single click, clicked *File* located on the menu bar, and a menu as shown in Figure A.2 displayed all shortcuts.

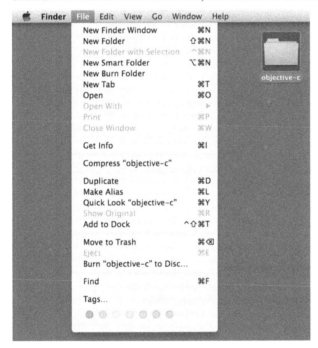

**Figure A.2** More shortcuts available from the *File* menu

For example, note the shortcut *Command-I* shortcut for *Get Info*. With my *objective-c* folder selected, pressing *Command-I* brought up a window as shown in Figure A.3. You can exercise more if you want.

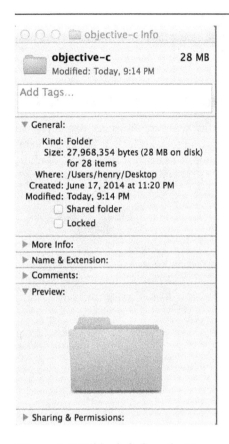

**Figure A.3** Folder info from the *Command-I* combination

These are all I'd like to share with you. Hopefully you find them helpful.

# Appendix B An Introduction to Objective-C

It's imperative to have a minimal understanding of Objective-C in order to be able to develop iOS apps effectively and efficiently. This appendix helps you achieve this objective with a brief introduction to Objective-C. We first introduce basic elements such as data types, variables, expressions, statements, loops, decisions, that you should be able to grasp easily, if you are familiar with at least one other programming language such as Java, C++ or C#. Then, we focus on the objective part of Objective-C, which is about *Classes* in Objective-C.

Let's start with some basic programming elements of Objective-C first.

## B.1 BASIC PROGRAMMING ELEMENTS OF OBJECTIVE-C

In this section, we cover data types, statements, variables, expressions, loops, decisions, and so on. These are basic programming elements common to every programming language. They are presented in Objective-C, and you can compare them with any other programming language(s) you are already familiar with.

Let's start with data types that Objective-C supports first.

### B.1.1 DATA TYPES

The four basic data types that Objective-C supports include:

1   **char**: This data type is designed for representing a single character such as 'a', '\n', and so on, where a character needs to be included in a pair of single quotes. In addition to regular characters, the character set also includes special characters, such as '\n,' which is a new-line character designated with the regular character "n" preceded with a back-slash symbol "\" to distinguish it from the regular character "n."

2    **int**: This data type is used for representing an integer. This type can be extended with *short, unsigned short, unsigned, long, unsigned long, long long,* and *unsigned long long* to represent smaller or larger numbers as needed.

3    **float**: This data type is used for representing floating-point numbers.

4    **double**: This data type is used for representing double-format numbers.

In addition, there is an *id* type that is used to store an object of any type. It is essentially a generic object type, which is very useful for implementing polymorphism and dynamic binding features of Objective-C, as discussed later.

## B.1.2 VARIABLES AND STATEMENTS

A variable is a placeholder for a data item for a given type. It could also be an address in memory, in which case, it is called a *pointer*. For example, the following statement declares a variable of *int* type that is assigned an integer number 100. (Note the semi-colon at the end, which makes it a statement in a program unit.) In this case, all we know and care is that a variable named `intVar` has an integer value of 100 somewhere in memory. Where it is located in memory is managed by the system and is beyond the programmer's control.

```
int intVar = 100;
```

On the other hand, we may also be interested in address variables, such as the following:

```
int *intPtr;
```

In this case, the variable `intPtr` is a pointer pointing to a memory location that stores an integer number. The difference is that it stores the address of an integer data item rather than the value of an integer data item. Unlike Java or some other programming languages, Objective-C supports the concept of pointers due to its deep root in C.

## B.1.3 EXPRESSIONS

An expression represents some kind of operation on at least one or more items. Like many other programming languages, Objective C supports the following types of expressions with their corresponding operations:

■ Arithmetic Expressions. This type of expressions support arithmetic operations such as addition (+), subtraction (-), multiplication (*), division (/), and modulo (%). For example, given two integer type variables i and j, i + j is an expression that represents the addition operation on two integer variables. Associated with arithmetic operations, Objective-C supports *compound assignment operations* such as the following:

   o   x += y: Adds x to y and assigns the result to x.
   o   x -= y: Subtracts y from x and assigns the result to x.
   o   x *= y: Multiplies x by y and assigns the result to x.
   o   x /= y: Divides x by y and assigns the result to x.
   o   x %= y: Performs modulo on x and y and assigns the result to x.
   o   x++: Increments x by 1 and assigns the result to x.
   o   x--: Decrements x by 1 and assigns the result to x.

- Boolean Expressions. This type of expressions support relational operations with various comparison operators applied, such as equal (= =), less than (<), larger than (>), not equal (!=), and combinations of less than and larger than with equal (<=, >=). The Boolean type in Objective-C is designated with BOOL, which takes one of the two values: true or false, equivalent to 1 or 0.

Compound Boolean expressions can be formed by combining multiple Boolean expressions with the logical operators of OR (||), AND (&&), and XOR (^). For example, the Boolean expression ((x < 1) && (y <1)) represents both x and y smaller than 1, and the Boolean expression ((x < 1) || (y <1)) represents either x or y smaller than 1. The XOR (^) operator means *exclusive* OR, namely, the Boolean expression ((x < 1) ^ (y <1)) returns *true* if either x < 1 is true or y < 1 is true, but not both.

Finally, it's helpful to remember the following *ternary operator*, which first evaluates the *condition* part, then the part following the question mark (?) if the condition evaluates to true or the last part if the condition evaluates to false.

```
<condition> ? <execute if condition is true> : <execute if condition is false>;
```

Note that in the above expression, angular brackets are not part of the syntax.

## B.1.4 Decisions

Decisions are one of the mechanisms for directing execution flow in a program. Objective-C supports if and if-else code blocks, similar to other programming languages. For example, if a block of code is supposed to be executed only if a condition turns out to be true, it can be expressed as:

```
if (condition) {
   //code to be executed
}
```

If different code is supposed to be executed based on the outcome of a condition, it could be expressed as

```
if (condition) {
   //code to be executed
} else {
   // code to be executed
}
```

In the above examples, "//" represents comment that will be ignored by the compiler. Objective-C also supports multi-line comments such as:

```
/*
This is a comment
You can have as many lines as you want here
*/
```

## B.1.5 Loops

Objective-C supports `while`, `do-while` and `for` loops, similar to many other languages. For example, the `while`-loop is supported as follows:

```
while (condition) {
    //code to be executed here
}
```

The code within the loop designated by a pair of curly brackets ({...}) is executed until the `condition` becomes `false`.

Unlike the `while`-loop, the `do-while`-loop is executed at least once, as the condition part is moved to the end as shown below:

```
do {
    //code to be executed here
} while (condition);
```

Note that you must have the semi-colon (;) sign included to end the do-while loop block.

A `for`-loop is composed as follows in general:

```
for (initializations; condition; loop-expression) {
    //code to be executed here
}
```

The *initializations* part initializes loop with one or more variables, the *condition* part determines when to stop looping, and the *loop-expression* part increments or decrements the value of the variable that controls looping so the *condition* will become `false` eventually to allow the loop to terminate. A trivial `for`-loop could be as simple as

```
int i = 0;
for (i = 0; i < 10; i++) {
    //code
}
```

Namely, the integer variable `i` starts with zero, and the code within the loop will be executed 10 times until the value of `i` becomes larger than 9.

Of course, you can re-direct the execution flow specified within a loop by using `break` or `continue` statements. A `break` statement is used to exit the loop at the point where the `break` statement is placed, while a `continue` statement returns control to the beginning of the loop.

Before concluding this section, let us use an example to help you solidify what you have learnt so far about Objective-C. You can create the `obj-c-demo0.m` file using Xcode *OS X/Application/CommandLine Tool* template, and enter the code as shown in Listing B.1. Make sure you save the file in a new project and group. (Refer to project *Obj-C Demo* from the download for this book. If you jumped here directly, refer to chapters 1 and 2 about how to set up Xcode on your OS X.)

Now, note a few things about this program:

- We first declared an integer variable named numOfLoops to be used for limiting the number of loops to run. An NSLog function call is made to prompt the user to enter an integer value for the numOfLoops variable.
- The scanf is a C-function for entering an input parameter on the command line. Its first argument specifies the type of data to be entered and the second argument specifies the address of the variable as the destination for the number to be entered. When the symbol (&) precedes a variable, it means the address of the variable in memory.
- The for-loop is very obvious except that the loop variable i is declared and initialized within the for loop rather than before the for loop. This is one of the *clean* ways to write high quality code.

**Listing B.1 The obj-c-demo0 program**

```
#import <Foundation/Foundation.h>

int main(int argc, const char * argv[])
{

    @autoreleasepool {

        int numOfLoops;
        NSLog (@"Enter the number of loops:\n");
        scanf ("%i", &numOfLoops);

        for (int i = 0; i < numOfLoops; i++) {
            NSLog (@"Loop # %i", i);
        }
    }

    return 0;
}
```

Now, change to the directory where main.m file is located, and execute the following command to compile the program:

```
clang -fobjc-arc main.m -o obj-c-demo0
```

The above command instructs the *clang* compiler to use Automatic Reference Counting (ARC) for memory management for the program named *main.m* and name the executable to be *obj-c-demo0*. Then enter at the command line

*./obj-c-demo0*

to run the program. When prompted for a number that specifies how many iterations the loop will run, enter a number, for example, 5, and you should see an output similar to Figure B.1.

```
henrys-mbp:obj-c-demo0 henry$ clang -fobjc-arc main.m -o obj-c-demo0
henrys-mbp:obj-c-demo0 henry$ ./obj-c-demo0
2014-07-11 18:55:36.726 obj-c-demo0[17637:507] Enter the number of loops:
5
2014-07-11 18:55:41.945 obj-c-demo0[17637:507] Loop # 0
2014-07-11 18:55:41.946 obj-c-demo0[17637:507] Loop # 1
2014-07-11 18:55:41.946 obj-c-demo0[17637:507] Loop # 2
2014-07-11 18:55:41.946 obj-c-demo0[17637:507] Loop # 3
2014-07-11 18:55:41.947 obj-c-demo0[17637:507] Loop # 4
henrys-mbp:obj-c-demo0 henry$
```

**Figure B.1** The output of running the obj-c-demo0 program

You can also run this program within Xcode by pressing the *Run* icon and get the expected output as shown in Figure B.2. The entire structure of this simple program is shown here as well in case you want to try it on Xcode and encounter issues.

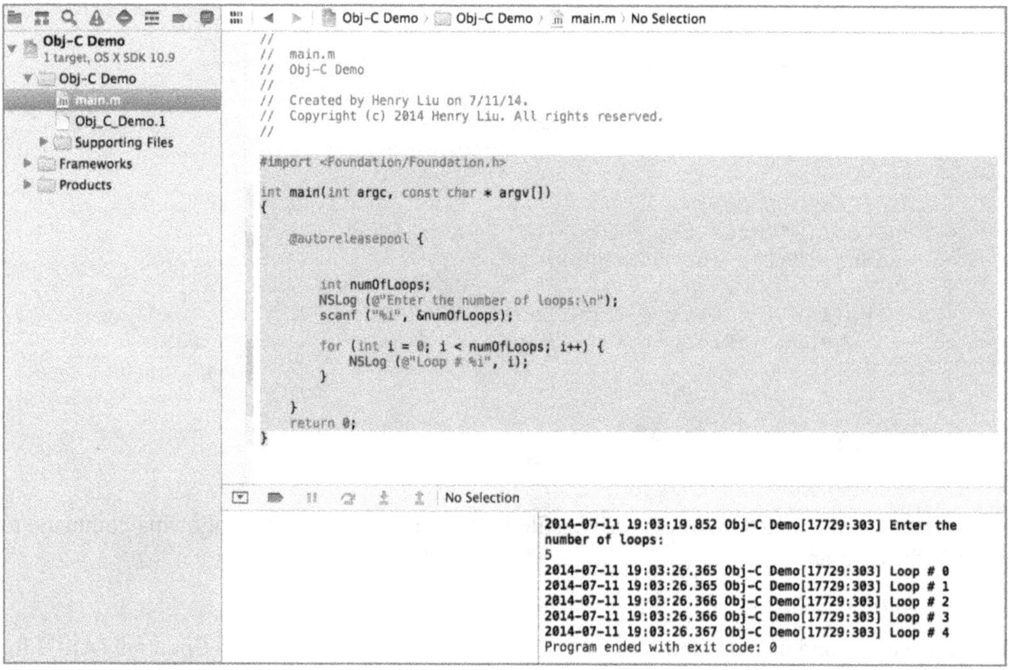

**Figure B.2** Running the *obj-c-demo0* program within Xcode

## B.2 OBJECTIVE-C CLASSES

Objective-C provides extensive support for developing object-oriented applications on iOS and OS X. However, it is patterned on SmallTalk, the first object-oriented language. Therefore, if you are familiar with other OOP languages, such as Java, C++ or C#, Objective-C's syntax for supporting classes may look unique to you initially. This section helps you learn and get used to how Objective-C supports classes, just like any other OOP languages, except for its uniqueness in syntax.

## B.2.1 Objective-C Class Interface and Implementation

An Objective-C class typically has two parts: the interface with a `.h` extension and the implementation with a `.m` extension. The syntax for an Objective-C class interface begins with `@interface` and ends with `@end` as follows:

```
@interface ClassName : ParentClass {
//properties;
}
//ClassMethods;
@end
```

In this section, we use a bank account example to illustrate how to create an Objective-C class named *Account*.

To begin with, if you like, you can use Xcode *OS X/Application/CommandLine Tool* template to create the *Account* project. For example, Figure B.3 shows how to create an initial project named *Account*. Note its type to be specified as *Foundation* by default. The other types include *C*, *C++*, *Core Data*, *Core Foundation*, and *Core Services*, which are irrelevant to us at this point.

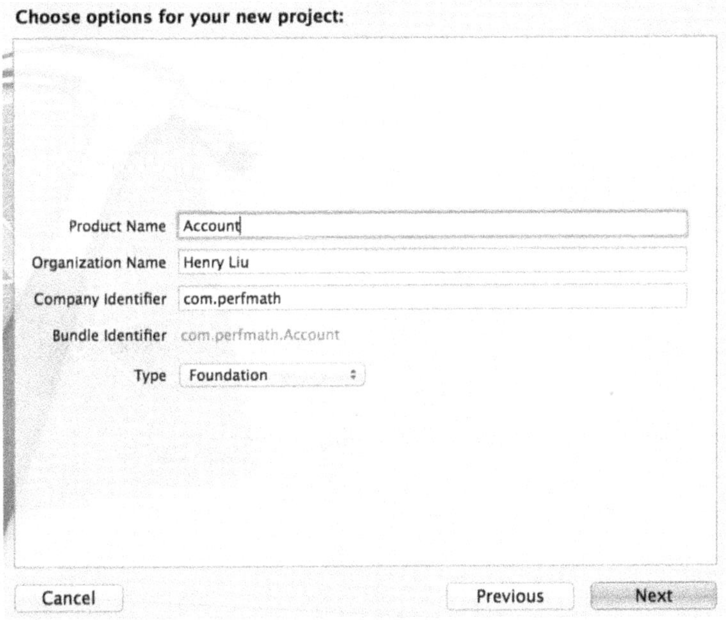

**Figure B.3** Choosing options for creating the *Account* class project using Xcode

The above step creates a *main.m* file without actually creating the *Account* class we are interested. To add the *Account* class, choose *File > New > File ...* and select *OS X/Cocoa/Objective-C class*, as shown in Figure B.4. As you see, this template will help create an Objective-C class, with header and implementation files created automatically.

After clicking on *Next* as shown in Figure B.4, you're prompted for entering the name of the class. Enter *Account* for this exercise as shown in Figure B.5. Note that our *Account* class subclasses the Foundation framework *NSObject* class by default, which is sort of a mother-of-all class for all iOS and OS X application classes.

Click *Next*. Then select *Account* for *Group* and *Targets* as usual. Click *Create* to complete the process of creating our *Account* class. For a large project, you can use this process to add more classes. However, for now, we only need this one class.

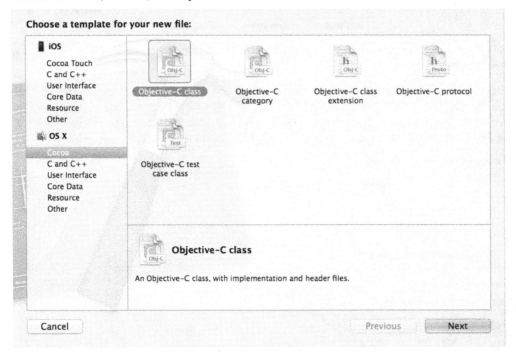

**Figure B.4** Choosing a template for creating the *Account* class using Xcode

**Figure B.5** Adding an *Account* class that subclasses *NSObject*

After the above steps, we now have the skeleton *Account.h* interface file as shown in Listing B.2 and *Account.m* file as shown in Listing B.3.

**Listing B.2 Account.h interface file**

```
#import <Foundation/Foundation.h>

@interface Account : NSObject

@end
```

**Listing B.3 Account.m interface file**

```
#import "Account.h"

@implementation Account

@end
```

As you see from Listing B.3, the *Account* class implementation file begins with an import statement, followed by @implementation *ClassName*, and ends with @end. Next, let's add some properties and methods to our *Account* class.

## B.2.2 ADDING INSTANCE VARIABLES AND METHODS

In object-oriented programming, a class is a type, while an object is an instance of a class. As a type, a class defines properties or attributes or instance variables as well as methods that define the possible operations to be applied to an object. An object is constructed by giving it specific attributes in conjunction with intended methods applied. Using the *Account* example discussed in the previous section, this section explains how to add instance variables and methods to an Objective-C class.

Let's say we want to add *account ID*, *status*, and *balance* attributes at a minimum to our *Account* class. We also want to add the corresponding methods for getting and setting those attributes as well as a deposit method and a helper method, showAccountInfo. Listing B.4 shows the complete *Account.h* interface file with the above attributes and methods added. (Refer to the folder named *Account* in the project download for this book.) Note that all attributes are added in a {...} block following the @interface declaration. Each attribute is designated with a type, followed by an attribute name and ended with a semi-colon. All methods are declared in the form of

```
<method type> (<return type>) <method name>: (<argument type>) <argument
name> <argument 2 label>: (<argument 2 type>) <argument 2 name>
```

Each part of the above form is explained as follows:

- <method type>: This has to be a plus (+) or minus (-) sign. A plus sign tells the compiler that the method is a class method, while a minus sign tells the compiler that the method is an instance method. The difference between the two is that a class method operates on the class itself, while an instance method operates on an instance of the class or object. With this example, we have all instance methods with no class methods, so as you see, every method is preceded with a minus sign.

■ (<return type>): This is the return type for a method enclosed in a pair of round brackets. If the method does not return a data item, the void type should be used; otherwise, use the type that matches the type of the data item to be returned.

■ <method name>: This is the name of the method, which must be a valid Objective-C identifier. It is not very different from many other programming languages.

■ The remaining part declares the arguments for the method. A few rules here:

  o Like the method name, each argument must begin with a colon (:), followed by a type enclosed in a pair of round brackets and the argument name.

  o The second argument (if any) follows the same syntax except that you can precede it with a label optionally to help make it clear what it is for. For example, we have a setAccountId:andStatus method to indicate that this method can set an account ID, plus the status attribute.

■ Unlike some other languages like Java, a method argument name cannot be the same as its corresponding attribute name.

Next, we see how those methods are implemented.

**Listing B.4 Account.h interface file with attributes and methods added**

```
#import <Foundation/Foundation.h>

@interface Account : NSObject
{
    long accountId;
    double balance;
    int status;
}
- (long) getAccountId;
- (void) setAccountId : (long) i;

- (double) getBalance;
- (void) setBalance : (double) b;

- (int) getStatus;
- (void) setStatus : (int) s;

- (void) setAccountId : (long) i andStatus : (int) s;
- (void) showAccountInfo;
- (void) deposit: (double) d;

@end
```

Listing B.5 shows the *Account.m* implementation file. Note that each method implementation follows the method signature defined in the corresponding interface file, with the method body enclosed in a block designated with a pair of curly brackets {...}. Since most of the methods for this example are *getters* and *setters*, we don't have much to explain.

Next, we explain the test driver for this example, which shows how an Objective-C object can be instantiated and how its methods can be called.

**Listing B.5 Account.m implementation file**

```
#import "Account.h"

@implementation Account

- (long) getAccountId
    {
        return accountId;
    }
- (void) setAccountId : (long) i
    {
        accountId = i;
    };

- (double) getBalance
    {
        return balance;
    };
- (void) setBalance : (double) b
    {
        balance = b;
    };

- (int) getStatus
    {
        return status;
    };
- (void) setStatus : (int) s
    {
        status = s;
    }

- (void) setAccountId : (long) i andStatus : (int) s
    {
        accountId = i;
        status = s;
    };
- (void) deposit:(double)d
{
    balance = balance + d;
}
- (void) showAccountInfo
    {
        NSLog (@"account id:  %li balance: %f status: %i ",
```

```
accountId, balance, status);
    }
```

@end

Listing B.6 shows the driver named `main.m` for testing the *Account* class example we explained above. This driver demonstrates the following:

- The interface `Account.h` has to be imported. This is accomplished with the second import as shown there. Note that the interface file name *Account.h* is enclosed using double quotation marks, as the <...> form is for importing interfaces that are *global* and reachable in *System's* path.
- At the beginning of the `autoreleasepool` block, an *Account* object is declared with a statement `Account *account;`, which designates a pointer named `account` pointing to an *Account* object. The next two statements use `alloc` and `init` class methods to allocate memory for the `account` object and initialize the `account` object, subsequently.
- The subsequent statements show how an Objective-C class method is called in the following form (of course, use the argument label as well if any):

```
[classOrObject methodName : argument values (if any)];
```

**Listing B.6 main.m driver for the Account example**

```
#import <Foundation/Foundation.h>
#import "Account.h"

int main(int argc, const char * argv[])
{

    @autoreleasepool {

        Account *account;

        account = [Account alloc];
        account = [account init];

        [account setAccountId: 123456789 andStatus: 1];
        [account setBalance: 500];

        [account showAccountInfo];

        NSLog (@"Account ID %li , Balance %f.", [account getAccountId],
                [account getBalance]);

        [account deposit : 100];
        [account showAccountInfo];

    }
    return 0;
}
```

If you run the above example, you should get an output similar to Listing B.7. You can verify the output by walking through the *main.m* file line by line.

**Listing B.7 Output of running the Account example driver main.m**

```
2014-07-14 06:46:57.518 Account[1693:303] account id:  123456789 balance:
500.000000 status: 1
2014-07-14 06:46:57.520 Account[1693:303] Account ID 123456789 , Balance
500.000000.
2014-07-14 06:46:57.520 Account[1693:303] account id:  123456789 balance:
600.000000 status: 1
Program ended with exit code: 0
```

Before moving to the next section, I'd like to draw your attention to some of the built-in edit-assistant features available from Xcode. You should take advantage of those features as much as possible in order to increase your productivity. For example, if you declared the instance variable account0 as accout0 with a typo of missing letter n there, the edit-assistant would warn the *use of undeclared identifier account0* and ask "*did you mean 'account0?*" This feature can help you identify typos or errors more quickly than using a plain text editor.

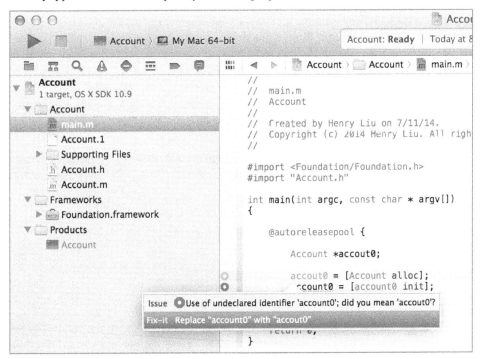

**Figure B.6** A warning about a typo from the Xcode built-in edit-assistant feature

Another example is that if the *Account.h* header were not imported as shown in Figure B.7, an error would appear warning the *use of undeclared identifier 'Account'*. The error would disappear if that interface were imported. You can try it out by removing the comment "//" preceding the import statement as shown in Figure B.7. You may find more examples like these as you use Xcode more. As such, I strongly recommend that you start using Xcode rather than a plain text editor as early as possible.

```
#import <Foundation/Foundation.h>
//#import "Account.h"

int main(int argc, const char * argv[])
{

    @autoreleasepool {

        Account *account0;                    ! Use of undeclared identifier 'Account'  2
```

**Figure B.7**A warning about using an unimported class displayed by the built-in edit-assistant from Xcode

### B.2.3 SYNTHESIZED ACCESSOR METHODS

Notice the getters/setters methods from the previous section about our *Account* class example? As of Objective-C 2.0, we can eliminate those hand-written getters/setters using something called *synthesized accessor methods*. The idea is that we declare those instance variables in the interface file using @property marker as shown in Listing B.8 without including any getters/setters; in the meanwhile, in the implementation file, we declare those instance variables using @synthesize marker without including type information, as shown in Listing B.9. This is enough information for the compiler to generate those getters/setters for us. (Refer to the folder named *BNKAccount* in the project download for this book for this project.)

However, in the driver program *main.m*, each property should be accessed using the dot operator. For example, instead of using the following statement to get the accountId for the NSLog function

```
[account getAccountId]
```

we use

```
account.accountId
```

to get the accountId. Similarly, we use the following form to get the balance information for the account object:

```
account.balance
```

In fact, it would result in an error if the method were still based on the *receiver-message* format. However, the unsynthesized methods should still be accessed using the *receiver-message* format. If you run this example, you should get the same result as shown in Listing B.7.

### Listing B.8 XAccount.h interface file

```
#import <Foundation/Foundation.h>
```

```objc
@interface XAccount : NSObject
@property long accountId;
@property double balance;
@property int status;

- (void) setAccountId : (long) i andStatus : (int) s;
- (void) showAccountInfo;
- (void) deposit: (double) d;
@end
```

## Listing B.9 XAccount.m file

```objc
#import "XAccount.h"

@implementation XAccount
@synthesize accountId, status, balance;
- (void) setAccountId : (long) i andStatus : (int) s
{
    accountId = i;
    status = s;
};
- (void) deposit:(double)d
{
    balance = balance + d;
}
- (void) showAccountInfo
{
    NSLog (@"account id:  %li balance: %f status: %i ",
        accountId, balance, status);
}
```

```objc
@end
```

## Listing B.10 main.m driver for testing XAccount class

```objc
#import <Foundation/Foundation.h>
#import "XAccount.h"

int main(int argc, const char * argv[])
{

    @autoreleasepool {

        XAccount *account;

        account = [XAccount alloc];
        account = [account init];

        [account setAccountId: 123456789 andStatus: 1];
        [account setBalance: 500];
```

```
        [account showAccountInfo];

        NSLog (@"Account ID %li , Balance %f.", account.accountId,
                account.balance);

        [account deposit : 100];

        [account showAccountInfo];

    }
    return 0;
}
```

## B.3 ADVANCED OBJECTIVE-C CLASS ASPECTS

This section briefly introduces some advanced Objective-C class aspects, such as *inheritance*, *polymorphism*, *categories* and *protocols*. You might know that encapsulation, inheritance, and polymorphism are the three pillars that object-oriented programming languages support, including Objective-C. However, categories and protocols are unique to Objective-C.

Let us start with inheritance first next.

### B.3.1 INHERITANCE

The concept of *inheritance* in OOP's parlance refers to the feature that one class can inherit the properties and methods of the class from which it inherits, forming a child-parent relationship. Inheritance is also termed *subclassing*, which is called for when you need to:

■ Extend the functionality of a class by adding some new properties and/or methods.
■ Make a specialized version of a class.
■ Change some of the default behavior of a class by overriding one or more of the parent class's methods.

This section illustrates how to subclass a class using the *Account* example we discussed in the previous section, stored in the folder of *BNKAccount*. To begin with, open your Xcode and select the existing *BNKAccount* project. Then, add a *SavingsAccount* target by selecting *File > New > Target > OS X > Application > Command Line Tool* to bring up the *Choose options for your new target* dialog. Enter *SavingsAccount* for *Product Name* as shown in Figure B.8 and click *Finish*. Your newly-created project should look similar to Figure B.9. Note that we now have two targets, each of them having its own folder with its own *main.m* file.

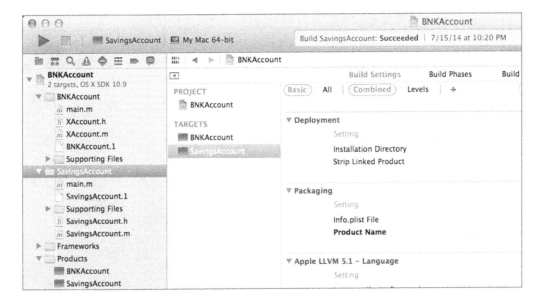

| Product Name | SavingsAccount |
| Organization Name | Henry Liu |
| Company Identifier | com.perfmath |
| Bundle Identifier | com.perfmath.SavingsAccount |
| Type | Foundation |
| Project | BNKAccount |

**Figure B.8** Settings for adding a new target to the existing *Account* project

**Figure B.9** *SavingsAccount* target

Now select your *SavingsAccount* folder. Press *Command-N* to bring up the *Choose a template for your new file* dialog. Select *OS X > Cocoa > Objective-C class* and click *Next*. Enter *SavingsAccount* for *Class* and *Account* for *Subclass of* and click *Next*. Make sure you select *SavingsAccount* folder and *SavingsAccount* Group and *SavingsAccount* target as shown in Figure B.10. Click *Create*. After this step, you should have a *SavingsAccount.h* file and *SavingsAccount.m* file created under your *SavingsAccount* folder on Xcode.

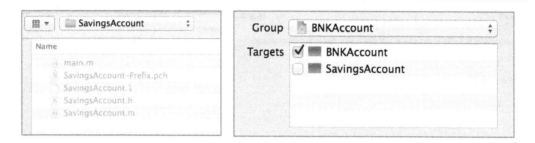

**Figure B.10** Settings for creating the SavingsAccount class

At this point, we have two files created for the *SavingsAccount*: *SavingsAccount.h* interface file and *SavingsAccount.m* file as shown in Listings B.11 and B12, respectively. Although they are skeleton files only at this point, you should already notice that @interface SavingsAccount is followed by its parent class *XAccount*, separated by a semi-colon sign (:), which represents the relationship that *SavingsAccount* class inherits *XAccount* Class. Note that in the *SavingsAccount.m* file, there is no direct expression that the *SavingsAccount* inherits any class. Instead, the inheritance (if any) is reflected through its interface file imported at its beginning.

**Listing B.11 SavingsAccount.h skeleton**

```
#import "XAccount.h"

@interface SavingsAccount : XAccount

@end
```

**Listing B.12 SavingsAccount.m skeleton**

```
#import "SavingsAccount.h"

@implementation SavingsAccount

@end
```

As we mentioned previously, we can add properties and/or methods to a subclass to extend the functionality of its parent class. In this case, we demonstrate the following:

- Adding an interestRate property for the SavingsAccount class
- Overriding the showAccountInfo by adding the interestRate to the NSLog function of its parent class.

Listings B.13 and B.14 show the addition of the interestRate property and the new overridden method showAccountInfo. Note that we used super and self to designate which class a property belongs to, with super indicating the parent object and self the object itself. Next, we discuss the *main.m* driver for testing the *SavingsAccount* class implementation.

**Listing B.13 SavingsAccount.h (formal)**

```
#import "XAccount.h"

@interface SavingsAccount : XAccount
@property double interestRate;
@end
```

**Listing B.14 SavingsAccount.m (formal)**

```
#import "SavingsAccount.h"

@implementation SavingsAccount
@synthesize interestRate;
- (void) showAccountInfo
{
   NSLog (@"account id:  %li balance: %f status: %i interest rate: %f",
super.accountId, super.balance, super.status, self.interestRate);
}
@end
```

Listing B.15 shows the *main.m* driver program for testing the *SavingsAccount* class implementation. As you see, we declare a *SavingsAccount* object rather than an *XAcount* object. Also, note the use of the setInterestRate method, which was absent in the base or parent class.

At this point, you might wonder how a method is resolved? Is it the parent's method or the object's own method that gets invoked? The rule is very simple: The object itself will be searched first, and if not found, then the next immediate parent object is searched until the method is found or an error is thrown. This is so intuitive so that we would not explain any further.

**Listing B.15 main.m for testing SavingsAccount class**

```
#import <Foundation/Foundation.h>
#import "SavingsAccount.h"

int main(int argc, const char * argv[])
{

    @autoreleasepool {

        SavingsAccount *account;

        account = [SavingsAccount alloc];
        account = [account init];

        [account setAccountId: 123456788 andStatus: 1];
        [account setBalance: 500];
        [account setInterestRate: 0.01];

        [account showAccountInfo];
```

```
    NSLog (@"Account ID %li , Balance %f.", account.accountId,
        account.balance);

    [account deposit : 100];

    [account showAccountInfo];

  }
  return 0;
}
```

At this point, if you want to run the *main.m* program for testing the *SavingsAccount* class implementation, you have to make sure that the *SavingsAccount* scheme is selected by choosing it at the tool bar. However, if you just click the *Run* icon located at the tool bar, you will see the "*Build Failed*" indicator and then a red mark at the activity bar indicating how many errors have occurred. If you click on that red mark, it will show you the errors generated from attempting building the target. The errors occurred because Xcode could not find the *XAccount.m* file. In order to resolve those errors, you have to add the *XAccount.m* file to the *Build Phases* as shown in Figure B.11. After this step, you should be able to run the *main.m* driver for testing *SavingsAccount* class implementation successfully, with an output similar to Listing B.16.

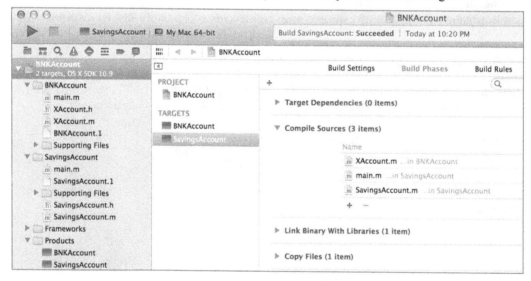

**Figure B.11** Compiled Sources for SavingsAccount Build Phases

**Listing B.16 Output of running main.m for testing SavingsAccount class**

```
2014-07-15 22:20:08.006 SavingsAccount[22037:303] account id:  123456788
balance: 500.000000 status: 1 interest rate: 0.010000
2014-07-15 22:20:08.008 SavingsAccount[22037:303] Account ID 123456788 ,
Balance 500.000000.
```

```
2014-07-15 22:20:08.008 SavingsAccount[22037:303] account id:   123456788
balance: 600.000000 status: 1 interest rate: 0.010000
Program ended with exit code: 0
```

Next, we introduce polymorphism supported by Objective-C.

## B.3.2 POLYMORPHISM

*Polymorphism* is a word derived from Greek, which means *many forms* or *shapes*. Objective-C supports polymorphism in the sense that a method with a given signature, i.e., identical method type, return type, method name and argument list, can be invoked on different objects of different types that all subtype or subclass a common superclass. Thus, this typically has something to do with inheritance. Next, let's use our *Account* example to illustrate what it means by polymorphism in Objective-C.

In the previous sections, we created an *Account* class and a *SavingsAccount* class to help illustrate how Objective-C supports inheritance. Now let's add a *CheckingAccount* class that also subclasses the *Account* class so that we would have an inheritance structure as shown in Figure B.12. The final project structure is shown in Figure B.13. Next, I'll describe how this project was created to illustrate how Objective-C supports polymorphism.

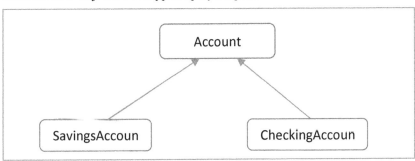

**Figure B.12** Account inherited by SavingsAccount and CheckingAccount

Given the experience you had with the previous examples, I assume that by now you know how to create a project on Xcode and then add targets and Objective-C classes. Here is the high-level procedure used to create the project and targets as shown in Figure B.13:

1   First, create an umbrella project named *BankingAccount* using the *OS X/Application > CommandLine Tool* template. Then, add an Objective-C class using the file template *OS X/Cocoa > Objective-C class* named *Account* which subclasses *NSObject*.
2   Then, create a target named *SavingsAccount* using the *OS X/Application Cocoa Application* template. Add an Objective-C class using the file template *OS X/Cocoa > Objective-C class* named *SavingsAccount* which subclasses *Account*.
3   Then, create a target named *CheckingAccount* using the *OS X/Application Cocoa Application* template. Add an Objective-C class using the file template *OS X/Cocoa > Objective-C class* named *CheckingAcount* which subclasses *Account*.

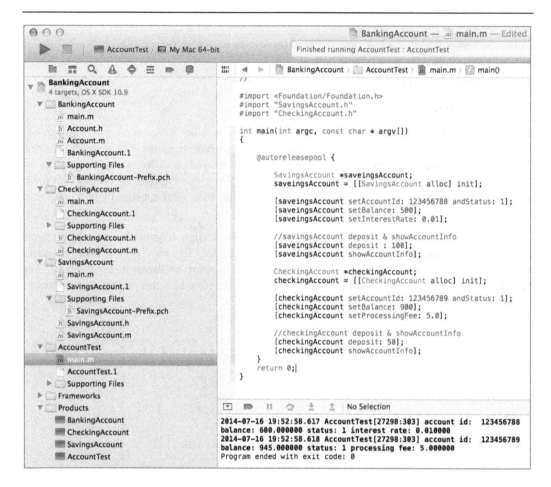

**Figure B.13** Account inherited by SavingsAccount and CheckingAccount

4    Finally, create a target named *AccountTest* using the *OS X/Application Cocoa Application* template. This will be our test driver, so there is no need to add an Objective-C class as we did with *SavingsAccount* and *CheckingAccount*.

Now we need to fill in those skeleton classes and the *main.m* test driver. For the *Account* class, the interface and implementation should be the same as Listings B.8 and B.9, respectively, except that we want to name it *Account* instead of *XAccount*. For the *SavingsAccount*, the interface and implementation should be the same as Listings B.13 and B.14, respectively. Our next task is to fill in the *CheckingAccount* interface and implementation.

Listings B.17 and B.18 show the *CheckingAccount.h* interface file and *CheckingAccount.m* implementation file. As you see from the interface file, we added a property named processingFee, intended for charging the customer whenever a deposit is made. You can verify this from the overridden method of deposit: shown in Listing B.18. Note also that we have overridden the showAccountInfo method so that the last item it outputs will be processingFee, which is specific to the CheckingAccount class only.

Given the above setup for the *CheckingAccount* subclass, next, we need to fill in the testing logic as shown in Listing B.19. Here, polymorphism is illustrated with the deposit: method. When this method is called on the savingsAccount object, it's the implementation found in the parent class that will be called, since it's not overridden in the SavingsAccount class. However, when this method is called on the checkingAccount object, it's the implementation found in the *CheckingAccount* subclass that will be called, since it's overridden in the CheckingAccount class. One method is called on more than one type of object with different implementations is what it means by *polymorphism*. The other method showAccountInfo also illustrates the concept of polymorphism in Objective-C, as it is switched between the two different types of objects derived from the common superclass. This kind of switching in method execution between the child and parent classes or among sibling subclasses is what it really means by polymorphism in Objective-C.

To verify that polymorphism illustrated with the above example works, build and run the example. The output obtained on my machine can be found in the console area shown in Figure B.13. However, you need to add the two subclass implementation files to your *AccountTest* target *Build Phases* as we demonstrated previously before running it. In addition, make sure you change the scheme to *AccountTest* before you hit the *Run* icon.

**Listing B.17 CheckingAccount.h**

```
#import "Account.h"
@interface CheckingAccount : Account
@property double processingFee;
@end
```

**Listing B.18 CheckingAccount.m**

```
@implementation CheckingAccount
- (void) deposit:(double)d
{
    self.balance = self.balance + d - self.processingFee;
}
- (void) showAccountInfo
{
    NSLog (@"account id:  %li balance: %f status: %i processing fee: %f",
super.accountId, super.balance, super.status, self.processingFee);
}
@end
```

**Listing B.19 main.m for testing the polymorphism example**

```
#import <Foundation/Foundation.h>
#import "SavingsAccount.h"
#import "CheckingAccount.h"
```

```
int main(int argc, const char * argv[])
{

    @autoreleasepool {

        SavingsAccount *saveingsAccount;
        saveingsAccount = [[SavingsAccount alloc] init];

        [saveingsAccount setAccountId: 123456788 andStatus: 1];
        [saveingsAccount setBalance: 500];
        [saveingsAccount setInterestRate: 0.01];

        //savingsAccount deposit & showAccountInfo
        [saveingsAccount deposit : 100];
        [saveingsAccount showAccountInfo];

        CheckingAccount *checkingAccount;
        checkingAccount = [[CheckingAccount alloc] init];

        [checkingAccount setAccountId: 123456789 andStatus: 1];
        [checkingAccount setBalance: 900];
        [checkingAccount setProcessingFee: 5.0];

        //checkingAccount deposit & showAccountInfo
        [checkingAccount deposit: 50];
        [checkingAccount showAccountInfo];
    }
    return 0;
}
```

This concludes our introduction to polymorphism in Objective-C. Next, we explain the concept of dynamic typing and binding in Objective-C.

### B.3.3 DYNAMIC TYPING AND DYNAMIC BINDING

A variable is dynamically typed when the type of the object it points to is not checked until runtime. In contrast, a variable is statically typed when the type of the object it points to is checked at compile time. Objective-C has a special data type named id for dynamically typing a variable.

On the other hand, *dynamic binding*, which is also termed *late binding*, is about determining the method to call at runtime instead of at compile time. Internally, dynamic binding is implemented using the concept of a selector, which is the name used to select a method when it's called upon an object. When the source code is compiled, a method name is replaced with a unique selector. For example, with our polymorphism example discussed in the previous section, the *SavingsAccount* class and *CheckingAccount* class inherit the same method deposit:, for which a selector is designated. At runtime, this selector acts like a dynamic function pointer that automatically points to the implementation of that method for whichever object it is assigned to. Next, we use an example to help illustrate these concepts.

Let's re-use our previous polymorphism example to construct a new example that demonstrates the concept of dynamic typing and dynamic binding. Instead of creating a new project from scratch, let's copy it to a new project and rename it to *DynamicBinding*. Here is the procedure to copy and rename a project on Xcode, in case you are not familiar with it:

1   Locate the *BankingAccount* project in your Xcode workspace folder (not on the Xcode IDE), right-click on it and select *Duplicate*. Now click on the *BankingAccount Copy* folder, follow it by another quick click and hold it down for a second and release your mouse. It should allow you to rename it now. Rename it to *DynamicBinding*.

2   In your newly-renamed *DynamicBinding* folder, locate the *BankingAccount.xcodeproj* file. Right click on it and select *Open With Xcode …*

3   Your *DynamicBinding* project should now appear on your Xcode IDE. In the right-most *Utility* pane, identify/select the *Standard* editor at the top (the left most icon), then the *File* inspector icon (the first icon at the next level). You should now see a *Name* text field under *Identity and Type*. Change the project name from *BankingAccount* to *DynamicBinding* now. If you encounter a dialog prompting *"Rename project content items?"* as shown in Figure B.14, you can select the items you want to rename, but for this example, select *Don't Rename*, as we just want to have a project that has a different project name – we'll use the same classes we used for the previous polymorphism example.

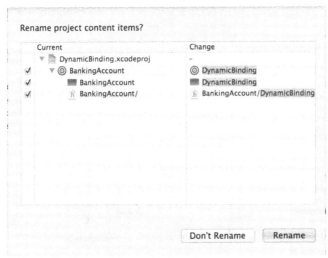

**Figure B.14** Rename project content items

Since all classes (*Account*, *SavingsAccount*, and *CheckingAccount*) remain the same, we just modify the *main.m* file from the *AccountTest* target. Listing B.20 shows the modified *main.m* file for the *AccountTest* target. As you see, previously, we used static typing that two separate objects, *savingsAccount* and *checkingAccount*, were introduced. Now, dynamic typing is used with the statement

```
id account;
```

located right under @autoreleasepool block. What that means is that account is a variable of type id, which could point to any object later. Then, if you look down further, you should see the following statements:

```
account = savingsAccount;
[account deposit : 100];
[account showAccountInfo];
```

As you see now, the savingsAccount object is assigned to the account variable, and the deposit: and showAccountInfo are called through the account variable rather than the savingsAccount object itself. This is the part of *dynamic binding* through a variable of type *id*. You can also find similar statements further down for the checkingAccount object as shown below:

```
account = checkingAccount;
[account deposit: 50];
[account showAccountInfo];
```

You might wonder why we couldn't just live with the *savingsAccount* and *checkingAccount* objects without getting involved with dynamic typing or dynamic binding at all? As you already saw from the previous polymorphism example, using those two objects directly were just fine. However, using dynamic typing and dynamic binding gives you some extra flexibility. To prove that's the case, if you look further down in Listing B.20, you should see the following statements:

```
NSLog (@"\nDynamic Binding 2:");
NSArray *accounts = [NSArray arrayWithObjects:savingsAccount,
 checkingAccount, nil];
id accountObj;
for (int i = 0; i < 2; i++)
{
    accountObj = [accounts objectAtIndex:i];
    [accountObj showAccountInfo];
}
```

As you see now, by putting both accounts into an NSArray, you can declare an *accountObj* object of type *id* and loop through the savingsAccount and checkingAccount objects with their common method of shownAccountInfo. This would be extremely convenient if you have thousands or millions of accounts that you need to apply a same operation. In summary, dynamic typing becomes handy when you have a large collection of objects to iterate through with some same operations.

To verify that dynamic typing and binding work, you can run the *AccountTest* target on your Xcode IDE. You should get an output similar to what I did as shown in Listing B.21.

**Listing B.20 main.m file for testing dynamic typing and dynamic binding**

```
#import <Foundation/Foundation.h>
#import "SavingsAccount.h"
#import "CheckingAccount.h"

int main(int argc, const char * argv[])
```

```
{

    @autoreleasepool {

        id account;

        SavingsAccount *savingsAccount;
        savingsAccount = [[SavingsAccount alloc] init];

        [savingsAccount setAccountId: 123456788 andStatus: 1];
        [savingsAccount setBalance: 500];
        [savingsAccount setInterestRate: 0.01];
         NSLog (@"Dynamic Binding 1:");
        //savingsAccount deposit & showAccountInfo
        //[saveingsAccount deposit : 100];
        //[saveingsAccount showAccountInfo];
        account = savingsAccount;
        [account deposit : 100];
        [account showAccountInfo];

        CheckingAccount *checkingAccount;
        checkingAccount = [[CheckingAccount alloc] init];

        [checkingAccount setAccountId: 123456789 andStatus: 1];
        [checkingAccount setBalance: 900];
        [checkingAccount setProcessingFee: 5.0];

        //checkingAccount deposit & showAccountInfo
        //[checkingAccount deposit: 50];
        //[checkingAccount showAccountInfo];
        account - checkingAccount;
        [account deposit: 50];
        [account showAccountInfo];

        NSLog (@"\nDynamic Binding 2:");
        NSArray *accounts = [NSArray arrayWithObjects:savingsAccount,
            checkingAccount, nil];
        id accountObj;
        for (int i = 0; i < 2; i++)
        {
            accountObj = [accounts objectAtIndex:i];
            [accountObj showAccountInfo];
        }
    }
    return 0;
}
```

**Listing B.21 Output of the dynamic typing and dynamic binding example**

```
2014-07-17 08:45:37.788 AccountTest[29519:303] Dynamic Binding 1:
```

```
2014-07-17 08:45:37.790 AccountTest[29519:303] account id:  123456788
balance: 600.000000 status: 1 interest rate: 0.010000
2014-07-17 08:45:37.790 AccountTest[29519:303] account id:  123456789
balance: 945.000000 status: 1 processing fee: 5.000000
2014-07-17 08:45:37.790 AccountTest[29519:303]
Dynamic Binding 2:
2014-07-17 08:45:37.791 AccountTest[29519:303] account id:  123456788
balance: 600.000000 status: 1 interest rate: 0.010000
2014-07-17 08:45:37.791 AccountTest[29519:303] account id:  123456789
balance: 945.000000 status: 1 processing fee: 5.000000
Program ended with exit code: 0
```

Next, we discuss categories and protocols supported by Objective-C.

## B.3.4 CATEGORIES AND PROTOCOLS

This section covers two more unique OOP (object-oriented programming) features that Objective-C supports: *categories* and *protocols*. We cover categories first and then protocols.

## B.3.4.1 CATEGORIES

In the previous sections, we learnt that one can extend the functionality of a class by subclassing it. On the other hand, the concept of categories is about grouping, but grouping of methods, not properties. For example, we could have a category that groups all transactional methods together, such as deposit and withdraw, etc. In this sense, categorizing is one of the mechanisms for refactoring the methods of a class. However, categorizing is for convenience or working around, for example, dividing the methods of a class into multiple categories so that more developers can work on them simultaneously. In this sense, categorizing is also a mechanism for modularizing a component.

Next, let us retrofit our previous *Account* example to illustrate how the concept of categories works in Objective-C.

First, follow the procedure given in the previous section on dynamic typing and duplicate our *BNKAcount* project into a *Categories* project. After you're done, add a target named *XAccount+TxOps* and then add an Objective-C class with the name *XAccount+TxOps*. (Make sure you save the class in the *XAccount+TxOps* folder.) Then, do the following:

1   Change the interface definition from `@interface XAccount_TxOps: NSObject` to `@interface XAccount (TxOps)`, namely, the name of the interface to be categorized, followed by the name of the category enclosed in parentheses ( ). This tells the compiler the interface to be categorized and the name of the category.
2   Change the implementation declaration line from `@implementation XAccount_TxOps` to `@implementation XAccount (TxOps)` for similar reasons as stated above.
3   Add `#import "XAccount.h"` in the *XAccount+TxOps.h* file.
4   Remove the `deposit:` method from the *XAccount.h* and *XAccount.m* files.
5   Make changes to the *XAccount+TxOps.h* and *XAccount+TxOps.m* files so that they would look like Listings B.22 and B.23, respectively. We explain next how *category* works with this example.

First, note that in the category interface file Listing B.22, the `#import` statement imports *XAccount.h*, the interface from which categorization is derived. The category name `TxOps` is enclosed in parentheses, following the interface name. Other than that, the method declarations are not very different from what we see in a regular interface file.

Similarly, the implementation file shown in Listing B.23 imports the category's interface file, *XAccount+TxOps.h*. The category (`TxOps`) is also included in the `@implementation` line. However, as is commented out, a category implementation file is not allowed to have an `@synthesize` line, as that belongs to the original class implementation. The rest of it is similar to what we typically find in a regular class implementation file.

Next, we discuss the *main.m* test file for this example, following Listing B.23.

### Listing B. 22 XAccount+TxOps.h

```
#import <Foundation/Foundation.h>
#import "XAccount.h"

@interface XAccount (TxOps)
- (void) deposit: (double) d;
- (void) debit: (double) d;
@end
```

### Listing B.23 XAccount+TxOps.m

```
#import "XAccount+TxOps.h"

@implementation XAccount (TxOps)
//@synthesize accountId, status, balance;
- (void) deposit:(double)d
{
    self.balance = self.balance + d;
}
- (void) debit:(double)d
{
    self.balance = self.balance - d;
}
@end
```

Listing B.24 shows the *main.m* file for testing the *TxOps* category associated with the class *XAccount*. Once again, *XAccount+TxOps.h* must be imported first. The rest of it is quite self-explanatory except that the `deposit :` and `debit :` methods are used as if they were from the original `XAccount` class. Listing B.25 shows the output of running this example on my MacBook Pro.

### Listing B.24 main.m for XAccount+TxOps

```
#import <Foundation/Foundation.h>
#import "XAccount+TxOps.h"
```

```
int main(int argc, const char * argv[])
{

    @autoreleasepool {

        XAccount *account;

        account = [XAccount alloc];
        account = [account init];

        [account setAccountId: 123456788 andStatus: 1];
        [account setBalance: 500];

        [account showAccountInfo];

        NSLog (@"Account ID %li , Balance %f.",
               account.accountId, account.balance);

        [account deposit : 100];
        [account showAccountInfo];

        [account debit : 100];
        [account showAccountInfo];

    }
    return 0;
}
```

**Listing B.25 Output of running main.m for XAccount+TxOps target**

```
2014-07-18 12:14:04.343 XAccount+TxOps[31666:303] account id:  123456788
balance: 500.000000 status: 1
2014-07-18 12:14:04.345 XAccount+TxOps[31666:303] Account ID 123456788 ,
Balance 500.000000.
2014-07-18 12:14:04.345 XAccount+TxOps[31666:303] account id:  123456788
balance: 600.000000 status: 1
2014-07-18 12:14:04.346 XAccount+TxOps[31666:303] account id:  123456788
balance: 500.000000 status: 1
Program ended with exit code: 0
```

Another advantage with category is that a category can be declared for any class, even if the original source code, such as for standard Cocoa or Cocoa Touch classes, is not available. As far as accessing methods defined in a category is concerned, any methods declared in a category will be available to all instances of both the original class and any subclasses of the original class. At runtime, a method added by a category and one that is implemented by the original class are indistinguishable. To prove that's the case, we continue with the above example by modifying the *SavingsAccount* class and its *main.m* file as described below.

If you subclass a superclass that has one or more categories, you don't do anything different except that you should import the category's interface file rather than the superclass's interface file. Listing B.26 shows the *SavingsAccount.h* file, while the *SavingsAccount.m* file is not listed as it remains the same.

Listing B.27 shows the *main.m* file, which tests *SavingsAccount* class that subcallses the *XAccount* class with a category named *TxOps* as discussed above. Once again, note that the interface header file *XAccount+TxOps.h* must be imported, as the *deposit* : and *debit* : methods are contained in it. At this point, if you just run the *SavingsAccount* target, you would encounter an error like *unrecognized selector sent to instance ...*, as shown in Listing B.28. That's because the *XAccount+TxOps.m* is not added to the *Build Phases* of the *SavingsAccount* target. After fixing that issue, that error should disappear and you should see a normal output similar to Listing B.29.

**Listing B.26 SavingsAccount.h interface file that imports the category interface file XAccount+TxOps.h**

```
#import "XAccount+TxOps.h"

@interface SavingsAccount : XAccount
@property double interestRate;
@end
```

**Listing B.27 main.m for testing SavingsAccount class that subclasses a class that has a category**

```
#import <Foundation/Foundation.h>
#import "SavingsAccount.h"
#import "XAccount+TxOps.h"

int main(int argc, const char * argv[])
{

    @autoreleasepool {

        SavingsAccount *account;

        account = [SavingsAccount alloc];
        account = [account init];

        [account setAccountId: 123456788 andStatus: 1];
        [account setBalance: 500];
        [account setInterestRate: 0.01];

        [account showAccountInfo];

        NSLog (@"Account ID %li , Balance %f.", account.accountId,
                account.balance);

        [account deposit : 100];

        [account showAccountInfo];
```

```
    }
    return 0;
}
```

**Listing B.28 Output of running main.m for the XAccount+TxOps target**

```
2014-07-18 15:23:19.946 SavingsAccount[32488:303] account id:  123456788
balance: 500.000000 status: 1 interest rate: 0.010000
2014-07-18 15:23:19.947 SavingsAccount[32488:303] Account ID 123456788 ,
Balance 500.000000.
2014-07-18 15:23:19.948 SavingsAccount[32488:303] -[SavingsAccount
deposit:]: unrecognized selector sent to instance 0x100108b70
2014-07-18 15:23:19.949 SavingsAccount[32488:303] *** Terminating app due
to uncaught exception 'NSInvalidArgumentException', reason: '-
[SavingsAccount deposit:]: unrecognized selector sent to instance
0x100108b70'
*** First throw call stack:
(
    0    CoreFoundation                      0x00007fff90c2425c
__exceptionPreprocess + 172
    1    libobjc.A.dylib                     0x00007fff9023be75
objc_exception_throw + 43
    2    CoreFoundation                      0x00007fff90c2712d -
[NSObject(NSObject) doesNotRecognizeSelector:] + 205
    3    CoreFoundation                      0x00007fff90b823f2
___forwarding___ + 1010
    4    CoreFoundation                      0x00007fff90b81f78
_CF_forwarding_prep_0 + 120
    5    SavingsAccount                      0x0000000100001b65 main + 389
    6    libdyld.dylib                       0x00007fff865b25fd start + 1
    7    ???                                 0x0000000000000001 0x0 + 1
)
libc++abi.dylib: terminating with uncaught exception of type NSException
Program ended with exit code: 9
```

**Listing B.29 Output of running SavingsAccount class's maim.m file after
XAccount+TxOps.m file added to the Build Phases for the SavingsAcount target**

```
2014-07-18 15:31:32.868 SavingsAccount[33278:303] account id:  123456788
balance: 500.000000 status: 1 interest rate: 0.010000
2014-07-18 15:31:32.870 SavingsAccount[33278:303] Account ID 123456788 ,
Balance 500.000000.
2014-07-18 15:31:32.870 SavingsAccount[33278:303] account id:  123456788
balance: 600.000000 status: 1 interest rate: 0.010000
Program ended with exit code: 0
```

This concludes of discussion on categories. Next, we discuss protocols.

## B.3.4.2 PROTOCOLS

A *protocol* declares an interface that any class may choose to implement, namely, it's meant for other classes to implement. For a protocol, implementing all methods is mandatory by default except those put below the line marked with @optional. If a class implements all required methods of a protocol, it's said that the class conforms to or adopts that protocol. This section presents a simple example to help illustrate how the concept of protocols in Objective-C works.

First, follow the procedure given in the previous section and copy the *Categories* project and rename it to *Protocols*. Then, add an Objective-C protocol named *AccountCheck* by using the *OS X/Cocoa Objective-C class* template, which should create an *AccountCheck.h* interface file at the first level of the *Protocols* project. Let's say we want to have a method that would lock an account if certain conditions are met, for example, when its balance becomes negative. Listing B.30 shows the *AccountCheck* protocol created using the Xcode Objective-C protocol template. As you see, it's not much different from defining an interface except that it has its own marker of @protocol and it is set to conform to the <NSObject> protocol. In addition, a protocol contains methods only with no properties.

**Listing B.30 AccountCheck.h for defining an AccountCheck protocol**

```
#import <Foundation/Foundation.h>

@protocol AccountCheck <NSObject>

- (void) lockAccount : (XAccount *) a;

@end
```

Now, let's modify the *SavingsAccount* class so that it adopts the *AccountCheck* protocol. For this example, it's easy: just import the protocol header file, add the lockAccount method in its interface, and implement it as shown in Listing B.32 as if it were a regular method.

**Listing B.31 SavingsAccount.h**

```
#import "XAccount+TxOps.h"
#import "AccountCheck.h"

@interface SavingsAccount : XAccount <AccountCheck>
@property double interestRate;
- (void) lockAccount : (XAccount *) a;
@end
```

**Listing B.32 SavingsAccount.m**

```
#import "SavingsAccount.h"

@implementation SavingsAccount
@synthesize interestRate;
- (void) showAccountInfo
{
```

```
    NSLog (@"account id:  %li balance: %f status: %i interest rate: %f",
       super.accountId, super.balance, super.status, self.interestRate);
}
- (void) lockAccount : (XAccount *) a
{
    if (a.balance < 0) a.status = -1;
}
@end
```

Listing B.33 shows how the above protocol can be tested. Note that the account had a $500 balance to begin with. Then, a debit transaction of $600 was made, which put the balance to an amount of -$100. Then, after the lockAccount method was called, the account status became negative, which was the outcome of a lockup operation. You can verify the result by examining Listing B.34.

**Listing B.33 main.m for testing the protocol example**

```
#import <Foundation/Foundation.h>
#import "SavingsAccount.h"
#import "XAccount+TxOps.h"

int main(int argc, const char * argv[])
{

    @autoreleasepool {

        SavingsAccount *account;

        account = [SavingsAccount alloc];
        account = [account init];

        [account setAccountId: 123456788 andStatus: 1];
        [account setBalance: 500];
        [account setInterestRate: 0.01];

        [account showAccountInfo];

        NSLog (@"Account ID %li , Balance %f.", account.accountId,
               account.balance);

        [account debit : 600];
        [account showAccountInfo];

        [account lockAccount : account];
        [account showAccountInfo];

    }
    return 0;
}
```

**Listing B.34 Output of running the protocol example**

```
2014-07-18 19:39:48.548 SavingsAccount[37612:303] account id:  123456788
balance: 500.000000 status: 1 interest rate: 0.010000
2014-07-18 19:39:48.550 SavingsAccount[37612:303] Account ID 123456788 ,
Balance 500.000000.
2014-07-18 19:39:48.550 SavingsAccount[37612:303] account id:  123456788
balance: -100.000000 status: 1 interest rate: 0.010000
2014-07-18 19:39:48.550 SavingsAccount[37612:303] account id:  123456788
balance: -100.000000 status: -1 interest rate: 0.010000
Program ended with exit code: 0
```

This concludes our introduction to the concept of protocols in Objective-C.

### B.3.4.3 DELEGATIONS

In the previous section, we used only one class, *SavingsAccount* to illustrate how to adopt a protocol. You could do the same with a *CheckingAccount* class as well. Yet, as you see, a protocol is not part of a super-class. This gives some extra flexibility for implementing a set of common operations without resorting to subclassing a common superclass.

A protocol can also be considered an interface definition between two classes. The protocol class, for example, *AccountCheck* from the preceding example, functions as a delegate that delegates the work defined by the methods in the protocol to the class that implements it, for example, the *SavingsAccount* class from the preceding class. You'll see more delegate examples as you work through the remainder of this text.

This concludes our brief introduction to Objective-C. To summarize, you have learnt:

- How to create Objective-C projects on Xcode
- Some basic concepts of Objective-C
- How Objective-C supports OOP in general
- Some advanced Objective-C aspects, such as inheritance, polymorphism, dynamic typing/binding, categories, protocols, and so on.

With the solid foundation established so far, you should be able to continue to learn Objective-C yourself by frequently and carefully studying the two high quality, comprehensive references given in the next section.

## B.4 RECOMMENDED OBJECTIVE-C REFERENCES

Apple provides many references to help developers learn their technologies for developing various applications on OS X and iOS X fast. I found that the following two are particularly useful:

1  Search online for *Cocoa Core Competencies* in *iOS Developer library*. To give you an idea about this reference, here is its Table of Contents (TOC):

2    Search online for *Programming with Objective-C* in *Mac Developer Library*. To give you an idea about this reference, here is its Table of Contents (TOC):

Of course, these are not the only references that you can find from Apple's developer libraries. Whenever you want to find out more about a concept or technology in the context of OS X and/or iOS, most likely you'll end up with finding an article from Apple's developer libraries. Consult those references often during your learning journey to grasping iOS programming!

# Index